# The
# Modern American Novel
# of
# Violence

# The
# Modern American Novel
# of
# Violence

by

Patrick W. Shaw

The Whitston Publishing Company
Troy, New York
2000

"The Kid's Fate, The Judge's Guilt: Ramifications of Closure in Cormac McCarthy's *Blood Meridian*." *The Southern Literary Journal*, 30 (Fall 1997), 102-119.

# Contents

# Introduction

I need first to define two crucial terms as they are used in this study: violence and novel of violence. As an indication of how difficult that defining task can be, we might recall that George Bush set up a President's committee called the Federal Violence Initiative. Though the initiative was widely supported, not only did the committee fail to define "violence" but its efforts to do so created such political turmoil that the Initiative was soon dissolved.

My own working definition is less volatile. It derives from several commonsensical definitions of violence that have been offered over the years. Leonard D. Eron quotes from John Dollard's *Frustration and Aggression* (1939) to note that violence is "an act whose goal-response is injury to an organism (or organism-surrogate)" (Huesmann 4). In *The History of Violence in America: Historical and Comparative Perspectives* (1969), editors Hugh Davis Graham and Ted Robert Gurr define violence as "behavior designed to inflict physical injury to people or damage to property" (xxxii). Hans Toch, in *Violent Men* (1984), says that "the behavior we shall deal with [i.e., violence] *is* injurious is rarely planned, and almost invariably is affect-laden" (1). Michael Kowalewski, in *Deadly Musings: Violence and Verbal Form in American Fiction* (1993) says that "Violence is thus popularly understood as an act of aggression that is usually destructive, antisocial, and degrading in its consequences and that usually seems deliberate" (7). Benjamin B. Wolman defines violence as "physical or verbal behavior that aims at harming and/or destroying someone or something. Violent behavior is a part of nature, and nature is violent" (xv). Laura E. Tanner, in her study of sexual assaults against women entitled *Intimate Violence: Reading Rape and Torture in Twentieth-Century Fiction* (1996), concludes that in such attacks "the forceful imposition of the assaulter's form on the victim may serve as a means of empowerment for the violator; the victim's body acts as a blank text on which an insecure individual's world view may be written" (4).

Therefore, either explicitly or implicitly, the definitions agree that violence is an act by one human being that causes pain and injury to another human being. While this a reliable core definition, the word "injury" itself needs to be amended. "Injury" is a wound that shows up as physical, pragmatic evidence: bruises, blood, cuts, abrasions, contusions. "Injury" is the kind of hurt a medical doctor can treat or that a qualified pathologist can point to and say "that's what killed this person." Assuming the validity of this modified and specific meaning of "injury," therefore, I define violence as *any action, premeditated or not, that is performed with the purpose of injuring or killing another living creature, especially another human.*

A secondary characteristic of human violence affects the novels that I discuss. Unlike other species, human violence is not consistently beneficial to the species Homo Sapiens. Once evolution burdened them with violent instincts, species other than humans made the most efficient use of those instincts to insure their survival and advance their kind. Humans, however, did not make such suitable or rational adaptations. Some studies, such as Richard Wrangham and Dale Peterson's *Demonic Males: Apes and the Origins of Human Violence* (Boston: Houghton Mifflin, 1996), suggest that various large apes kill their own kind to secure females and territory. Humans do the same. However, as Erich Fromm and others have noted, Homo Sapiens "is the only primate that kills and tortures members of his own species without any reason . . ., and who feels satisfaction in doing so" (26). Luigi Valzelli, author of *Psychobiology of Aggression and Violence*, further clarifies the distinctions between humans and other animals: "man, among the thousands of species that fight, alone fights destructively, with cruelty and malice, and is capable of becoming a mass murderer" (62). From a legacy of "many past and present atrocities," Valzelli concludes, "man has achieved the distinction of being the only misfit in his own society. . ., and the wicked seed from which his own destruction will likely stem" (62). As Benjamin Wolman observes, "Human beings are ahead of all other species in intraspecific murderous violence. In war and in peace people are killed by people" (xv). This self-destructive phenomenon and the sense of puzzlement that it causes mark the subtext of each novel discussed in this study.

Though no one can explain why human beings direct their violence predominantly at each other, several theories have tried to explain why some *individuals* act more violently than others. As Barbara Fawcett and other editors of *Violence and Gender Relations: Theories and Interventions* (1996) note, "violence takes on many forms, involves many different types of relationships, and attracts countless theories that attempt to explain it" (1). Benjamin Wolman, editor of the *International Encyclopedia of Psychiatry, Psychology, Psychoanalysis and Neurology*, makes the important point that

> There are two main sources of violence, namely, the fear of death by starvation and the fear of death by being killed. The fear of having nothing to eat leads to offensive violence, and the fear of being eaten up leads to defensive violence. To eat and not to be eaten, this is the question. (xv)

Because "Fight for survival is the chief motivation of human behavior," Wolman continues, "the chances for survival depend mainly on one's power, that is, the ability to get food and shelter and to fight off one's enemies" (xvi). Though such concepts as "power" and "enemies" sound simple, when used in theories that seek to codify human behavior, especially in a sophisticated technological culture, they become complex and conflictive. As Fawcett notes, the violence theories

> are many and various: Biological, psychological, social psychological, sociological, political, economic. More precisely, specific theories have attempted to explain violence through individual pathology; psychodynamic developments; stress, frustration and blocked goals; socialization and learning theory; family system processes; social structures and sociopolitical critique.(1)

Two general theories emerge from this confusing mass to explain why some humans are violent and others are not. One: human violence results from physiological damage or alteration to the brain itself, especially to the frontal lobe. Two: violence is a trait acquired through evolution and serves a definable role in the struggle to survive. This theory, which may generally be termed neo-Darwinian, also encompasses Freud's idea that violence originates in the Oedipus complex, with the son wanting to displace the father. From that impulse, Freud argued, all civilization began. Thus, violence was "good." Quite similarly, the neo-Darwins argue that violence is the aggressive male's way of getting females and thus keeping his genetic heritage current in the species. Violence or the lack of violence is determined by the degree to which chemicals (especially serotonin) are present in the blood.

The most obvious shortcoming of both these theories is that neither explains all forms or instances of human violence. While the group of humans that include homicidal maniacs, serial killers, and explosively violent individuals may contain many case histories of child abuse and physical traumas, most individuals who have been abused or suffered head injuries are not violent. In fact, as many tend to be noticeably passive rather than aggressive. The notorious practice of lobotomizing patients, so abused in the 1950s and 1960s and attacked in such novels as Ken Kesey's *One Flew Over the Cuckoo's Nest*, attests to the truth that clinical "damaging" of the brain can subdue rebellious individuals. On the other hand, neo-Darwins argue, as did Freud, that violence serves an ultimate benevolent purpose in human evolution. Gang violence, for example, may be seen as the positive expression of males who have been denied access to the economic sources of our society and who thus revert to fundamental violence as a way of demanding their place in society—especially their access to females. Therefore, a repressive culture is bad and violence is good. However, little rational evidence supports such a theory. If evolution is working, it should take us away from violent behavior, not to it, because violence often destroys the strongest and most able of the species (as those killed in wars). Moreover, while a noticeably small amount of serotonin may be found in excessively violent men, equally small amounts are as often found in men who are ordinary, good citizens. On a more abstract level, as Cynthia Ozick phrases it, how are we to account for the "philosophical criminal of exceptional intelligence and humanitarian purpose, who is driven to commit murder out of an uncompromising idealism" (114)? Obviously, none of the current theories answer such questions.

Leonard D. Eron concludes in *Aggressive Behavior: Current Perspectives* (1994) that "The factors involved in [violent human behavior] range from genetics, neuroanatomy, endrocrinology, and physiology through exogenous substances and firearms to gangs and community influences." However, Eron adds, "No one of these factors by itself can explain much of the variance in the extent and intensity of violent behavior in the population" (Huesman 9). Eron is correct in suggesting that no one theory or explanation adequately explains human violence. The authors of the novels I analyze do not subscribe to scientific explanations or to any theory of violence per se. They neither apply nor make efforts to account for any theory about the origin of violence in Homo Sapiens. Even in those books where a theory of violence may seem to explain behavior of the characters— such as *In Cold Blood*—the authors themselves make no attempt to connect actions to explanatory theory. They simply begin with the commonsense reality that violence dominates our activities. Violence is the catalyst for their creative imaginations, but arguing its origins or biological complexity does not occupy them. Thus, none of the novelists covered by this study espouses a favorite hypothesis or forces characters to live by presupposed dictums. This or that theory has no especial call upon the fictionist's imagination. Actually, the diversity and disagreement surrounding violence are what make it intriguing as a continual subject of fiction.

One final element of violence is pertinent to these theories. As Robert Wright points out in his summary of recent violence theories, "From an evolutionary point of view, the leading cause of violence is maleness" (72). Even a fanatic proponent of gender equality would be hard pressed to refute Wright's observation. Post-World War II technological developments in the art of making war, and recent skirmishes such as the Gulf War, suggest that females are just as capable of destroying a distant enemy so long as pushing a button is all that is required. Yet in the essential violence that instigates eye-to-eye, face-to-face killing, males are still by far the more capable. Males are better equipped physically and mentally to be violent, and—not surprisingly— most acts of violence are therefore committed by males. Quoting Martin Daly and Margo Wilson, Wright notes that "Men have evolved the morphological, physiological and psychological means to be effective users of violence" (72).

The "why" of this gender specifically is as perplexing as the question of why violence at all. Wright summarizes the neo-Darwin view that "During evolution, males have competed over this [female] resource, with the winners impregnating more than their share of women and the losers impregnating few or none." Consequently, males have acquired more genes that incline them "toward fierce combat" (72). As humans have become more "civilized," the direct combat over the female has been sublimated into status seeking or power; but the goal remains the same: to get the female. Of the novels discussed in my analysis, only Toni Morrison's *Beloved* has a female protagonist who directly and alone commits a violent act; and Sethe is reacting to a unique set of circumstances, as we will see.

The only rational conclusion to be drawn from the theories of violence is that they are interesting beginnings but do not explain to any great degree the immense complexity of the human behavior known as "violence."

I refer to the works I discuss as novels of violence. Clearly, the term belongs first to W. M. Frohock and his *The Novel of Violence in America* (1950). However, Frohock assumes "violence" is self-defining and makes no specific effort to fix the term. For my purposes, a novel of violence has violence as its central narrative focus and as the conflict that energizes the plot. This essential violence is distinct from incidental instances of violence that merely attend another major action that is not violent. Further, the novel of violence has a recognizable vocabulary of violence. That is, the text needs a vocabulary precise enough to make the audience immediately aware that violence is intended. Fundamentally the vocabulary is a matter of an author's choosing words that either denote or strongly connote violence. For example: agony, anger, attack, beat, bleed, blood, bones, break, chop, claw, cut, die, flay, gash, gore, groan, guts, hurt, mangle, scream, shredding, slash, stab, tearing, twist, and whip. Obviously many other words and phrases could be added to the list. As in all rhetoric, context is crucial. Consequently this vocabulary will be more meaningful when the individual novels are discussed.

Many novels are published that have this rhetoric of violence and in which violence is the central focus or force. I do not analyze them, however, because in them violence is gratuitous and operates in an aesthetic void. That is, I have not considered novels in which violence is an end in itself. The distinction between gratuitous violence and violence that directs a narrative to intellectual or aesthetic purposefulness is obviously a difficult line to draw. Yet, common sense and experience make that line discernible enough to serve as a guide. I have in mind, for example, such novels as Anne Rice's vampire series and Stephen King's *Rose Matter* (1996). Though these novels fulfill all or most of the criteria I establish for a novel of violence, and though they may have attributes that elevate them above "pulp" fiction, they share one important characteristic that disqualifies them: they use violence primarily or solely to shock or nauseate the reader. Excluding such novels as those written by Rice and King may imply a bias against science fantasy or horror-fiction. To some degree that may be true, for these genres depend heavily on the formula of fright and flight, the occult and the supernatural. Certainly those elements may be used effectively in fiction, as Henry James proved with *Turn of the Screw* or as Kurt Vonnegut shows by satirizing the genre. As a rule, however, their intent is to frighten the reader at the moment of contact rather than to induce any long-lasting aesthetic or intellectual response.

I also eliminate from consideration the "hard boiled" detective fiction emanating from Mickey Spillane and those numerous writers that developed from his influence. In this genre too, the formula calls for periodic violence that is meant primarily to further the plot and re-galvanize the reader's attention. The violence does not transcend the formula that dictates the narrative. Thus the characters are defined by the violence, rather than having the violence act as an adjunct element in a series of actions and responses that constitute a rounded fictional personality. To make another point, I might add that the violence does not reflect the narrative form of the novel. That is, the extratextual potential of the narrative form is flattened rather than expanded by the violence. Spillane's Mike Hammer may gut-shoot someone and then stand over the writhing victim to pontificate about how he has saved America from the Red Peril or his male pals from feminine wiles. Were the violence effectively integrated into the narrative scheme, such explanations (which in themselves ring false) would be superfluous. On the other hand, James M. Cain's crime story *The Postman Always Rings Twice* uses violence in ways that may at first appear gratuitous. Yet, as we will see, Cain uses objectified, emotionless violence to reflect a stark, amoral landscape that subtly combines with fictional style to involve the reader in moral and philosophical questions that neither Frank Chambers (the narrator) nor his violence alone could manage.

The point is that I omit no specific genre; but I do omit novels that in my judgment use violence only to frighten or nauseate the reader. Stephen King is quoted on the back cover of his 1983 Berkley Books edition of *Danse Macabre* as saying that if horror and terror fail to gain his readers' attention he will go for the "gross-out." The spirit of composition underlying King's intent to "gross out" his readers suggests the types of novels that I choose not to analyze.

Some novels that are otherwise outstanding examples of narrative fiction approach but do not fulfill the criteria I establish for a novel of violence. I need briefly to look at several of these "almost" novels so that I might further clarify the meaning of "novel of violence."

Joseph Heller's *Catch-22* contains the bloody, violent "Snowden" scene (chapter 41) in which Yossarian finally discovers the flak wound that is killing the turret gunner Snowden. The climax of the scene is these lines:

> Yossarian ripped open the snaps of Snowden's flak suit and heard himself scream wildly as Snowden's insides slithered own to the floor in a soggy pile and just kept dripping out. . . . Here was God's plenty, all right, he thought bitterly as he stared—liver, lungs, kidneys, ribs, stomach and bits of the stewed tomatoes Snowden had eaten that day for lunch.      (449)

This scene contains the rhetoric of violence and the appropriate horror and gore to fashion a lasting psychological impact on the reader. Consequently, the scene is artistically effective. Yet, *Catch-22* is not a novel of violence. If the entire novel revolved around the Snowden scene, if the novel duplicated similar descriptions of the various ways in which airmen are mangled or killed, and if such scenes were thematic or formed a rhetorical motif, the novel would be a novel of violence. Overall, however, *Catch-22* does not revolve around violence. The violence in Heller's narrative is best symbolized by "The Soldier in White," who is "constructed entirely of gauze, plaster and a thermometer" (171). Heller never divulges precisely what type of violence put this anonymous victim in the hospital. With "The Soldier in White," as with Snowden, we do not have a sense of a person or persons intentionally inflicting violence on another human. We simply see the consequence of some anonymous viciousness. Though foreshadowed, the Snowden scene is incidental to the larger context of the 463 page novel, not essential.

The same incidental violence is true of Larry McMurtry's epic western *Lonesome Dove*. Its most graphic scene of violence is in chapter 57, which presents the half-breed Blue Duck and his cutthroats. Dog Face has been shot and the others are tired of listening to his dying complaints:

> Dog Face continued to moan. Then the Kiowa sat on his chest. . . . One Kiowa cut his belt and two more pulled his pants off. Before Lorena could even turn her head, they castrated him. Another slashed a knife across his forehead and began to rip off his hair. Dog Face screamed again, but it was soon muffled as the Kiowas held his head and stuffed his own bloody organs into his mouth, shoving them down his throat with the handle of a knife. (498)

Here too the rhetoric or violence and the psychological impact are evident. Too, we do see one person intentionally inflicting violence upon another. However, though the consequences are gruesome, the scene is incidental rather than essential to the narrative. No other scene in the novel approaches its graphic depiction of human-to-human violence. While other characters die from snakebite, gunshot, Indian attack, hanging, and other calamities, violence remains secondary in a 945-page narrative that is more a frontier domestic comedy than a western novel of violence.

In a somewhat different vein, the trait that prevents a novel such as Walter Van Tilburg Clark's *The Ox-Bow Incident* from being a novel of violence is that it implicitly promises to concentrate on violence but ultimately reneges on that narrative obligation. The entirety of Clark's narrative builds up to and revolves around a disturbingly violent act: the lynchings of three innocent men. Clark emphasizes the hangings for 64 pages, from the time the victims are caught till they are hanged. However, when confronted by the brutal physiological reality of what occurs when three men are lynched, Clark becomes rhetorically demure. He says two of the men died instantly, which is unlikely in such a jury-rigged hanging, and that only Martin was "squirming up and down like an impaled worm, his face bursting with compressed blood" (266). This is aseptic rhetoric for such an appalling context, especially since Clark is trying to make a strong case against the horrors of vigilantism. Moreover, the narrator Art Croft, is a hardened cowboy, a veteran of western justice, and an experienced brawler. He would hardly describe a face as "bursting with compressed blood." Because of such authorial squeamishness, *The Ox-Bow Incident* loses narrative power and credibility. Consequently, a narrative that could have been energized by the violence that is innate to its plot is diminished by authorial failure to commit creative energy to that violence.

The title of Flannery O'Connor's *The Violent Bear It Away* suggests that it should be analyzed as a novel of violence. However, though O'Connor alludes to rape, gunshot wounds, child abuse and several other actions that typically qualify as violence, her allusions are incidental rather than central to the narrative design and purpose. Actually, *The Violent Bear It Away* may stake greater claim to violence but evoke it less than many other American novels. It is grotesque, but it is not a novel of violence. It especially lacks a specific rhetoric of violence. Further, it fails to attain the artistic integrity of O'Connor's best fiction. Her *Wise Blood* is perhaps one of the three or four great American short novels; and short stories such as "A Good Man is Hard to Find" help define the genre. By comparison, *The Violent Bear It Away* is a noble experiment at combining theological satire, Southern Gothic, and Faulknerian humor, but succeeds only partially as an articulated work of art. When compared to a novella such as Katherine Anne Porter's *Noon Wine*, *The Violent Bear It Away* is noticeably disordered in structure and conception. Moreover, O'Connor's significant gifts of Negative Capability and biting irony are better demonstrated in her other works.

As for the novels I do analyze, I have focused on those written after 1930. That somewhat arbitrary beginning date is chosen for two reasons. First, no modern American novel written before that year conforms to my definition of the "novel of violence." By my estimate, William Faulkner's *Light in August* is the first modern American novel of violence. I do not presume, however, that Faulkner is the first American novelist to use graphic violence as a fundamental narrative element. Frank Norris probably holds that distinction. However, in his most violent novel *McTeague* (1899), Norris makes violence more incidental than central to narrative form and style. Moreover, though Norris clearly understood that violence is bequeathed to us by genetics, he was determined to chronicle the naturalistic trap in which human beings struggle. That single-mindedness blinded him to the full potential of literary violence. As a result, his novels are thesis-driven. Jerome Loving states the case for Norris sympathetically when he notes that Norris depicted "the interior struggle in which the 'brute' of prehistoric man fought with his better, socialized self" (x). Even a character as memorable as McTeague is psychologically oversimplified because he is made to serve as persona for the irrepressible brute-self. Not until Faulkner do we encounter the irony that results when multidimensional characters such as Joe Christmas, Joanna Burden, and Percy Grimm are set "free" to deal as best they can with violent instincts that control their sexual, social, and familial lives.

I also choose 1930 as a beginning date because W. M. Frohock in *The Novel of Violence in America* attended to the American novel from its beginning up to 1950 (his revised edition was 1957). Though it remains useful, Frohock's study is out of date and lacking in several significant areas. He does not, for instance define "violence" or "novel of violence," assuming incorrectly that "violence" is a self-defining term. Nonetheless, he presents a serviceable background discussion of violence as it generally appears in American fiction before 1950 and as earlier critics perceived it. I have chosen, therefore, not to reexamine the few "violent" texts that mark pre-1930 American literature and that have been previously termed novels of violence and analyzed under that rubric. I reexamine only two of the novels Frohock discusses (*Light in August* and *The Postman Always Rings Twice*) because each uses violence in ways that Frohock does not discuss and that had not previously been seen in American fiction. Each novel also heralds the novels of violence that follow it.

Another study of literary violence, Frederick J. Hoffman's *The Moral No: Death and the Modern Imagination* (1964), simultaneously analyzes war novels and explains why I do not extensively include that seemingly violent genre. While Hoffman neither defines "violence" nor limits his commentary to American literature, he does focus intelligently on the war novel. His observations are wide-ranging, but his primary thesis is that "The two major wars of our century are the focus of any discussion of modern violence. From every point of view, sociological, psychological, and aesthetic, they have helped severely to dislocate the forms according to which force in the past was contained" (139). The value of Hoffman's analysis vis-à-vis violence is his survey of and commentary on the novels of World War II and his effort to understand the moral questions raised by individual and cultural violent behavior. His discussion of such novels as Lawrence Kahn's *Able One Four*, Peter Bowman's *Beach Red*, Colin McDougall's *Execution*, William Hoffman's

*The Trumpet Unblown*, and Glenn Sire's *The Deathmakers* is the best available material on novels that are now seldom read. Hoffman recognizes, borrowing from Freud, that violence is an instinct, not learned behavior, and that war is the highest expression of that cultural phenomenon. "All men instinctively desire to act violently," Hoffman says, "but it is only in time of war that this desire is released and 'used'" (205). Hoffman probably should modify his war statement to read "released and used with society's or the state's blessings," but otherwise his observation is a clear summary of an important point regarding the origin and method of human violence. Ironically, like *Catch-22*, none of the war novels Hoffman discusses is expressly violent and does not satisfy the definition of novel of violence as used in this study.

Another important element of both the Frohock and Hoffman studies in that they (and practically all others who previously wrote of violence) presume that violence is evil, a Great Negative that obstructs the road to human perfection. That traditional view, however, is now open to question and I do not presuppose its validity in any of my analyses.

The critical premise underlying my analyses is that much can be learned from the texts of good literature, that the critic should never allow his or her ego to obscure the creative imagination that produced those texts, and that clearly stated and reasoned textual analysis still matters. I am a pragmatic pluralist in that I employ any methodology that facilitates understanding of the novel at hand. New Historicism, Feminism, Marxism, Deconstructionism, Lacanianism, Freudianism and all other critical theories fascinate me. Admittedly, some of the fascination comes from the ego-centered superciliousness of the writers who advocate such theories, but the theories nonetheless intrigue me. In other words, no one methodology or one theory is to blame for what I think or write about a text.

I sympathize with Frank Lentricchia, who recently confessed his feelings for literary criticism:

> Over the past ten years, I've pretty much stopped reading literary criticism, because most of it isn't literary. But criticism it is of a sort—the sort that stems from the sense that one is morally superior to the writers that one is supposedly describing. This posture of superiority is assumed when those writers represent the major islands of Western literary tradition, the central cultural engine—so it goes—of racism, poverty, sexism,

homophobia and imperialism: a cesspool that literary
critics would expose for mankind's benefit. . . . It is impossible, this much is clear, to exaggerate the heroic
self-inflation of academic literary criticism.    (3)

Like Lentricchia, my own allegiance remains to fictional
texts such as those that animated my imagination and curiosity
long before I began to read academic criticism. *Light in August,
For Whom the Bell Tolls, Blood Meridian, Beloved*: those are
the kinds of texts that still serve as my intellectual and spiritual
mentors. Humbled by such texts, I try to write some readable,
thoughtful analyses of several fascinating novels that epitomize
the "novel of violence" published in the United States since
1930.

Another crucial adjective appears in the title of the study:
American. That word, too, adds a dimension to my definition of
violence that needs some clarification. H. Rap Brown, a popular
black activist of the day, coined a familiar quotation in 1967: "Violence is as American as cherry pie." Rap Brown was correct, of
course. He would have been equally correct if he had interna-
tionalized his observation: Violence is as human as veinal
blood. America has no exclusive claim to violence. Yet violence
seems more closely identified with and acutely felt in the American personality than in any other culture. As Michael
Kowalewski notes, "American writers have persistently, almost
obsessively, turned violence (and I refer here to depictions of
physical violence or pain and its aftermath, not psychological
violence or examples of metaphorical, 'discursive' violence)
into an imaginative resource" (4). Perhaps this assessment is
true because the American novelists have tried to expose a harsh
truth about the American character that the general population
does not wish to confront. Americans have pretended from the
nation's beginning that when we emigrated to the New Eden we
closed out our genetic bank account in the Old World and freed
ourselves to pursue happiness across the meadow lands of tranquillity. The truth is, those genes that made us intrepid enough
to venture into the wilderness were the same genes that intensified the natural tendency to violence. Mixed, mingled, and re-
generated, those genes have made America's history a
hemophile's delight.

Yet, we have refused to admit that we are a bloodthirsty
nation. To admit, in other words, that we are human. A few
years ago, Cormac McCarthy noted the dangers of such refusal:

There's no such thing as life without bloodshed, . . .
I think the notion that the species can be improved in
some way, that everyone could live in harmony, is a really dangerous idea. Those who are afflicted with this
notion are the first ones to give up their souls, their
freedom. Your desire that it be that way will enslave
you and take your life vacuous.

(Quoted in Woodward, 36)

This refusal to acknowledge violence is reflected in our literature. Considering the thousands of novels written by Americans
since 1823 when James Fenimore Cooper published *The Pilot*
and *The Pioneers*, surprisingly few deal directly with violence.
While many *contain* violence, most treat violence incidentally,
casually. Seldom it is the central focus of the narrative. Those
relatively rare novels in which violence *is* central come closer
than any others to being The American Novels. Those are the
ones this study analyzes.

# William Faulkner's
# *Light in August*

Richard Chase recognized many years ago that no novel is "more characteristically American" than *Light in August* (210). Chase likens Faulkner's masterpiece to *The Prairie, Moby-Dick, Huckleberry Finn*, and other American standards that are full of romance, melodrama, comedy, and symbols of light and dark. Since 1957, when Chase made his assessment of its epitomizing qualities and the elements that mark it as typically American, *Light in August* has been scrutinized and analyzed from every conceivable perspective and from the viewpoint of every possible critical bias. Despite such thorough dissecting, however, the one element that accounts for its fascination and durability has remained comparatively unexamined. The uniqueness of *Light in August* stems from Faulkner's development of an archetypal protagonist who exploits violence to certify his membership in the human race. That little noted but original use of violence as a method of narrative control and character analysis greatly influenced subsequent American novels of violence. For that reason, I want briefly to revisit Faulkner so that his place at the forefront of the modern American novel of violence might be definitively established.

Thought limited in scope, and despite the glaring error of consistently referring to Percy Grimm as Percy Grime, W. M. Frohock's analysis of *Light in August* helps locate it within the milieu of violence where it attains its most meaningful significance. Frohock notes the ten days in which the plot of the narrative unfolds, then realizes that "on the other plane, we have had the tortuously unfolded stories of how the principal characters got the neuroses which have brought them here, each according to the inexorable law of his own personality, to make the catastrophe inevitable" (154). These characters are tortured, Frohock implies, because they "feel the impact of the violence which they perform, like Christmas—or witness, like Hightower." Frohock's most useful observation vis-à-vis violence, however, is his comment that characters such as Christmas "are aware of being either the agents, or in danger, of an evil which is always abroad in the world, incarnate sometimes in an individual, sometimes in a mob, sometimes in nature itself" (156). Though Frohock does not elucidate this lurking "evil," and though he implies a moral judgment about violence that recent studies do not support, his observation touches on the essential question we raised earlier about the source and purpose of human violence.

Faulkner develops two simple but ingenious narrative techniques to make *Light in August* the foremost pre-World War II novel of violence. First, he constructs his text so that the incidental scenes of violence lead like spokes to the definitive center—the scene in which Christmas decapitates Joanna Burden. Second, he arranges the major characters in pairs. This pairing device is especially pertinent in a study of violence because Faulkner is careful to make one member of the pair more violent than the other. This unique coupling technique in turn foreshadows the action of and directs the narrative into the central scene with Christmas and Joanna.

Let us look first at the incidental scenes of violence. These foreshadowing scenes entail most possible types of violence: child abuse, sexual assault, filicide, castration, and suicide, to name a few. As Harold Hungerford correctly recognizes, "*Light in August* is a kind of private war among strangers" (193). One crucial feature we should note about this "private war" is that these incidental scenes of violence are empowered by a significant rhetoric of violence. Two short and quotable, yet typical, examples of this rhetoric of violence will suffice to make the point. One is Christmas's assault of the young Negro whore and the second is Grimm's attack on Christmas. As the added italics point out, the matrix of these quotations is filled with words that connote violence:

> He *kicked* her hand, *kicking* into and through a *choked* wail of surprise and *fear*. She began to *scream*, he *jerking* her up, *clutching* her by the arm, *hitting* at her with wide, wild *blows*, *striking* at the voice perhaps, feeling her flesh anyway, enclosed by the womanshenegro and the haste.                    (116)

> When they approached to see what [Grimm] was about,
> they saw that the man was not *dead* yet, and when
> they saw what Grimm was doing one of the men gave a
> *choked cry* and stumbled back into the wall and began
> to *vomit*. Then Grimm too *sprang* back, *flinging* behind
> him the *bloody* butcher *knife*. 'Now you'll let white
> women alone, even in *hell*,' he said. . . . For a long mo-
> ment [Christmas] looked up at them with peaceful and
> unfathomable and unbearable eyes. Then his face,
> body, all, seemed to collapse, to *fall* in upon itself, and
> from out the *slashed* garments about his hips and loins
> the pent black *blood* seemed to rush like a released
> breath. It seemed to *rush* out of his pale body like the
> rush of sparks from a rising *rocket*; upon that black
> *blast* the man seemed to rise soaring into their memo-
> ries forever and ever.                      (345-346)

Faulkner uses these and other powerful incidental scenes
of violence as spokes leading to the murder of Joanna Burden.
He does not, however, do the predictable and locate this essential
scene of violence in the literal center of the text. Instead, he reveals the first segment of the murder early, then lets carnage
wind through the narrative, gaining details incrementally. This
incremental technique helps control a text that follows no traditional organizational methods. Though we learn early of the
beheading, only later do we see Christmas with the straight razor
in hand, hear Joanna trying to make him pray, and learn of the
old Civil War pistol with which Joanna had hoped to kill them
both. The power of the murder scene rests in its understated
horror, in the myriad of psychological nuances and narrative
foreshadowing that lead to it, and in its contrast with the incidental scenes of violence. Ironically, this essential scene of violence is opaque when compared to these incidental scenes. Furthermore, although it contains the rhetoric of violence typical of
the other scenes, it lacks their concentrated impact. Like the two
columns of smoke that rise above Joanna Burden's burnt
home—"one the heavy density of burning coal" and the second
"a tall yellow column" (21)—the murder is as nebulous as a
cloud and as beguiling.

Significantly, the scene is first described by an inarticulate
farmer whose droll account introduces the macabre humor that
thereafter attends the murder and enhances its horror:

> She was lying on the floor. Her head had been cut
> pretty near off; . . . he was afraid to try to pick her up
> and carry her out because her head might come clean

> off. . . . And he said that what he was scared of hap-
> pened. Because the cover fell open and she was laying
> on her side, facing one way, and her head was turned
> clean around like she was looking behind her.   (66, 67)

The verbal inarticulateness with the macabre and ironic "look-ing" motif suggests that we as readers must articulate the mur-der with its surrounding moral complex.

How well we realize that process depends in large mea-sure on how clearly we understand Faulkner's pairing tech-nique. The significant pairs that require analyzing are Lena Grove and Joanna Burden; Byron Bunch and Lucas Burch; Gail Hightower and Percy Grimm; and the furniture repairman and his wife who close out the narrative. Faulkner depends upon this pairing technique to further his psychological evaluation of Christmas and Joanna, the conjoined figures around whom the entire narrative revolves.

Using a pair of mules plodding "slow and terrific" (4) in the fictive distance as an associative metaphor, Faulkner imme-diately introduces Lena Grove and Joanna Burden. Lena waits in very real time and space for the mules to overtake her so that she may catch a ride, while Joanna's presence is symbolized by the ominous smoke standing like a sentinel on the horizon. Though the two women do not know each other and do not meet, their sisterhood is later confirmed when Lena occupies Joanna's cabin, where she gives birth to baby "Joey." It is signifi-cant that Lena's bastard child is born at the site of Joanna's mur-der because the function of this mismatched pair is to emphasize the sexuality of the two women and the reader's ironic judg-ment of that sexuality.

Faulkner uses a subtle visual motif to stress the moral, psychological differences between the two women and to fix the reader's attitude toward them. Quite simply, he uncovers much more of Joanna than of Lena. He depicts Joanna thrashing about in all her naked lust, assuming "erotic attitudes and gestures as a Beardsley of the time of Petronius might have drawn" (193). We see her in "the wild throes of nymphomania" with "her clothing torn to ribbons" and "her hair wild." We hear her lustful cries of "Negro! Negro! Negro!" (192-193). Her "fits of jealous rage" and her ability to love "with such fury" (192) astonish even Christmas—certainly no stranger to violence and aberrant sexual behavior. He is terrified by the "imperious and over-riding fury of those nights" (193). Such graphic scenes—filled with the rhetoric of violence—compel us to make moral judgments about Joanna. Once we get past our own erotic response, we appropriate society's moral norm and judge her sexual outbursts rather harshly.

On the other hand, we have no opportunity to play voyeur to Lena's sexual activity. All of Lena's trysts occur beyond the open window, in the dark, far offstage. We have nothing but her self-serving recollections of the assignations as our source of information. We see only the consequence of Lena's acts, not the acts themselves. Both physically and figuratively, she remains unexposed. We do not know whether the sexual encounters that led to her pregnancy were passionately violent or bland as mating clams of if she was the seducer or the seduced. Moreover, we do not much wonder about the details of her sexuality as we advance through the narrative. Joanna's graphic sexuality and numerous other compelling actions demand our attention, and we suspend judgment of Lena altogether or see her, like Irvin Howe says, as "the good unruffled vegetable" (209). We see Joanna, on the other hand, as the corrupt fruit from a decayed Puritan vine.

A moment's reflection tells us that Lena's illicit affair with Burch is no less reprehensible than Joanna's affair with Christmas. That one affair culminates in comedy and the other in tragedy should not affect the moral basis on which we make our judgment against fornication. Yet we judge Joanna's acts to be more licentious. We make such judgment first of all because Faulkner dictates our responses with his over-exposure of Joanna. On a more subtle plane, however, we make such harsh judgment because Joanna's sexuality is not a natural consequence of biological compulsions that overwhelm a naive rustic. Joanna is an educated, middle-aged, and very subtle woman. Unlike Lena, who simply copulates without attaching any ulterior motives to the act. Joanna's sexuality is part of a complex agenda of revenge and redemption. She envisions her pregnancy as proof to a hostile community that she has flaunted two of its greatest taboos: non-marital sex and cohabitation with a Negro. Eupheus Hines, we recall, has murdered one man and facilitated his own daughter's death for breaking these same rules. True to her family name and tradition, Joanna imagines that she stoically will bear the black man's burden, as she has borne years of ostracism and insults. Like a modern Hester Prynne, she wants to flaunt her sin and force society to change its attitude toward her, thereby to celebrate her final victory over that society. Unlike Hester, however, Joanna's desire for revenge and redemption becomes violently destructive, and we cannot forgive that excess.

We especially disapprove of her violent manipulation of Christmas, who has been a victim of white female vindictiveness since infancy. To Joanna, his death is the fulfillment of her earlier prophecy that "it would be better if we both were dead (206). She knows that brandishing the inoperative Civil War pistol will lead to her own murder and that Christmas will be executed for that murder. No matter what Christmas has done to Joanna, we sympathize with him as a victim of female neuroses and because of the alienation that such treatment has caused. He is, as W. M. Frohock recognized years ago, one of those doomed characters who suffer "under an unholy amount of stress" (156). As citizens of a post-modernist madhouse, we empathize with that predicament. Therefore, when Joanna exploits Christmas, we lose sympathy for her, no matter what justifications she may have for her actions. This disapproval is of course ironic because we judge Joanna's manipulating Christmas as being more reprehensible than his cold-bloodedly murdering her. Such an ethical contradiction is another example of how Faulkner continually goads us about our ambiguous attitudes toward violence, especially violence in the context of male and female relationships.

Of the two women, Lena and Joanna, Faulkner clearly favors the less violent Lena. He champions her, however, only to the point where her behavior does not counteract his own epistemology of violence. Though he admires her innocuous tranquillity, he makes her pay dearly for it. To attain such serenity she must sacrifice her intelligence. Lena has little awareness of history and place—two elements vital in shaping the personalities of the other characters. Consequently, she has no consciousness of the past and little concern for the future. In polar contrast to Joanna Burden who is tied to the past and determined to manipulate the future, Lena exists in the present moment. Reminiscent of Robert Burns' mouse, Lena is blessed by being touched only by immediate concerns, untroubled by backward glances and future prospects. She is blissfully stupid and stupidly blissful.

Faulkner shows how little regard he has for Lena's high-priced tranquillity by placing her between the two dumbest characters in the narrative: Lucas Burch and Byron Bunch. Superficially very dissimilar, Burch and Bunch are joined because of their relationships with Lena, because of her disingenuous refusal to distinguish their names, and because of their ultimate battle over her. Neither can match the violence that Christmas personifies. Of the two, however, Burch is distinctly more aggressive in fulfilling his goals and quite willing to resort to violence when he knows that his own violence will not be countered by superior violence. He is aggressive enough to pursue and impregnate Lena, a sexual drive that is lacking in the meek and mild Byron Bunch. Moreover, Burch's seductive use of violence is demonstrated by his responses to Christmas and Bunch: he passively accepts Christmas's assaults, one almost homicidal, but is quick to "beat the hell" out of Bunch to avoid commitment to Lena.

The entirety of the Burch-Bunch-Lena romantic triangle is a seriocomic counterpart to the vicious "love" affair between Christmas and Joanna. Lena Groves does not care whether she gets a Burch or a Bunch, since she has no abiding emotional involvement with either man. In contrast to Joanna Burden's calculating, violent manipulation of Christmas, Lena's "pleasant-faced" (368) disinterest in the two buffoons who attend her sets the tone for the comic substructure of the text. It is a comic light that makes the violent narrative only darker by contrast.

Byron Bunch's ludicrous affair with Lena is a vaudevillian version of the eternal male-female conflict, in contrast to the deadly violence of the Christmas-Joanna affair. Just as Christmas cannot bring himself to separate from Joanna, so too is Byron enthralled by Lena the teenage earth mother. Why Byron is so attracted to her, however, remains unclear, even to him. Whereas Christmas's slavery to Joanna's sexuality is graphically convincing, growing from biological laws and compulsions, Byron's servitude to Lena is farcical. Byron does not even have carnality to explain his servitude to Lena, considering that his libido is minuscule and that she has no intention to accommodating it in any case. He seems at best asexual, and his one pathetic attempt as copulation with Lena (chapter 21) is a comedy of Eros. The scene is a narrative counterpoint to Christmas's brutal rape of Joanna and to Burch's all too obvious past success with Lena. It is, significantly, an episode told by the furniture repairer who has himself just copulated with a willing and satisfied mate. He describes Bunch as "the kind of fellow you wouldn't see the first glance if he was alone by himself in the bottom of a empty concrete swimming pool" (369). He finds Byron's emasculating subservience to Lena humorously incredible. Like us, he knows that Lena is perhaps estrous, but hardly worthy of such enchantment.

Burch's salvation is that he is immune to Lena's country charms. Shiftless, greedy, and marked for comedy by his little popcorn scar, Burch is a dime-store dandy—one of those indigenous Southern no accounts that Faulkner, Flannery O'Connor, Eudora Welty and other Southern writers delight in parodying. Faulkner toys with rather than condemns such sawdust Casanovas. In fact, Faulkner sees some redeemable qualities in Burch. Using an ironic reversal of natural law, he brings Burch and Bunch together in a violent mating ritual:

> It does not last long. Byron knew that it was not going to. But he did not hesitate. He just crept up until he could see the other where he stopped, looking at the crouching and unwarned figure. 'You're bigger than me,' Byron thought. 'But I dont care. You've had every other advantage of me. And I dont care about that neither. You've done throwed away twice inside of nine months what I aint had in thirty-five years. And now I'm going to get the hell beat out of me and I dont are about that, neither.'
>
> It does not last long. Brown, whirling, takes advantage of his astonishment even. He did not believe that any man, catching his enemy sitting, would give him a chance to get on his feet, even if the enemy were not the larger of the two. He would not have done it himself. And the fact that the smaller man did do it when he would not have, was worse than insult: it was ridicule. So he fought with even a more savage fury than he would have if Byron had sprung upon his back without warning: with the blind and desperate valor of a starved and cornered rat he fought.          (326-327)

The scene is a comic rendering of a serious biological ritual. One of the most prevalent explanations for the origin and purpose of violence is that the violent male impregnates the most women and thereby instills his genes into the race. In other words, to the violent go the mates. Nowhere in that theory, however, does it say that the violent must linger to assist in the rearing of the offspring. Thus, in the biological sense, Burch is the ideal mate. As the violent male, he makes his genetic deposit. Then he leaves the worry and fret of childbearing to the female and whomever else she might procure to assist.

Thus Faulkner passes no severe judgment against Burch for impregnating Lena and subsequently deserting her to bear his bastard child. That scenario is neither rare nor prosecutable, and Lena is as much to blame as he. Though a scoundrel, Burch does not fall prey to Lena's dedicated search for a mate. He flees, thus clearing the way for Byron to be appropriated as a surrogate father, traveling companion, and provider. In his relationship with Christmas and in his groveling desire to gain the $1000 reward, Burch (as Brown) is harshly portrayed; yet he ultimately has the strength and wits to escape the biological trap. Like Lena, he flies when gender and social roles threaten to confine him. In that flight, he avoids the sexual servitude that stifles Byron's freedom and that kills Christmas. Burch's moves are instinctive acts of self-preservation, like Lena's travels. In a violent world, such self-preservation is to be applauded.

Percy Grimm and Gail Hightower are paired in their blind allegiance to historic tradition and to war, and by being present at the scene of Christmas's death. They also both experience a period of sloth, from which only one emerges. Again we see the violent-passive combination that distinguishes Faulkner's pairing technique. Hightower is the most submissive male in the narrative, whereas Grimm in one brief, sharply focused scene surpasses even Christmas in his explosive violence.

Given their polar opposite personalities we need to remind ourselves that the same Southern myth of brave warriors and frail womankind that shapes Grimm and offers the rationale for his castration of Christmas also shapes Hightower. Adrift in the haze of the past, dreaming of a grandfather who fought to preserve Southern maidenhood, Hightower has no defense against life's terrifying actuality. His own Fair Damsel is a wife who prefers sexually aggressive males over an impotent visionary. Because neither her husband nor the quaint Jefferson society can accept this biological imperative, Mrs. Hightower dies a very real death shattered on a Memphis street.

Hightower, however, never assimilates this violent experience into any kind of cognitive reasoning or responsible action. He loses himself instead in a stubborn resolve to escape real violence by glorifying the chicken-stealing exploits of his long-dead ancestor. A moral and physical coward, he ponders the abstractions of sin, redemption, and epic bravery to a point near madness. He dies with wife and church lost, and with his stale, flaccid corporeity mocking the imaginary, violent warriors on fiery steeds that he values more than wife and worships more than God. Above all others in the novel except Christmas, Gail Hightower personifies the tragedy of American idealism permeated by Calvinist dogma. His Christian meekness disguises a deadly failure to act. Ironically, Hightower never suspects that even the violence of active chicken thievery is glorious when compared to his own moral and physical stagnation.

Like Hightower, Grimm too was once "lazy, recalcitrant, without ambition" (336). Unlike Hightower, however, Grimm is saved—not by God's grace but by culturally sanctioned violence. Grimm is redeemed from his sloth by "the new civilian-military act" (335). Resurrected by military training in the National Guard, he now has "a sublime and implicit faith in physical courage and blind obedience, and a belief that the white race is superior to any and all other races" (336). Grimm is the 1930s resurrection of the mythic ancestor that Hightower worships, though his name suggests how the Gray Ghost of the Confederacy has transmogrified into the Grim Reaper. Superficially he personifies the ideal patriotic American, simultaneously strengthened and flawed by traditional American ideologies. He espouses the rhetoric of the Republic and is eager to fight for Woodrow Wilson's illusion of a safe world and democracy. His life's major disappointment is having been too young to kill and die in World War I. Now in the Depression, his patriotism has ossified into nazism—the politics that result when zealots mix chauvinism with violence.

In Christmas Grimm discovers the "foreigner" against whom he can legally vent his rage. Ostensibly setting out to guarantee Christmas a fair trial as promised by the democratic state, Grimm is overjoyed when the facades of peaceful and honorable justice fall away to reveal a primordial, violent hunt. He despises Christmas because by being poor and "black" and the victim of Calvinist absolutism Christmas has no delusions about conventional society and is thereby freed from its strictures. Christmas is, in short, a walking denial of Grimm's militaristic, quasi-religious gore. Worse insofar as Grimm is concerned, Christmas's living with Brown hints at a homoeroticism that Grimm represses in himself and for which his martial bravado is partially a mask. His castrating Christmas is the ultimate and predictable psychic explosion of the volatile mix of sexual, political, and social conflicts that fuel his energies. It is with fine irony that he tries pathetically to rationalize his violence in terms of the romantic Southern past, claiming to be an errant knight protecting Southern maidens. In reality he is a morally—and probably sexually—impotent killer.

Taken at his best, Grimm could be admirable—another Robert E. Lee or John J. Pershing. This potential is suggested by the fact that Jeffersonians "had suddenly accepted Grimm with respect and perhaps a little awe and a deal of actual faith and confidence, as though somehow his vision and patriotism and pride in the town, the occasion, had been quicker and truer than theirs" (340). The males "were almost at the pitch where they might die for him" (340). However, when Grimm castrates Christmas, he loses their allegiance. The men literally separate themselves from his action, one even vomiting in revulsion. Nothing in the text proves that these men are rabid or abnormal in their original support of Grimm and certainly nothing suggests they are wrong in their subsequent rejection of him. Furthermore, the sober tone of the passage, especially when contrasted to previous contextual ironies such as the scene in which the Mottstown idlers "clotted about the square" to gossip endlessly about the white "nigger" (259), strongly suggests that Faulkner agrees with the Jeffersonians in this particular instance.

Unlike Eupheus Hines and Christmas, both who also focus their violence on individuals, Grimm is neither a lunatic who is drunk on the sour mash of religion nor an alienated psychopath. Especially if we accept Jean Paul Sartre's premise that the individual is often violent so that he or she will be recognized as human and accepted into the group, Grimm is a well-adjusted, productive member of society. He keeps the violence that identifies him as animal confined to the limits of society's values. Thus Faulkner, himself a frustrated warrior, does not condemn Grimm's militarism or violence per se. It is certainly preferable to Hightower's odious lethargy. What Faulkner does unilaterally oppose is the narrow focus that Grimm's violence assumes or the degree to which it is specifically targeted.

Grimm's unforgivable flaw, then, is the racism that results when his violence is not adequately diffused by significant motive. He directs his violence at Christmas not because Christmas threatens anarchy or even a major disruption in civil routine. Gavin Stevens' quick legal deal to give Christmas life in prison implies how readily the townspeople are willing to get "justice" done and resume their mundane lives. They will miss neither Christmas nor Joanna Burden, who are mere aberrations. Grimm turns his violence toward Christmas not because he is a public threat, therefore, but because he is (supposedly) black and because he activates the homophobic guilt that Grimm suppresses. Neither motive justifies the degree to which Grimm specifies his violence. Only much larger callings, such as Casting Satan from Heaven, Protecting Southern Womanhood, Keeping the World Safe for Democracy warrant the type of violence that Grimm microcosmically demonstrates.

This distinction between targeting a cause or hating a crime and singling out an individual to execute for that crime is a rather vague line of moral demarcation. Yet it seems to be the border that Faulkner sets between civilization and savageness. This border is not marked as an absolute criterion for behavior (not like a county line or a state boundary), but is seen only in the traces left by human actions and our reactions to those traces. We simply *know*, for instance, that Eupheus Hines is wrong to let his daughter Milly die in childbirth and that Percy Grimm is wrong to castrate Christmas. The certainty of "wrongness" is less distinct, however, when grandfather Hightower is shot in the chicken house or Joanna Burden is decapitated in her ante-bellum home. Just how we *know* these distinctions, however, is as nebulous as the dust raised by wagon wheels on a hot August day or the smoke wafting above a burning house. Faulkner seems to imply that civil danger ensues when we so blur this line between hating the action and the actor that, like Percy Grimm, we fail to see when we have crossed it. Later Hemingway will have Robert Jordan contemplate the same dilemma and decide that "no man has a right to take another man's life unless it is to prevent something worse happening to other people" (304). Though cast in entirely different circumstances, Robert Jordan's aphorism seems to clarify Faulkner's attitude toward Percy Grimm.

We could continue the analysis of more traditional pairings in the narrative, such as the marriage pairings of Simon and Mrs. McEachern and Eupheus and Mrs. Hines. In these pairing also the divisions between violence and passivity are pronounced. The husbands are fanatically violent whereas the wives are little more than incarnated acquiescence. We need not restate the data already garnered from the other marriage pairings. There is, however, one final pair that requires some explanation: the furniture repairer and his wife. Because the furniture repairer and his wife occupy the crucial valedictory episode (chapter 21), the foremost question is how do they complement what we have already learned about violence in *Light in August*? There are two feasible answers to that question, neither of which contradicts the violence or pairing motifs previously developed. The first is that the repairer and his wife duplicate characteristics already established in the narrative but bring us back to a comic equilibrium to offset the horror of the earlier chapters. The second is that they offer a spurious sense of the familiar that reemphasizes the degree of violence and incompatibility confirmed by the earlier pairs.

First, the furniture repairer and his wife obviously coincide with the other pairs in the violence motif in several fundamental particulars. They are paired by the pun in the name of his profession (repairer) and by marriages like the Hightowers and others. They continue and conclude the sexual motif that begins with Lena's pregnancy and then permeates the narrative construct. Moreover, the husband is a member of a rather large club of otherwise secondary characters who assume crucial roles as narrators, such as Byron Bunch, Mrs. Hines, and Gavin Stevens. Like the other wives, the repairer's wife is subservient. In psychology and attitude, however, the repairer and his wife do not fit the paradigm established in the earlier text for partners. Here in closure we suddenly have the only harmonious pair—married or otherwise. We need only glance back at the Hightowers, the McEacherns, and Christmas-Joanna relationships to prove this point. The psychobabble buzz word "dysfunctional" comes nowhere close to describing the collective pain caused by these "love" relationships. That the repairer and his wife do not fit the paradigm is quite the whole point. They communicate with each other, they share a sexual relationship that is mutually satisfying but not abusive, and they have a sense of humor. They are, in other words, the exceptional partners in the narrative.

They are not, however, the exception in American society. They bring us back to the everyday world with which we are familiar and more comfortable. We do not routinely encounter the violence that we see in Christmas or Joanna or Grimm or McEachern. This violence demands introspection, creates tension, forces agonizing reappraisals of our own violent natures. The prevalent tone of the narrative before chapter 21 is mordant.

Even the comedic elements of the Byron Bunch and Lucas Burch characterizations are negatively cast. That is, there is a comedy based on buffoonery and social crassness. It is elemental comedy, with no verbal wit or subtlety and considerable violence. With the repairer and his wife, however, we are relieved of the violent tensions that dominate the other pairs. We move to a comfortable, familiar setting where the tone is loving and gentle and the repartee is spiced with puns, innuendo, and double entendre. It is a very private, intimate scene. The repairer and his spouse may be rustic folk like many others we meet in the narrative, but they are youthful, bright, freely erotic, emancipated from Calvinistic repressions and the Southern past. They enjoy the present moment. They are, in a word, happy. In closure, they take us away from the horrific world of rape, castration, and murder and transport us back to a calm, sane environment. We may not identify with them in all social and moral particulars, and they may not even be the most intriguing pair. They are, however, the only couple in the narrative with whom we would choose to relax. Like us, they are "normal."

The second explanation of the repairer and his wife, however, is less reassuring. The very characteristics that make them seem loving and normal also may make them appear as abnormal and terrifying as the other psychoneurotics. Just as we do not daily encounter knife-wielding killers such as Christmas and Grimm, neither do we routinely meet loving couples such as the repairer and his wife. To use Faulkner's image, they are the flip side of the same rare coin. There is an image that we only delude ourselves into thinking of as normal. They are a Norman Rockwell cover from the *Saturday Evening Post* or a scene from a Hollywood movie meant to cheer us in the midst of Depression. Maybe they are a flashback to our prepubescent past when we had not yet encountered our own Dietitian in the Bedroom; back before the sweet toothpaste turned to vomit. We see them as fleetingly and as imprecisely as we see ourselves: in one fixed moment blurred by hope rather than in the context of life's long travail.

Our life's daily routine is not ordinarily violent. Then again, it is not ordinarily happy and comedic. It is something in between, like the existence the citizens of Jefferson and Mottstown demonstrate: mundane, boring, a sequence of acts that lead to other acts and back again. At rare moments the sequence is agitated by a rape or a murder or a glimmer of happiness. It is this rare glimmer that Faulkner presents with the furniture repairer episode. What he does not tell us in the episode per se is that violence lurks in the dark. The rest of the text, however, has already etched that warning on our psyches. It is in our genes. No matter how pleasant a moment may seem, it is but a part of the camouflage of terror. The peaceful times are the aberrations.

We catch the young repairer and his wife in post-coital repose, momentarily content, momentarily happy. As we watch, we might recall how the theme of defenestration winds through the text: Lena sneaks through the window to her assignations with Burch; Burch jumps through a window to flee from Lena and his baby; Christmas climbs out a window to meet his whore; Mrs. Hightower leaps from a window in the Memphis hotel. We might also recall the ends to which all those window exits lead. Then, we might note that jumping, high hotels, and adultery are alluded to in the furniture repairer's table. These associations serve to remind us of what tomorrow might hold for the happy young couple talking in the bedroom. Such is the ambiguity with which Faulkner leaves us in chapter 21, in the dark with anonymous strangers.

Faulkner, then, with the possible exception of the repairer and his wife, unites those characters who represent varying degrees of violence. He does so to gain perspective on a variety of social and ethical issues and to probe various psychological responses to violence. If he were to group rather than pair the characters according to violence and nonviolence only, the associations would be entirely different from what they are. Christmas, Grimm, Hines, McEachern, Burch, and Joanna Burden, plus several other minor characters would be aligned on the side of "violent." Hightower, Bunch, Mrs. Hines, Mrs. McEachern, and Lena, plus several other minor characters would be aligned on the side of "nonviolent" or passive. What novel we would have as a result of such realignment is senseless to contemplate, but the point is that violence and pairing are an essential combination that determines the shape and scope of the novel that we do have.

Like no other American novel before it, *Light in August* exploits the aesthetic power of sheer violence. Using violence as his narrative matrix, Faulkner not only creates memorable and uniquely American character types but also inculcates nearly every distinctive and formative element of American society.

The Burden family chronicles take us back to the colonial and revolutionary era, as does the very name of the town in which the central violence occurs—Jefferson. From that past, we follow the American chronology, through Hightower's obsession with the Civil War to the topicality of Grimm's nazism. Calvinism, racial conflict, militarism, capitalism, Freudianism, sectionalism—all interfuse text and subtext. Moreover, America's wars dot the narrative background: the Revolutionary War, the Civil War, the frontier Indian wars, World War I, and (with some prescience) the beginnings of World War II. All these violent elements stem from Faulkner's effort to develop an American epistemology. Only by accepting the reality that America is a violent, martial nation populated by violent individuals, Faulkner proposes, can we begin to know what America is all about. *Light in August* is the first novel to make violence essential rather than incidental and the first to argue that violence uniquely defines the American personality. In the presentation of that harsh truth and in the implication that we may still possess enough frontier spirit to explore it, *Light in August* may arguably be the first purely American novel.

# James M. Cain's
## *The Postman Always Rings Twice*

Few would insist that James M. Cain's *The Postman Al-ways Rings Twice* (1934) has aesthetic perception and sensibility enough to qualify as a great novel. W. M. Frohock declared in 1950 that "nothing [Cain] ever wrote was completely outside the category of trash" (13). Joyce Carol Oates, after suggesting that Cain's writing is "sleazy," "vulgar," and "disappointing" (110), grants that "he is an entertainer with an uncanny knowledge of the perversities of his audience, the great range of their vulgar-ity" (114). Less obliquely, James T. Farrell called his contempo-rary a Hollywood writer who aimed only at "yokels" (quoted in Madden, 59). Even a critic as astute as Alfred Kazin categorizes Cain as an exploitative writer "pandering to the same taste which enjoyed the synthetic violence of the murder mystery and drugstore treatises on lesbianism" (303). The prolixity that marks (or mars) the styles of both Oates and Farrell may well ac-count for their disapproval of Cain's brief, skeletal novels, and Kazin's unfriendly evaluation may be pardoned because he was writing contemporaneously, without the advantage of aesthetic distance. In the early 1940s he perceived Cain as being merely one of the "less-talented Broadway-Hollywood novelists" (302). Frohock was simply too dismissive. Given the multitude of prejudices and biases that color all criticism, these critics' failure to appreciate Cain is understandable. Their emphasis upon and their judgmental attitude toward Cain's audience, however, is surprising in that it assumes an intellectual, aesthetic superiority that relegates to the realm of the vulgar and salacious any novel that attracts the kind of popular attention *Postman* received.

Granted that *Postman* may be meretricious. Of the hard-boiled novels that proliferated in the 1930s, however, it is among the few to transcend its pulp heritage and become a minor classic of violence. More so than *The Maltese Falcon* or *The Big Sleep*, *Postman* gave life to Mike Hammer and the countless other tough guys that appeared after World War II. Unlike these testosterone heroes, however, Cain's protagonist communicates a metaphysic of violence that demands more than passing attention. Furthermore, the narrative style so subtly reflects this ontology, and vice versa, that the two seem a near perfect integration of form and function. Albert Camus had this narrative coherence in mind when he noted *Postman*'s influence on *The Stranger* (see Madden, 171).

Camus's oft-noted attribution is appropriate, because in several important respects *Postman* is America's *Stranger*. In both tales, the traditional moral codes have gone haywire, and the behavior the codes once directed has been short-circuited. Individuals such as Mersault, Frank Chambers, and Cora Papadakis therefore operate sui generis because the civilizing messages no longer register. Joyce Carol Oates, obviously no great admirer of Cain, admitted that "Frank and Cora are representative of a competitive society that has bypassed them" (120). Cut off from external, societal controls, they look inside themselves for guidance. There they find only the instinctual drives that have dictated animal responses since the days of the primordial slime. Thus, ironically, they are genuine specimens of human behavior before it was slathered over by eons of social conditioning. Encountering them is like finding an Australopithecus afarensis in our bathtub: we are not comforted by the meeting, but we are extremely curious.

What *Postman* sets out to do, it does extremely well: using a variety of subtly developed narrative techniques, it fuses the two most basic and fascinating animal instincts, sex and violence, into an eroto-violent tour de force. This singularity of purpose is precisely why *Postman* demands a place in any study of the novel of violence. If we examine Cain's technique closely and without prejudice, we see that *Postman* is a much better example of the fictionist's art than Frohock, Oates, and other detractors have conceded.

Granted, everything about *Postman* and Cain's career in general superficially suggests that he consciously directed his talents not at the literati but at the reader who was willing to spend two dollars and a couple of hours on what the blurbs call a good read. "If you ask me," Cain wrote to a friend, "a simple tale, told briefly, is what most people really like" (quoted by Hoopes 2). His insight was proven valid by the phenomenal success of *Postman* and the later failure of the much longer and pretentious *The Moth. Postman* did not come easy, however. The ideas that eventually took shape in the violent story of Frank Chambers and Cora Papadakis gestated for a long time, nurtured by Cain's own erratic life as a sometimes drifter around Maryland's Eastern Shore and his sporadic experiences at journalism and movie scripting. Enamored of automobiles, particularly a 1932 Ford roadster in which he rambled about California, Cain literally drove into the experience that finally inspired him to write the novel he had long avoided. Roy Hoopes reports the chance encounter at a filling station:

> 'Always this bosomy-looking thing comes out—commonplace but sexy, the kind you have ideas about,' he later told an interview. 'We always talked while she filled up my tank. One day I read in the paper where a woman who runs a filling station knocked off her husband. Can it be the bosomy thing? I go by and sure enough the place is closed. I inquire. Yes, she's the one—this appetizing but utterly commonplace woman.'
>
> (8)

This event, coupled with recollections of the sensational accounts of the 1927 Ruth Snyder—Judd Gray murder case, forms the heart of *Postman*. It is a novel that epitomizes the popular formula Cain had been seeking: A "simple tale, told briefly," based on the actions of "commonplace" people, with a sex-and-murder plot that had already proven itself with the popular audience.

In dire need of funds to support himself and a recently acquired wife and two children, Cain made no pretense about his primary motivation as a writer: to make money. His pragmatism, however, did not eradicate his art. Years later he would reflect upon the level of art he had displayed in *Postman* and regret that he had afterward denied his own creative birthright for the lucre of Hollywood. "I parked my pride, my esthetic conviction, my mind outside on the street," he lamented toward the end of his career, appropriately using a common automobile metaphor to express how he felt about deserting his art for the movie "whorehouse" he hated (quoted in Hoopes 13).

Ironically, in writing for an audience Oates calls perverse and Farrell terms yokels, Cain created not only his own individual masterpiece but an enduring example of the novel of violence. "With *Postman*," Hoopes notes, "Cain had produced the rarest of literary achievements—a best-seller widely acclaimed by the critics" (12). The apparent paradox of popular and academic praise can be explained by how adeptly Cain uses symbols to convey the philosophy of violence he wishes to impart. His automobile motif is especially well managed, and exemplifies his adherence to and success with the "commonplace." The motif offers a good point of demarcation for an analysis of how his "popular" craftsmanship disguises his aesthetic accomplishments in *Postman*.

When Cain came to write *Postman* (1934) during the midst of the Great Depression, he was certainly aware of the myriad of ironic and sometimes conflicting images that the automobile had acquired since its introduction. He was aware also of the "Okies" arriving hourly in California in jalopies of every size and shape, the symbols of a culture falling to pieces. Furthermore, Cain knew previous literary works that had made use of the car and had established themselves with portions of the popular audience he wished to reach. Among the best known of these works at the time was Aldous Huxley's *Brave New World* (1932), in which the automobile and its most famous proponent Henry Ford are elevated to godhood, with all the irony and satire that attach to such deification. Popular also was Robert Sherwood's *The Petrified Forest* (1934), a play set, like *Postman*, in a desert gas station cafe. Such filling station diners were a mini-institution established solely as a satellite of the automobile. The car functions as a microcosm of a world composed of hitchhikers, drifters, and other assorted wanderers cut loose from society's central core. Cain was aware also of F. Scott Fitzgerald and his *The Great Gatsby* (1925), a novel that was a popular failure but that was later to become an American classic, in part because of its adept use of automobile symbology. The point is not that Cain borrowed from any specific work, but that he was well aware of the trends such works reflected. In short, he knew how popular modern icons could be used in art and had a good idea of what the car-crazy public was buying to read.

He no doubt sensed that despite the relative popularity of such works as *Brave New World* and *The Petrified Forest*, even they were a tad more cerebral than he felt appropriate. Himself a failed playwright before migrating to Hollywood, Cain knew the limits and relatively specialized tastes of the theater's audience. Too, he sensed that the audience he wanted to reach was not prone to overt political or social satire and not given to polemics and literary allusions. The readers whose pockets he wanted to tap, while neither stupid nor perverse as Oates and Farrell suggest, were unsophisticated. Moreover, gaining life's necessities left them with little idle time. Burdened by bad troubles, they could find some solace in reading about people who had life worse. Though certainly not intellectual, such an audience was not hopelessly dense. Cain, always with a hint of the didactic, wanted to communicate with that audience not only in hopes of reaping his share of the wealth that fed the Capitalist machine but also in hopes of making that audience (ironically) aware of what the system was doing to it. Thus, what better vehicle than the ubiquitous and popular auto to carry him?

The action of *Postman* moves full cycle, like the sun rising and setting over the desert or the car wheels rolling past the Twin Oaks Tavern. The narrative begins with a simple, violent act that is magnified by Frank Chamber's Ishmael-like tone: "They threw me off the hay truck about noon" (1). It ends very violently with the "big truck" (116) that smashes Cora and her unborn baby. Within this cycle, Frank and Cora play out their own tawdry yet tragic life cycles. Tangential scenes of violence that do not directly involve automobiles are present, such as Frank and Cora's brutal treatment of Kennedy the blackmailer. Yet, even that beating occurs at the Twin Oaks Tavern with cars parked all around. Other than these several tangential scenes, however, the automobile is pivotal in every important act they perform and an implement in every disaster that befalls them.

Three major instances of the automobile stand out in the narrative structure, however, and serve to show how carefully Cain uses the common but artistically useful symbol as an element in his philosophy of violence. The first of these vital scenes appears in chapter 3, when Frank and Cora intentionally plunge Nick's car "into a little eucalyptus grove" (11) and violently make love. Their lust temporarily satiated, they then discuss for the first time Cora's desire to kill her husband. Frank reacts to Cora's proposal with typical hard-boiled understatement: "They hang your for that" (14). The scene foreshadows Frank's own death sentence and advances the plot very effectively. More important than these mechanical functions, however, is how the scene reiterates that the sexual instinct and the violent instinct are inextricably combined. This is a crucial point we will return to later. The scene also introduces an irony that becomes increasingly apparent as the narrative progresses. In the scene Cain reveals that Frank not only does not want to kill his benefactor Nick but that he innately wishes to avoid automobiles. He comes as close to pleading as he can come, asking Cora to go away with him. "Just blow," he says. He wants her to leave the car, the cafe, and Nick, and trust their feet and fate to take them away. Later, in chapter 5, they do attempt to walk away; but Cora, too accustomed to the modern paradox of cars that facilitate a sedentary life, cannot go more than a  quarter of a mile. She refuses to move further, and they both collapse in tears. Cora cries in relief that her pedestrian pain has ended; but Frank cries because he inarticulately realizes that his last chance at escape has passed.

The second vital car scene can be termed The Drama of the Car. Frank refers to it as "the play" (39). It forms the entire middle section of the novel (chapters 7, 8 and 9). In this long central portion, Frank and Cora succeed in killing Nick, an act that previous events in the narrative demand; they expose the most bizarre elements of their lust when they fornicate immediately after the murder; and they prove how closely allied are their sexual and homicidal impulses. The automobile in "the play" literally becomes the stage for murder, the weapon of murder, and the escape from murder. Frank and Cora have very carefully orchestrated Nick's killing. They make sure that witnesses see the three of them together, that Frank and Nick appear drunk, and that the 2x4 that they use to lever the car over the cliff has been properly road beaten so no one will question its presence. Later Frank receives authentic wounds when he rolls part way down the cliff inside the car with Nick's body, an ironically fortuitous but unplanned bit of violence. Coupled with Frank's clever testimony that he was driving the car even though witnesses swear he was drunk and capable of neither driving nor murder, these wounds help exonerate Frank.

As in the previous episode, however, more is going on than is immediately visible. They kill Nick not to free Cora from him sexually. They have managed quite well to engage their mutual lust regularly and to keep Nick ignorant. Cora has determined before Frank appears in her life that Nick must die. Frank merely serves the dual function of lover and killer—roles that Cora sees as being almost indistinguishable. Nick, on the other hand, represents the system that has demeaned and tricked her, the system that promises Hollywood lights but delivers desert gloom. She is a sweetheart from the American Heartland, corrupted by Hollywood dreams. The same physical attributes and sensuality that took Clare Bow and Jean Harow to fame and fortune on the silver screen make Cora nothing but a "cheap Des Moines trollop" (12). The All-America, over-sexed girl, Cora pursues the American Dream westward into prostitution and desperation. Feeling the Capitalist system has misled her with its promises of happiness and that nature has fitted her for disaster, she ultimately looks to murder as a form of compensation. She becomes Cain's version of that "bosomy thing" in a cheap filling station: commonplace, sexy, and doomed.

In this middle section, Frank's history appears like the road map of a barren land. Reminiscent of Faulkner's *Light in August* and Joe Christmas, Frank has wandered the country as an outsider in a system he does not have the wits to comprehend. Born in San Francisco, he has spent his twenty-four years in vagabondage. Wichita, Tucson, Salt Lake City, New Orleans, Chicago: "I've seen them all," he says (57). Though he has frequently been arrested for petty crimes, he has escaped the system by presenting a moving target. By way of box cars, trucks, and automobiles (vehicles always owned by others and not himself) he has never remained in one place long enough to become a part of or a victim to the institutions, mores, and patterns of the Capitalist system that so readily traps Cora. By not owning anything, he is owned by nothing. Only when he lingers too long under the twinkling Neon sign of the Twin Oaks Tavern to sample the rewards of laissez-faire and fair damsel does this system finally claim him, permanently and fatally.

One of the worst accusations prosecutor Sackett uses against Frank is his sudden permanence. It is not suspicious, Sackett demands, "That after knocking around all these years, and never doing any work, or even trying to do any, so far as I can see, you suddenly settled down, and went to work, and held a job steady?" (58). Harassed as a wanderer by a system that cannot abide footlessness, Frank is suddenly condemned when he ceases to wander. Work and steady jobs are usually to be praised, especially in the midst of the Depression; but for Frank they crate only suspicion and threats. He learns about Catch-22 before there was a Catch-22. Unconsciously and inarticulately pursuing his own version of the American Dream (a woman to love, a place to work and live) he steps blindly into chaos. He knows innately that his tramping and road-love have kept him free of what Ken Kesey calls the Combine. When his primordial instinct for freedom loses out to his even stronger sexual instinct, he is damned, caught in the biological and economic trap that was set for him and his kind long ago. The rambling auto mechanic dies in the gears of the heartless state.

In the third significant car passage, Cain uses the automobile metaphor to summarize what exactly has happened to Frank and Cora. As usual, Cora and not Frank has the insight into what has befallen them. Despite all their clever planning and all the sinuous twists and turns the murder takes, the Capitalist system momentarily sets Frank and Cora free. That the big insurance companies find more profit in letting the killers go than in turning them over to the judicial system is the deciding fact in Frank and Cora's lives. Alive or dead, they simply are not worth the thousands of dollars the companies would lose. Significantly, Katz the lawyer uses an obscure clause in the California Vehicle Act to convince the companies of his strategy. Later, thinking about the hash house, the movies, and the murder, Cora uses an image straight from the automobile production line to express her rudimentary understanding of what Katz and the system have done to her:

> [God] gave us all that two people can ever have. And we just weren't the kind that could have it. We had all that love and we just cracked up under it. It's a big airplane engine, that takes you through the sky, right up to the top of the mountain. But when you put it in a Ford, it just shakes it to pieces. That's what we are, Frank, a couple of Fords. God is up there laughing at us.     (88)

Cora's reference to God is ironic, since she has so far done nothing pious nor seen any indication that God still operates within the mechanistic ethic signified by the automobile. Moreover, her describing her relationship with Frank as "love" is equally ironic in that it severely tests the reader's credulousness. Yet the essential irony of the comment is her Ford comparison. The point she is making, unconsciously perhaps, is that a mechanized state cannot produce citizens capable of spiritual greatness or transcendent love. It can only produce citizens as incapable of greatness as the commonplace Flivvers that roll profitably out of Detroit. A few years after *Postman*, John Steinbeck would celebrate Tom Joad riding the old Hudson Super-Six and Jim Casy's high-octane transcendentalism to spiritual, humanistic heights.

Cain, however, denies such romantic optimism. Fords cannot carry one through the skies of great expectations, love, or transcendent ideas. They travel only over the asphalt and through the deserts of mundane and quotidian drabness. Aspirations to truly brave new worlds will simply shake the individual to pieces. Having sensed this, Cora joins Frank in a prolonged drunk that numbs all but her basic biological drives and that carries her through to death, the final violent escape.

Cain uses the automobile to emblematize the removal of the people from the earth, from basic contact with the only medium in which moral roots can grow. As Erskine Caldwell writes in *Tobacco Road* (1932), another Depression novel in which the automobile and violence figure prominently, cars are "all right to fool around in and have a good time in, but they don't offer no love like the ground does" (158). Cain demonstrates this tragic uprooting not only in Cora and Frank, but in the general population, the auto-mobilized people who pause only briefly at the Twin Oaks Tavern seeking "a chance to sit out under the trees for a half hour . . . before they got in their cars and went on" (91). Referring to these "shabby, gray days" of the 1930s and of the proletarian novelists, Leslie Fielder spoke years ago of "the dream of violence [that] possessed the American imagination like a promise of salvation. Politics was violent and a-politics equally so; whatever else a man publicly accepted or denied, he did not deny terror" (457). No writer of the period more expertly tapped into the terror than Cain. Though no proletarian or agrarian, and certainly no propagandist, Cain was acutely attuned to the age in which he had to pursue his art and livelihood. He borrowed the common violence metaphor from many other popular and not-so-popular works of the period, grafted it like Caldwell, John O'Hara, and others to the ever-commercial sex and lust. His instincts were good, and he knew what would sell. More than that, however, he used the "commonplace" symbols of the Depression to convey the terror and desperation upon which he ironically fed.

One of the notable ironies that Cain manages is to make us have less compassion for Nick than for his killers. That transference of sympathy culminates in the central scene of violence, which lies at the heart of the "Drama of the Car":

> . . . I braced my feet, and while he still had his chin on the window sill I brought down the wrench. His head cracked and I felt it crush. He crumpled up and

> curled on the seat like a cat on a sofa. It seemed a year
> before he was still. Then Cora, she gave a funny kind of
> gulp that ended in a moan.                               (42-43)

> . . . My left arm was shooting pain so bad I would
> yell every time I felt it, and so was my back. Inside my
> head was a bellow that would get big and go away
> again. When it did that the ground would fall away,
> and this stuff I had drunk would come up. I was there
> and I wasn't there, but I had sense enough to roll around
> and kick.                                                (49)

This murder is the thematic and structural center of the narrative, bringing the three major characters and the reader together in one bloody, erotic melee in which conventional moral attitudes are redefined. Here when we should rebel against such violence and sympathize with the victim, our sympathies actually shift to the killers.

We realize that Nick is little more than a victim in waiting. He is benign but foolish, rendered unsympathetic by his coarse desire and simplistic vision of American life. Superficially generous and likable, Nick is actually lustful, slothful, greedy, gluttonous, and obtuse. In William Maring's phrase, *Postman* "narrates the end of the open road, the penalties for lust and failure to work" (1). Nick personifies that narrative quality. So eager is he to have a handyman assume his workload that he invites a violent criminal into the cage with his little "white bird" (6). Though he has wed Cora mainly to satisfy his own carnal appetites, Nick is conveniently blind to her fiery sexuality. He naively chooses to believe, for example, that a swinging door caused her sex wounds. Such willful obtuseness implies a moral impotency that adds a psychological counterbalance to the potent overt sexuality that dominates the text. We are so beguiled by the characters' sexual violence that we downplay their homicidal violence.

The ornate sign Nick hangs in front of the Twin Oaks Diner accurately conveys the extent of his mental dullness. Nick's drawing of this twinkling wonder amazes even Frank: "It had a Greek flag and an American flag, and hands shaking hands, and Satisfaction Guaranteed. It was all in red, white and blue Neon letters . . ." (10). When Nick hurries off to have the sign built, Frank seizes the interlude to guarantee his own satisfaction with Cora. Later they plot his murder in its glow. Nick is so blinded by the sign and his pride in it that he has no perception of the dire events its Neon illuminates. Moreover, the

gaudy, benign patriotism implied by the sign is particularly odious in an era when the national infrastructure verged on collapse and political rhetoric rang acutely false. Nick, however, is
unaware of the verbal and political nuances of the sign of the so-
cioeconomic atmosphere in which it flickers. Nick denies the
"terror" that fuels what Fiedler called "the dream of violence
[that] possessed the American imagination like a promise of salvation" during the Depression.

Americans overindulge the youthfully naive, as shown by
our mythicizing Huck Finn, Holden Caulfield, and Billy the
Kid—two pathological liars and a homicidal maniac. Though
our toleration of Congress may suggest otherwise, we are less
patient with adult stupidity. Thus we have little tolerance for
Nick's shortcomings, and tend to judge him rather severely.
One of those hapless suckers who is born every minute, he
seems to deserve the cuckoldry and violence that befall him.
The Greek's fate also seems less tragic because Frank and Cora's
eroto-violence is more dramatically compelling than Nick's dull
life. Although Nick's murder is the focus of the narrative and is
explicitly detailed, it pales in the glare of the lover's white-hot
passion. Moreover, while we expect murder to be gory and
vicious, we still venerate the illusion that love is sweet and
tender, much as Cora deludes herself into thinking that the
vicious lust she shares with Frank is "love." We are therefore
alarmed by love attacks that force us to redefine ardor and
violence: "I sunk my teeth into her lips so deep I could feel the
blood spurt into my mouth. It was running down her neck
when I carried her upstairs" (9). This combat amour leaves the
strapping 24-year old Frank "dead" for two days. Not only does
such a lengthy post-coital convalescence fall outside the
experiential pale for most of us, we cannot recall its equal
anywhere else in literature. Frederic Henry needed only a few
more days than Frank to recuperate from his trench mortar
wound. The point is that we are so captivated by such war zone
sex that Nick's murder seems almost pastoral.

Moreover, the dramatic tension of the murder scene is intensified by the disharmony that Cain accomplishes by interject-
ing lust into a setting that has been carefully prepared for violence. As noted, Frank arranges the murder scene in cold,
meticulous, logical details. Frank's remorseless tone and these
details produce an ideal matrix for the killing that we know is
imminent. Yet, just after Frank crushes Nick's skull with the

wrench and they push the car over the edge, uncontrolled lust suddenly erupts. "Rip me! Rip me" Cora screams (46). She and Frank then violently fornicate, while Nick's bloody corpse is still warm inside the car. This outburst of passion wrenches our attention away from the murder to remind us that lust is the main reason we are here late at night on "the worst piece of road in Los Angeles County" (40). At first we are drawn like voyeurs to Frank and Cora's primitive eroticism. We are also perturbed, however, because their elaborate murder scheme may be foiled at any moment. We do not much like Nick and are ironically, rooting for his killers. In a sense, we have become their rational selves who are otherwise absent from the action. Calm and reasonable, we know what dangers their uncontrolled lust presents. We worry that while they are fornicating in the rocks and blood below, another nosy cop may appear, just as he did at their first murder attempt. For several nerve-wracking minutes, therefore, we actively participate in the world of the eroto-violent. Our own instincts and reason have been put in conflict. The scene stands as a powerful example of how Cain combines sexuality, violence, and audience into one ironic, dynamic melange.

After we regain our "civilized" equilibrium and realize that Cain has just placed us in league with two murderers, we might wonder how such collusion came about. We can hardly deny that we have vicariously allowed our own sexual and violent instincts to direct us. Admitting that, we might then rationalize our actions by claiming that two mean people with deadly charisma have kidnapped us emotionally. Logic quickly tells us, however, that Cora Smith Papadakis and Frank Chambers are ordinary, street-variety killers. Hundreds like them walk the boulevards and alleys of Los Angeles, twenty miles down the road. Consequently, we can only conclude that either we are as innately vicious and lustful as these two commonplace erotomaniacs or that the power of the scene as Cain renders it is responsible for a momentary loss of reason that plunges us into raw sex and killer blood. In a sense, we either admit to being gullible fools or acknowledge the success of Cain's art of violence.

Another notable element of the scene is that it causes us to contravene our most sacred social codes to take the sanguinary plunge. Nothing we learn about Frank and Cora before the central murder scene justifies a moral or intellectual commitment to them. Cora readily prostitutes herself when her

Hollywood schemes fail. She marries Nick to escape a trollop's life and to avoid honest work otherwise. Bored, and dejected that she has not realized her leisure plan, Cora then rejects motherhood, beds Frank, and plots Nick's murder, all without remorse and with little cause beyond greed and carnal desire. In short, she does not meet the social and moral standards set for women, especially in an era before the words wife, nurturing, loyalty, and devotion became rhetorical Molotov cocktails to inflame the feminist heart. Cora is selfish, sexually aggressive, and a woman capable of molding a man into a violent killer. Even remembering that we see her through Frank's androcentric vision does not alter these facts about Cora.

Frank too is motivated essentially by lust and laziness. He wants only a willing woman and a labor-free life on the road. The ludicrous sentimentality shown when he gets "to blubbering" over Nick's grave (86) and his subsequent concern for love, marriage, and family are but domesticated variations of the eroto-violence and a ploy to get a stay of execution. In fact, Frank may have corrupted Father McConnell, the priest to whom he is confessing. Such superimposed sentiment and compassion suggest that the Father may have ameliorated Frank's confessional text as he found "places where maybe it ought to be fixed up a little, for punctuation and all that" (118). Frank has, after all, already persuaded us to judge others inside his moral codes, and is thus persuasive enough to have duped the priest into doing some select editing. Perhaps the same motives that caused us to join Frank and Cora in murder also explain why Father McConnell is so attracted to Frank. No matter what guise we assume and no matter how much we suppress lust and violence, they lurk in all our psyches and will somehow find their outlets. The idea that the Catholic Father also has joined Frank in his eroto-violent scheme suggests how totally Frank and his narrative concentrate on its singular deadly purpose.

More pertinent, though, is that no matter how clever Frank imagines himself, he is duped at every turn. His losing $250 to the pool hustler (31) is a minor signification of his essential gullibility. Cora, using her sexuality like a narcotic, easily persuades Frank to kill Nick. In an equally bizarre but less vicious scheme, Madge Allen uses her sexuality to lure Frank into a cat hunt. Then too, he is so much a pawn in the chess game between Sackett and Katz that he has no inkling of what has transpired (we might add that the reader often joins Frank in that confusion). Finally, the biggest con of all is how much nature's big pool game dictates Frank's every move. Driven solely by sexuality and violence, Frank is dumb to how completely those instincts direct his fate. The point is that little about Frank or Cora justifies our allegiance or sympathy—unless we abrade every criterion by which we judge civilized conduct. Cain's ability to make us to just that indicates a subtle artistry.

Finally, however, we might suspect that Cain wants us to realize that we are being too callous in our responses to his trio of victims. We see this possibility developed in our discussion of Frank and Cora's helplessness in face of a system that is complex far beyond their intellectual capacities to understand. This readers' callousness is especially seen in our attitudes toward Cora. A slightly more melodious voice, a bit more savvy, a kiss on the right lips at the right time and Cora could have been a movie star. We would be standing in line to see her image on the silver screen and fretting over who designed her dress for the Academy Awards ceremonies. The willy-nilliness of the naturalistic universe does not favor her, however, and she ends up married not to a movie czar but to a "greasy" Greek (14) whom she hates. Ripped away from dreams of celebrating with the Rich and Famous, she awakens to the realities of cooking in a hash-house. Society teaches her values that are superficial and unsustaining, then breaks all the connections that tie her to a viable moral standard. She must exist in the modern mechanical world of Fords, airplanes, fancy Neon signs, and a robotized legal system. Yet she must rely for survival on the same primitive instincts that tell an armadillo to cross the Interstate.

That Cora is so shallow may say much about Cain's weakness as a novelist. That we care so little about he and her cohort says much more about how innately mean and violent are our own instincts. Though a slight novel, and comparatively insubstantial as a work of art, *The Postman Always Rings Twice* nonetheless succeeds admirably as a novel of violence. It also anticipates questions raised by subsequent novels of violence. For instance, Cora is a very violent woman who does not actively kill but who sublimates her killer instincts into a violent sexuality that in turn metamorphoses into maternal desires (she is pregnant when she dies). How different is this scenario from the one that leads Sethe Garner to kill her child in Toni Morrison's *Beloved*. We will revisit that question later.

# Katherine Anne Porter's
## *Noon Wine*

Katherine Anne Porter's *Noon Wine* is more a nine-stanza prose poem than a novel. It is exquisitely balanced, phrased, and arranged. Its numerous motifs intersect, inter-twine, then disengage in choreographic harmony. Its text and subtext merge seamlessly. It is a near perfect example of the fic-tionist's art created by a writer who fashioned the purest aesthet-ics of her era. As Harold Bloom aptly notes, "She is a supreme lyricist among story writers" (1). Seen from a post-modernist, end-of-century perspective, however, this near perfection of *Noon Wine* (1936) is a damaging flaw. Its motifs are too appar-ent and predictable; its symbols too pat; and its Freudian psyche to luminous. Its journey and stranger-in-a-strange-land motifs do not thrill us any longer. Dilapidated houses and clogged springs seem symbolic collector items. Freud has been battered to a cliché by the cudgel of political correctness. In a phrase, *Noon Wine* is passé and too accessible. Like *Old Man and the Sea* or *Heart of Darkness*, it seems to serve best as a teaching text for Literary Fundamentals 101. Despite its meretricious artful-ness, however, *Noon Wine* develops the most powerful ironic contrast between beautiful form and horrific content of any American novel of violence. Reading it is like opening a Fabergé egg and finding Hell.

With the exception of Cormac McCarthy's *Blood Merid-ian*, *Noon Wine* is arguably the purest example of an American novel of violence. No other novel is so completely devoted to violence. Violence is essential to its narrative technique and its controlling philosophy. Violence dominates the language, set-ting, characterizations, plot, symbology, and every other element of the narrative. This dominance is especially pronounced be-

cause of the brevity of *Noon Wine* and its limited number of
dramtis personae. That brevity, perhaps, is what first suggests
parallels to Henry James' *Turn of the Screw*. *Noon Wine* has
the same unresolved question of what is real and who is truly
evil. Porter leaves us with a Jamesian angst and lingering nuances of guilt. In the words of Harold Bloom, James was "her
truest precursor" (1). Traces of T. S. Eliot are also discernible, in
the symbology of decay and the waste land setting, and in the
overwhelming sense of spiritual drought. Then too, *Noon
Wine* has elements of Gothic horror: an old dilapidated, two-
story house; isolation; darkness; madness; axes; knives; mysterious stranger with odd traits. The moment that the "tall bony
man with straw-colored hair" walks through the gate that no
longer swings to confront a man with "stiff black hair and a
week's growth of black whiskers" (324), we anticipate upcoming
polar conflicts and catch the dread that will dominate the text.
We sense that the several acres of this decrepit Texas farm will
soon become the killing fields.

The autobiographical basis for this violent tale has often
been recorded and needs no extensive review. Joan Givner has
conveniently outlined the autobiographical background. The
specific details stem from Porter's childhood stay with the
Thompson family in Buda, Texas. Her general attitude toward
violence is shaped by experiences with her own father. Porter
herself discussed the supposed inspiration for the story in
"'Noon Wine': The Sources," a 1956 essay that has been widely
reprinted. There she states that "By the time I wrote 'Noon
Wine' it had become 'real' to me almost in the sense that I felt
not as if I had made that story out of my own memory and real
events and imagined consequences, but as if I were quite simply
reporting events I had heard or witnessed" (Collected Essays 469).
Insofar as violence is concerned, the important autobiographical
element of Porter's writing was the personality of Harrison
Boone Porter and his daughter's response to him. After Porter's
mother died, her father became increasingly hostile and violent.
As Givner summarizes the situation, "He was given to violent
outbursts of hatred and he always wanted to kill someone" (50).
He expressed uninterrupted animosity to his sons, but seemed to
love whichever daughter happened to be the prettiest at the
moment. In Givner's words, "Porter knew that she had been
fundamentally affected by her relationship with her father. She
said that she had tried to love him but could not and that his af-

fection frightened her because it was based on incomprehensible motives and was likely to change for inexplicable reasons" (50). We see her father's personality reflected in Royal Earle Thompson. Moreover, the conflicted parental relationship helps explain her overall philosophy of violence, which was based on a polar conflict between hatred and love. I will elucidate this important point later. Though we do not want to overemphasize the autobiographical influences in Porter's fiction, Givner is correct in concluding that "The unpleasantness of [Porter's] outer world caused her to turn inward and develop remarkable powers of imagination" (62). Those powers and the impact violence had on them are my concern here.

I mentioned earlier that *Noon Wine* may now seem best suited for the undergraduate classroom. It is fitting, therefore, that the most lucid and thorough explication of *Noon Wine* remains one that appeared in a pedagogical text. Louis Leiter's "The Expense of Spirit in a Waste of Shame: Motif, Montage, and Structure in *Noon Wine*" appeared in the first edition of *Seven Contemporary Short Novels* (1969), a text designed for the undergraduate college student. Leiter's essay is a section-by-section, almost line-by-line explication of Porter's novella. It analyzes the interrelationships of the characters, the symbology, the motifs, the verbal series, the social and moral implications, and the violence. In a phrase, it is an excellent guide to be the literary conventions exemplified in *Noon Wine*. Though I do not agree with Leiter on several interpretative points nor that Porter was working with a moral agenda, I nonetheless appreciate his essay on many levels. It sets the standards for *explication de texte* insofar as the novella is concerned, especially for a text meant to be used by unsophisticated but inquisitive readers.

Somewhat ironically, Leiter may have been too successful with his explication. It is so thorough that it leaves little room for the novice reader to see past his commentary to the fiction it analyzes. Leiter and his co-editor Charles Clerc apparently realized the oxymoronic detrimental success of the essay. They dropped it from the second edition of *Seven Contemporary Short Novels* (1975), explaining that they wanted "to open up" the anthology and to "encourage freer application of its uses" (Preface, n.p.). Whether or not that wish was realized I have no idea. I do suspect, however, that Leiter's explication and the widespread use of *Seven Contemporary Short Novels* hastened the decline of critical publications about *Noon Wine* after the

mid-1970s, although it is Porter's masterpiece. This critical ne-
glect is indicated by the fact that Harold Bloom, editing the Modern Critical Views collection of essays on Katherine Anne Porter
in 1986, chose not to include any essay that specifically addressed
*Noon Wine*, though essays on *Ship of Fools* and several of the
short stories are included (two on "He"). In any event, Leiter's is
an excellent analysis and I acknowledge my debt and appreciation.

The nine sections of *Noon Wine* are balanced four-one-
four. The first four sections form one distinct unit and the second four sections form another distinct unit. These sections are
neither numbered nor indicated as chapters, but are set off only
by interposed white space. To facilitate discussion, therefore, I
will refer to sections 1-4 as Unit One and sections 6-9 as Unit
Two. Section five is a short transition statement about time
passing and children growing up, or the "bridge" section. The
textual image that Porter suggests for this narrative equilibrium,
and the one critics most frequently appropriate, is scales. In this
image, section five is the fulcrum. More appropriate, given the
title, section five is the "noon time" between the work hours of
morning and those of evening. It is like a break under the shade
tree before all Hell breaks loose. No matter what image we
choose, the point is that *Noon Wine* is meticulously arranged
and organized. So too are the scenes of violence within the narrative.

Those scenes in Unit One are scenes of secondary violence. By that I mean that they are scenes in which no overt
bloodshed or severe physical injury is visible. Considering
Porter's courtroom metaphor, we may categorize them as scenes
in which no prosecutable offense occurs and in which most of
the evidence is hearsay. Violence is alluded to, expressed ver-
bally, and manifested in one instance of aggressive behavior, but
no scene gives us an active view of hitting, stabbing, shooting, or
other graphic incident compatible with our definition of novel
of violence. The scenes we do have in Unit One, however, are
the circumstantial evidence that death and destruction are about
to occur. Those scenes of violence in Unit Two are scenes of
primary or manifest violence. They are overt and deadly. They
initially continue the secondary type violence of Unit One but
soon escalate into graphic, active violence. They convey violence that is indeed prosecutable by man's law and, if we choose
to view the novel in moral contexts, violence that is punishable

by God. In fact, the overriding metaphor that Porter develops in the narrative is crime and punishment. Evidence is presented, facts recorded, circumstances developed, eyewitness opportunities afforded. We are judge and jury, but the accuracy of our perceptions and the wisdom of our judging are severely tested.

In Unit One, Porter exhibits evidence of what happens when individuals fail to acknowledge that they are naturally violent animals. The dramatic irony that results when we realize how little these characters understand their desperate lives is easily identified. Moreover, as we will see, scenes of violence offer a telling vantage point from which to view the narrative per se. However, finding a philosophical or psychological base from which to study the Thompsons and their violence is another matter. Porter makes them so assiduously one dimensional that even the traumatic events of Unit Two do not shock them into self-awareness. She also purposely makes them frontier people, essentially uneducated and rustic. They are not barbarians, and neither are they without worth. Quite the contrary, they are most in need and thus most deserving of our tender mercies. Yet they themselves remain the raw material from which sensitive, thinking individuals might develop. Their remote farm and their inchoate minds constitute the literal and emotional boundaries within which we must join them. Instead of forcing them to operate on our relatively sophisticated level—a philosophical environment in which they simply cannot function— we understand them better by seeking a level of compassion commensurate with their own.

That level is best reached through the violence that defines the Thompsons' lives, even though they themselves comprehend practically none of the implications of that violence. As noted, this discrepancy between what we know about violence and what the Thompsons do not know about it forms the abiding dramatic irony that fuels the entire narrative. The violence of Unit One is mundane, the kind of violence that is common in any family, especially a rural South Texas family of the 1890s. Royal Earl Thompson is a typical male citizen of his time and place; and his personality, in Louis Leiter's phrase, is marked by an "incipient but always threatening violence" (211). As a textual element, this is background or expository violence. Using allusions to violence, Porter brings all the Thompson family members together in their various single and united relationships. Violence is the adhesive that holds the family together.

Royal Earle Thompson immediately introduces violence with his allusion to "two niggers" that worked for him and who "got into a cutting scrape up the creek last week, one of 'em dead now and the other in the hoosegow at Cold Springs" (325). Ellie Thompson is then seen lying in her cocoon of darkness, complaining that life was "such a battle" (328) and remembering all the "cranky," violent men in that life (330). Next, both Royal Earle and Ellie interact with their boys in a conversation with violent overtones. Hearing that the Sunday School Superintendent has reprimanded Herbert, Royal Earle becomes "a hurricane of wrath" and sends them to bed (334). Then, after the boys have sneaked away, Porter offers the only scene that suggests sexual intimacy between Mr. and Mrs. Thompson. Feeling his version of affection, Royal Earle gives his wife "a good pinch on her thin little rump" (335). Ellie responds:

> 'Why, Mr. Thompson, sometimes I think you're the evilest-minded man that ever lived.' She took a handful of hair on the crown of his head and gave it a good, slow pull. 'That's to show you how it feels, pinching so hard when you're supposed to be playing,' she said, gently. (335)

Robert Penn Warren stated (or probably created) the conventional interpretation of this scene. He sees the pinching as a form of "masculine, affectionate bragging and bullying and teasing" and Ellie's response as "shy and embarrassed playfulness." The entire scene, Warren says, is "a sudden brightness and warmth" in their otherwise "drab world" (14). To some extent, Warren's evaluation is correct. There is more to the scene, however, than his optimistic view reveals.

The short passage is a paradigm of how inextricably joined are sexuality and violence. The drawn shades, headaches, and perpetual illness indicate that Ellie may not have been sexually active for years. In a double entendre phraseology that shows how unaware he is of her basic instincts (and of verbal subtlety), Royal Earle notes that Ellie has "gone down" (336) on him years ago. Royal Earle is essentially ignorant as to why his wife has deteriorated and spends much time seeking darkness. He is dumb to a fundamental caveat: human relations, like gates and spring houses, require constant maintenance lest they deteriorate into uselessness. Still an intellectual juvenile, Royal Earle thinks of affection and foreplay in terms of aggressive rump pinching. Ellie's fundamentalist Baptist rearing has taught her that sex is associated with the "evilest" things, and Royal Earle has done no work over the years to modify that Calvinist dogma. Consequently, Ellie's own repressed sexuality has transformed into migraines and passive resistance. Rather than devote any effort to establishing an intimate relationship with Ellie—either sexually or intellectually—Royal Earle lets his sloth direct him to alcohol and prostitutes at the Buda Saloon, with its upstairs rooms. As his braying laugh signifies, where women and general human relations are concerned, Royal Earle is a jackass.

Ellie, however, must share the blame for the conditions under which her family lives. Just how tightly controlled she keeps her desire is signified by her response (or lack of response) to her husband's rump-pinching. She offers no squeals, no yelps, no exclamations of any type. She expresses no pleasure, no anger, and no surprise. To show just how inverted Ellie's emotional responses have grown, Porter reverses the usual relation between the rhetoric of violence and the message it conveys. The words Porter uses to describe Ellie's reaction to Royal Earle's pinching are studiously nonviolent, almost loving: good, slow, playing, gently. By juxtaposing the gentle words with the abusive action they describe, Porter emphasizes how much anger and dormant violence have been produced by Ellie's denying her two fundamental instincts. At this stage in the narrative, knowing the extent to which she has repressed her sexuality and her violence, we may well anticipate that Ellie is the character who will soon erupt into maniacal violence.

Unit One ends with three allusions that place violence closer to the surface and show how the Thompsons have been unable to acknowledge the violence that dictates their existence. All three allusions center on Arthur and Herbert's playing with Helton's harmonicas. Retaining the secondary violence typical of Unit One, Porter gives us this important scene retrospectively. Ellie does not recount it till years later, a fact that again illustrates how much the Thompsons refuse to acknowledge the importance of violence in their life. She remembers one day looking for "shade" in which to hide her eyes and having instead to see Helton attacking her sons:

> Mr. Helton was *shaking* Arthur by the shoulders, *ferociously*, his face most *terribly* fixed and pale. Arthur's head *snapped* back and forth and he had not stiffened in resistance, as he did when Mrs. Thompson tried to *shake* him. His eyes were rather *frightened*, but surprised, too, probably more surprised than anything

else. Herbert stood by meekly, watching. Mr. Helton
*dropped* Arthur and *seized* Herbert, and *shook* him
with the same methodical *ferocity*, the same face of
*hatred*.                                                    (340)

I have added the italics to emphasize how in this excerpt Porter
reverts to the more traditional usage of the rhetoric of violence.
It is a rhetorically harsh, violent passage that is compatible with
the anger it describes. Moreover, the passage reveals the immense violence that the placid, plodding Olaf Helton is repress-
ing. We do not know at this point just how violent he has been,
but his shaking of the two boys gives us a good indication of his
potential. Then too, as noted, the passage further shows how absolutely Mr. and Mrs. Thompson avoid any recognition of the
violence that boils just beneath the surface of  their mundane
lives and that is about to erupt to destroy those lives. This eruption is not merely forced upon the Thompsons "by the in-
tractable Hatch, is not sudden and unmotivated, but the local
conclusion of a life or oral lassitude on one hand and rigidly
fixed but limited morality on the other" (Leiter 212-213).

Finally, the passage plays a trick on readers who by this
point in the narrative may have begun to feel smug about understanding Porter's design and purpose. The violence motif so
far in Unit One has certainly become apparent. Continuing that
motif, this passage leads us to conclude that if not Ellie, then the
mysterious stranger will bring havoc to the Thompson's dull existence. If he can shake children, then perhaps he is capable of
slaying the entire family in their sleep. We too have had the
urge by now to shake the Thompsons out of their stupor. So
having the calm, silent, diligent savior of the dairy farm erupt in
destructive violence would be a clever ironic twist to the narrative. And one the self-congratulatory reader would applaud,
since he has anticipated such a turn. However, Porter does not
manage her art in conventional ways. "Her method of composition," Robert Penn Warren recognized years ago, "Does not, in
itself, bend readily to the compromise" (8). We soon learn that
after his original sin, and despite the capacity for violence that he
demonstrates with his attack upon the boys, Helton never again
raises his hand to harm another. Darlene Unrue oversimplifies
Helton when she concludes that he "is a dead man, simply waiting for law and order to catch up with him, just as he brings
death indirectly to other characters" (79). He in fact exemplifies
how controlled violence can lead to order and harmony. The

slothful, inert Mr. Thompson who seems so ripe for being victimized will be the one who surprises us.

Minutes after having been shaken by Helton, the boys forget the attack and return to their play.

> They galloped through their chores, their animal spirits rose with activity, and shortly they were out in the front yard again, engaged in a wrestling match. They sprawled and fought, scrambled, clutched, rose and fell shouting, as aimlessly, noisily, monotonously as two puppies. They imitated various animals, not a human sound from them, and their dirty faces were streaked with sweat.                                (341)

Here again Porter reverses the rhetoric of violence in relation to the message. Though the excerpt describes play, it describes it in violent language. More important, however, is the implication that children are more attune to instinctual violence than adults. Their encounter with Helton's violence has not visibly harmed them. On the contrary, it seems to have put them in closer contact with their own incipient violence. Forgetting his attack, they soon return to "play" that is a preparation for their own adult violence. That they imitate various animals and momentarily abandon human speech shows how close Homo Sapiens is to his primordial ancestry and how violence is an integral, natural part of his constitution. The "play" passage is perhaps Porter's most direct statement of her belief in a naturalistic universe.

The final ironic turn to the shaking episode is that the boy's father threatens to "take a calf rope to them" for dirtying Helton's harmonicas. He tells them how his own "pa used to knock me down with a stick of stove wood or anything else that came handy," and threatens to "break every bone in 'em" (342). He tells Ellie that "It's a wonder [Helton] don't just kill 'em off and be done with it" (343). The most apparent function of this outburst is to show us that Royal Earle's indignation is misdirected. He should be angry at Helton, not his sons, because Helton's attack on the boys is inappropriate if not dangerous. Yet, Royal Earle is so dependent on Helton that he will  not risk offending him. This dependence accounts in great part for the more violent events soon to follow.

The outburst also verifies something we have already suspected: Royal Earle himself was physically abused as a child. Now he passes that pattern of abuse on to his own children. Only his pathological laziness prevents him from actually picking up the stick of stove wood and breaking bones, as his own father did to him. That parental abuse may well help explain why Royal Earle denies his own violent instincts till they erupt fatally. Taken in context of the "play" passage, Royal Earle's outburst against his sons indicates that Porter saw both an environmental and a hereditary explanation for violence. Having witnessed her father's uncontrolled swings between violent hatred and superficially expressed love, Porter learned early that humans are caught in the double prongs of a naturalistic trap. They are programmed for violence genetically; and should they manage to control that genetic trait, they must then face the traumas of environment. It is a trap few humans totally avoid or survive.

Royal Earle's outburst is the final scene of violence in Unit One of *Noon Wine*. Immediately after the brief transitions of section five, the apotheosis of all this  unacknowledged violence will appear. The Thompsons are about to learn how deadly it is to deny violence till it has grown too big to redefine.

Along with several ancillary scenes of violence, three major scenes dominate Unit Two: Royal Earle's story of his insane aunt, his killing of Homor T. Hatch, and his suicide. The first echoes the secondary violence of Unit One, the second is overt violence, and the third is imminent overt violence. Unlike any scene of violence in Unit One, we witness two of these major scenes of violence in Unit Two. The secondary violence that creates such tension in Unit One escalates into active, bloody death—and thereby is more ironically cathartic for the audience than any other element in the narrative. Typical of the pathology of violence, all acts of fatal violence in Unit Two are performed by males.

Homer T. Hatch, who appears at the beginning of section six, is not Royal Earle's secret sharer or some suddenly transmuted other self. Consistent with the violence that dominates the text, Hatch is the incarnation of the dormant violence that marks Unit One. When Porter has the sardonic omniscient narrator note that Hatch "certainly did remind Mr. Thompson of somebody" (347), she implies that Hatch personifies the violence that psychobiologists trace back to the time when unicellular amoeboids began to consume other amoeboids to become multicellular and that anthropologists recognize in the chain of human development from Australopithecus afarensis to Homo Habilis to Homo Sapiens. In a phrase, Royal Earle is looking eye-to-eye with his own humanness. He cannot bring his physical or mental energy into focus long enough, however, to recognize that Hatch is presenting him with the rare opportunity of acknowledging his own violence. Too mentally and physically lazy to take advantage of the potential for self-discovery that Hatch's arrival offers, Royal Earle remains true to his pattern of behavior and continues to hide behind lies and social props.

Though we have already grown impatient with this unexamined behavior in Unit One, we should nonetheless recognize that Royal Earle is not totally to blame for his missed opportunity for self-discovery. Hatch is not easily recognizable because he also disguises his violent self. He camouflages his violence beneath the bunting of law and order, flies the banner of social good, and as a bounty hunter hides behind the violence of others. Like a social maggot, he lives off the wounds of a violent culture. His tricking Olaf Helton's mother into revealing her son's whereabouts then making her pay for his trip typifies his parasitic nature. That we view him as one of the most despicable characters in American fiction suggests how odious we judge those who thrive off violence without themselves acknowledging their own violence. More ironically, that he operates within the laws that our culture approves, that he is a good citizen by any definition that we can apply under those laws, and that he is a hale fellow with a gift for gab reminiscent of our politicians, proves that like Royal Earle, we too may not be astute in recognizing how desperately we construct disguises for our true instincts.

Royal Earle himself gives us the first tangible indication that Homer T. Hatch's arrival means that primary violence has finally strolled through the gate that Helton has readied for him. Hatch tells Royal Earle that Helton was once in a lunatic asylum. Not wanting to admit that he has already been harboring another persona of violence, Royal Earle diverts his thoughts by telling Hatch how his Aunt Ida "got vi'lent and they put her in one of these jackets with long sleeves and tied her to an iron ring in the wall, and Aunt Ida got so wild she broke a blood vessel and when they went to look after her she was dead" (349). This darkly humorous anecdote is a telling allusion to violence. It reminds us that Porter believes that violence generally and suicide specifically are hereditary; Aunt Ida's death foreshadows Royal Earle's own self destruction; and the indefinable catalyst that ignites Aunt Ida's explosion is the same catalyst that ignites

Royal Earle's own "crazy" violence. Given the act that Aunt Ida is the only female other than Ellie who seems to have had any lasting impact on Royal Earle's memory, Porter may be implying that the proper code of civil behavior lies somewhere between Aunt Ida's irrational, insane violence and Ellie's passive, whining subservience. Just where on that continuum or what that code is, however, remains unstated and problematic.

Royal Earle's murdering Hatch is the central scene of violence in the narrative. It is located in the middle of the text; it brings together the four major adult actors in the novel (Royal Earle, Ellie, Helton and Hatch); all previous actions foreshadow it; and all subsequent actions develop from it. Moreover, it is dramatic and beautifully written in that it remains true to the slightly sardonic tone of the omniscient narrative voice but takes the narrative to a higher and more complex plane. That is, Porter raises the objective correlatives several levels. For example, the same narrative facilitator who announces drolly, and with a tone of slight superiority, that Royal Earle can sit for hours fretting about who will take care of the ragweeds growing around his woodpile must now turn attention to what happens when that same man is forced out of lassitude and isolation to confront the judicial system, his neighbor's attitudes, and ethical questions that he is not prepared to answer. In other words, the grim humor that marks Unit One, with its tobacco-spitting crudeness, insensitive anecdotes of crazy aunts and dead Negroes, and double entendres, leads to but does not facilitate the dire consequences of Unit Two. The braying laugh and repeated inane joke about "giving beer to a goat" (332) no longer serve. That Porter manages this narrative shift from the comically trivial traits to the tragically vital ones without hesitation or obvious sign attests to the purity of her artistry. How she manages the violence, however, is our immediate concern.

This artfully managed central scene is not necessarily the scenario that we expected, based on evidence already given to us. We have thus far met three suspects who seem more suited to violence and who have better motives for killing than Royal Earle: Helton, the mysterious stranger who attacks children; Ellie the frustrated and abused wife; and Hatch the bounty hunter who thrives on other's blood. Royal Earle is the most torpid, least motivated of them all. Ironically, however, this moral and physical lassitude is precisely why Royal Earle turns out to be the killer. Quite simply, he wants to protect the slothful life that

Olaf Helton has made possible. Fearing to lose the man who does all his work and who keeps his veneer of respectability in repair—and having some sincere regard for a man who over nine years has become the nearest thing he has to a friend— Royal Earle refuses to let Hatch take Helton. Appropriately, the violent outburst is as surprising and confusing to Royal Earle as it is to us.

The added italics mark the rhetoric of violence that Porter applies to the scene:

> He saw the fat man with his long bowie *knife* in his hand, he saw Mr. Helton come around the corner of the run, his long jaw dropped, his arms *swinging*, his eyes *wild*. Mr. Helton came in between them, *fists* doubled up, then stopped short, *glaring* at the fat man, his big frame seemed to collapse, he *trembled* like a shied horse; and then the fat man *drove* at him, *knife* in one hand, handcuffs in the other. Mr. Thompson saw it coming, he saw the *blade* going into Mr. Helton's stomach, he knew he had the *ax* down on Mr. Hatch's head as if he were *stunning* beef.                    (358)

Royal Earle has shunned work most of his life, categorizing it vaguely as (1) unbecoming, (2) for women, and (3) proper for men. The last category is very small, filled with types so rare that Royal Earle fortunately has not encountered an example. Here at last, however, is the man's work that Royal Earle has sought: killing, murder, violence. He does it quickly and surprisingly well, in a classic martial encounter of ax, blade, slit stomach, and split head. We may regret that Porter avoids giving us the blood and gore that would make the scene even more authentic, but the scene nevertheless works as a powerful example of violence.

This single moment when physical exertion combines with instinctual drive offers Royal Earle his one chance for redeeming a worthless life. He proves, however, to know his neighbors no better than he knows himself. Having slain Hatch, his response should be to proclaim that he is indeed a wronged man capable of murder. Texans of the day did not condone intrusions into their private lives and admired honest violence more than mealy-mouthed excuses. Had Royal Earle said "The damned bounty-hunting outsider invaded my property and threatened my family and hired man, so I killed the SOB with my ax," he would be admired as a man who took care of his own. What is more important, he would be much more at peace with himself. Porter sets the story in her native state to empha-size this "community" connection. Moreover she exaggerates the importance of place by inserting a headnote that calls setting to our attention. She wants to make sure we are aware of pre-cisely where we are and when we are there: the society of Rural South Texas, 1896-1905. It was a violent society in a violent time. To reconcile himself to it and to himself, Royal Earle should therefore wash himself in the blood of his violence and broadcast his notoriety. By so doing, he would place himself in the violent tradition of the West, especially of the Texas frontier.

We may not rest comfortable with the message that this combination of community politics and unpunished violence conveys. However, we are probably more in agreement with the citizens of Buda, Texas, than we care to admit. Even if Hatch has tweaked our social consciousness with platitudes about moral and legal duties and society's safety, we still do not like him. We fear his taking of Olaf Helton as much as Royal Earle fears it, al-though for different reasons. Like Royal Earle we want Hatch "off this place" (358). We admire the order and sanity that the "lunatic" Helton has wrought and—especially from our fin de siècle retrospective—appreciate how difficult such accomplish-ments are. Even though Hatch is on the side of law and order, we know that he and not Helton is the threat to peace and tran-quillity. We consider the case of his murder and instantly con-done the destruction of this despicable intruder. We stand as judge and jury and exonerate his killer. Justifiable homicide, we reason.

Yet, not surprisingly, Royal Earle can neither understand nor share the logic that culminates in such a liberating attitude toward violence. Consequently, he mismanages his one poten-tially redemptive moment by turning it into a pastiche of ill-re-membered facts and outright lies. Worse, he hides his inadequa-cies behind a woman and further abuses his wife when he forces Ellie to carry his lies into the social arena. Like his family and neighbors, we are soon disappointed in Royal Earle, are next dis-gusted, and then hostile. Years ago, focusing on Porter's "power to make the common thing glow" (12) and talking specifically about the opening scene with the churn, Robert Penn Warren captured the essential flaw that leads to Royal Earle's suicide. Warren's remains the best summary of Royal Earle's undevel-oped personality:

> [Mr. Thompson] is the sort of man who ought, or thinks
> he ought, to be holding the reins of a spanking horse
> and not the cord of a churn, and his very gesture has a
> kind of childish play acting. Somewhere in his deep-
> est being, he is reminded of the spanking horse with
> the belly swishing in the trot, the horse such a fine
> manly man ought to have under his hand, if luck just
> weren't so ornery and unreasonable, and so he plays the
> game with himself. But he can't quite convince him-
> self. It is only a poor old churn, after all, woman's work
> on a rundown and debt-bit shirt-tail farm, with kids
> and an ailing wife, and so he spits his tremendous spits
> or masculine protest against fate, and the brown juice
> gleans with its silly, innocent assertiveness on the
> stones the woman's broom has, so many times, swept
> clean of this and that.                                    (13)

Ironically, this detailed look that Porter gives us of Royal Earle's self-satisfied stupidity distances him from us. In a sense, it "de-sympathizes" him. Thus, his suicide is as far removed from our conscience as the muffled shotgun blast that inspired Porter's violent tale.

Royal Earle's suicide is purposely anticlimactic. A pathetic conclusion to a wasted life, it is a cowardly act of violence that negates the potential good of the violent outburst that killed Hatch. His note is more revealing than his imminent suicide. With the stub of a moistened pencil, he writes:

> 'Before Almighty God, the great judge of all before who
> I am about to appear, I do hereby solemnly swear that I
> did not take the life of Mr. Homer T. Hatch on purpose.
> It was done in defense of Mr. Helton. I did not aim to
> hit him with the ax but only to keep him off Mr. Hel-
> ton. He aimed a blow at Mr. Helton who was not look-
> ing for it. It was my belief at the time that Mr. hatch
> would of taken the life of Mr. Helton if I did not inter-
> fere. I have told all this to the judge and the jury and
> they let me off but nobody believes it. This is the only
> way I can prove I am not a cold blooded murderer like
> everybody seems to think. If I had been in Mr. Helton's
> place he would of done the same for me. I still think I
> done the only thing there was to do. My wife—[he
> deletes these two words]. . . . It was Mr. Homer T.
> Hatch who came to do wrong to a harmless man. He
> caused all this trouble and he deserved to die but I am
> sorry it was me who had to kill him.'                      (371)

Numerous elements of this note require attention. Here for the first time we see Royal Earle invoke God. From the beginning of the narrative to the end, he has been confined to his own narrow perception. Other than for allusions to perfunctory church attendance and Ellie's once teaching Sunday School in Mountain City, religion plays no role in the novel or in the Thompsons' lives. For that matter, Porter generally shows little regard for religion as it is practiced. As Darlene Unrue summarizes the situation, "Although Porter held a belief in God and found beauty and power in some religious rituals, she was often critical of what she regarded as the abuses of institutional religion, which she said provided unsatisfactory answers to the most basic questions about life" (10-11). In any case, even assuming that Royal Earle's note is a prayer addressed to a God in whom he sincerely believes (which is problematic), his words are more damning than expiatory. His final plea to God for mercy is no more than a reiteration of the legal defense he learned to mouth from lawyer Burleigh. It continues the central lie on which that ploy was based. (Hatch did not aim a blow at Helton and Thompson knew that Helton was an escaped murderer.) His note further compounds the error by telling God who deserves to die and who does not. Royal Earle probably did not need to lie to the jury to get exonerated, but that he compounds the lie in his plea to "God" gives ultimate proof of his irredeemablility. He cannot distinguish between man's law and some higher law of nature (call it God or whatever one chooses), and that inability reveals the mindlessness by which his life is directed.

Rather than proving himself blameless in the eyes of man and God, therefore, Royal Earle's suicide note proves his absolute guilt. Two reiterated phrases from the note offer subtle clues to understanding Porter's intent vis-à-vis Royal Earle's personality. Both are repeated from his response to Arthur's threatening to "blow [his] heart out" (369) for mistreating Ellie. Ironically surprised that his sons should think he could abuse their mother, Royal Earle tells them "I never did your mother any harm in my life, on purpose" (370). In his note, Royal Earle insists that he did not kill Hatch "on purpose" and that he is a "harmless" man. In two crucial moments, therefore, Royal Earle depends on the two lame phrases "on purpose" and "harmless" for absolution. Because of acts he has done and acts he has left undone, Hatch is dead, Helton is dead, Ellie is hysterical and near catatonic, his sons view him as a threat, and Royal Earle himself has been humiliated by his fellows. His life is strewn with destruction like the battle ground that Ellie earlier imagines life to be. Yet Royal Earle refuses to accept responsibility for any of this devastation.

If at any stage of his trial (the legal one and the moral one), he had paused, like the questing knight facing the wasteland, to ask what does it all mean and what might I do to change it, Royal Earle's redemption would be possible. The harmony that Helton has brought to his literal landscape and the spring that he revitalized symbolize the moral possibilities that exist for Royal Earle. He is, however, incapable of making subtle transitions between literal and spiritual realms. Moreover, he is no Galahad. The only quest he can make is to wander pathetically among people embarrassed by his wheedling and who are often as vacuous as he. His quest is pointless and he asks the wrong questions. Had he accepted the cathartic power of violence properly directed through socially beneficial channels, he might well have become the upstanding citizen and happy man he has long pretended to be. Ellie would not have had to lie, she would not have reverted to insane hysteria, his sons would not hate him, and his community would embrace him. However, because of his refusal to accept responsibility and his insistence that nothing he did was on purpose, all the restorative work that Helton began and died for has been absolutely negated.

The core of Porter's philosophy of violence in *Noon Wine*, and elsewhere, is a complex elucidation of a statement that Porter herself made in "The Necessary Enemy." She says that "Love is taught" but hate "comes of itself" (Collected Essays 184). Though just how that belief is expressed is often difficult to articulate, the paradox itself lies at the heart of everything we might say about Porter and violence. As Joan Givner correctly notes, Porter wrote fiction "to try to wrangle the sprawling mess of our existence in this bloody world into some kind of shape" (18). In *Noon Wine*, Porter is stating a truism that we have already noted several times: violence is as natural to Homo Sapiens as two ears and the forward-facing eyes of a predator. Killing our fellows is what makes us human, and, sadly, what allows us to be a part of the human community. If we are not violent, we are not human. Porter obviously accepted that hard, biological reality. No amount of sentimentalizing, romanticizing, or sermonizing could alter that truth. Yet, Porter did not despair because of that truth. She realized, too, that although we are a species damned by violence, we are also a species damned by a brain capable of understanding that violence. That is, we are killers capable of understanding that we are killers. No other animals, though violent all, can make that connection between instincts and experiential knowledge. With that "gift," we can understand that an existence without constant brain-bashing, gut-tearing blood and gore might be possible.

That possibility is what Porter means when she says that love, unlike violence, must be learned. Moreover, that learning must be a constant, ongoing process, like building a dam one small stone at a time against the torrent. Violence is easy, but the opposite of violence is excruciatingly difficult. Louis Leiter is correct when he notes that "Among the chief themes of *Noon Wine* is that of the daily expense of moral and intellectual stamina, its attrition through the flabbiest kind of action and reaction to existence" (219). The irony that underlies this belief in a vigilant and staunch intellectuality is perhaps more promising than the philosophy itself may at first appear to be: violence forces us to love each other. Without the incentive that horrific pain and suffering bring to us, our fabulous brains would not develop the antidote to that pain and suffering. Perhaps, even, if we are pure evolutionists, we might argue that the violent instinct gave rise to the brain to frustrate the self-destructive course that violence had set. Without violence, therefore, we would not exist. Quite simply, as Porter implies, we must love one another or we die.

It is paradoxical that in order to understand the many implications of the hate-love quandary, we must search through the xenophobia, bigotry, ignorance, and self-absorbed mindlessness of a people who sorely test our patience and capacity for applying the love that Porter says we must learn. We are on philosophically safe ground, however, to conclude that Porter is not advocating or condoning undirected or unchanneled violence. She is neither a moral nor social anarchist. Most of her writing implies the blessed rage for order that inspired her. What she does advocate, however, is that we must accept the violence that distinguishes us as human. To deny that instinct is also to deny our humanness. We are violent animals for sure, but we are *reasoning* violent animals. We can be aware of our violence and thus direct it toward whatever end might keep us from ripping each other apart. Violence is negative only if it is repeated, irrational, and disrupts the social order.

Helton more so than any other character in the novel personifies this truth. He has channeled his violence into work and harmonica playing, has restored order to a disorderly place, and brought a modicum of satisfaction to a family that has done little to deserve his efforts. Those who deny or abuse the harmony that violence can produce (Royal Earle, Hatch, the sheriff, even Arthur and Herbert) are the destructive individuals. As a true aesthete, Porter knew that art can transform any experience, and in that transformation make the most horrible of life's elements enjoyable. It is this aesthetic appreciation that Helton silently personifies and that Porter brings to bear upon violence generally.

It is tempting to interpret the motif that Royal Earle highlights with his "I am blameless" defense as Porter's commentary on the sins of omission and commission. Doing so, however, too strongly suggests that Porter is on a theological crusade. Superimposing moral codes on texts that do not intrinsically support such weight is critically arrogant, however; and *Noon Wine* gives few clues from which to launch ex cathedra pronouncements. We risk the intentional fallacy by assuming that because Porter was Catholic and because other of her stories rely on that faith, then *Noon Wine* must be a theodicy too. In this short novel, however, she is more concerned with pragmatic human actions than with theological possibilities. Rather than extrapolate a theology and dissect Royal Earle's relationship with God, we profit more by concentrating on the mess he has made of his life here and now. His suicide is less a denial of the Church that happens to condemn self-slaughter and more the cowardly act of an individual who cannot cope with the pain caused by his own mindless actions. It is that mindlessness that Porter condemns.

# Ernest Hemingway's
## *For Whom the Bell Tolls*


In discussing violence and verbal form in American fiction, Michael Kowalewski chooses not to discuss *For Whom the Bell Tolls*, mentioning it only in passing. This is a regrettable omission, because *For Whom the Bell Tolls* is the novel in which Hemingway handles violence most convincingly and because Kowalewski otherwise makes intelligent comments about Hemingway's management of violence. In discussing *To Have and Have Not*, for instance, Kowalewski quotes the (in)famous passage in which Harry Morgan details the gut-shooting of Pancho by the "nigger" with a Tommy gun. "While the violence in this moment is random, disturbing, and explicit," Kowalewski notes, "the language of its depiction seems not only uncharacteristic of Hemingway (as does most of this novel) but fairly tame as well" (132-132). "Tame" is the key word here because Hemingway's writing about violence is generally tame. For a writer so intimately identified with violence in all its manifestations, Hemingway is surprisingly bland when he has to confront specific scenes of violence. That "tameness" in *For Whom the Bell Tolls* would have benefited significantly from Kowalewski's analysis.

In passing, and before risking my own critical skin by presuming to say something worthwhile about an author who has been over-analyzed into a literary cliché, I might note that Kowalewski's comments offer one of the sanest recent evaluations of Hemingway and of the existing criticism. Kowalewski writes a candid overview and conveys the thinking that long ago abandoned texts and turned Hemingway into a literary demigod—or demi-devil as some would have it. (In fact, the only weakness in Kowalewski's book is that he devotes too much time to summarizing the criticism and not enough to his own analysis.) Kowalewski aptly warns that "Biographical genuflections have not only impaired our awareness of the nature and function of [Hemingway's] writing, they have often willfully misconstrued it by subordinating his verbal behavior to extratextual concerns" (133). Kowalewski's warning that we should return to what Hemingway actually wrote should be posted above the word processor of every American literary critic.

I give attention to Kowalewski's words because they expose much of and offer a lucid corrective to the "critical tendentiousness" (139) that has marked Hemingway criticism. More importantly, however, they save my having to construct a lengthy synopsis of numerous tangential elements before being pardoned to speak about a very specific element of Hemingway's technique in one single novel. I agree with Kowalewski's observation that "There is a long tradition of disliking Hemingway's work" and that "Much of the disapproval is aimed at his preoccupation with violence" (131). I agree even more so that "neither the new nor the old approaches to violence in his work actually confront it" and that "Scenes of violence in Hemingway's fiction afford a telling vantage from which to discern what kind of perceptual seismograph we find wavering in his work" (133). Therefore, partially because Kowalewski has covered the criticism and the other novels so well, I concentrate only on scenes of violence as they appear in *For Whom the Bell Tolls*. They are obviously only one of many ways to access the novel, but they do indeed offer an excellent vantage point from which to judge what Hemingway wrote.

Considering how much Hemingway is identified with war, bullfighting, hunting, suicide and other topics conventionally defined as violent, it is surprising to realize that only *For Whom the Bell Tolls* (1940) actually qualifies as a novel of violence—and then only marginally. As noted, Hemingway's writing about violence is generally circumspect. *The Sun Also Rises*, for instance, details no violence aside from the one-punch fist fight between Robert Cohn and Jake Barnes. Cohn does pummel Brett Ashley's matador lover, Pedro Romero, but that scene is presented after the fact, and rather prudently. That is, we are not eyewitness to the violence but are only told about it later by Mike Campbell. In subtext, there is the "wound" that causes Jake Barnes's impotency, but Hemingway offers no explicit account of that trauma. It remains as enigmatic as Brett Ashley's sex appeal.

*A Farewell to Arms* is even more circumspect in its management of potentially violent scenes. Frederic Henry's out-of-body experience when the trench mortar hits and Catherine Barkley's dying in the hospital are certainly two scenes that offer opportunities to explore the various psychological and rhetorical possibilities of violence. They are nicely polar, for instance. One presents the violence of birth, the other the violence of death. Yet, as powerful as the scenes are, they nonetheless lack the rhetoric of violence. Frederic's scene is rendered in poetic metaphor and Catherine's death is recorded in the flat, emotionless tones of Frederic's depression. Over all, *A Farewell to Arms* has little blood, no guts, no screams of agony. The wounded suffer and die silently, as does Aymo or the anonymous soldier whose life blood drips slowly down on Frederic in the ambulance. Even Frederic's shooting of the fleeing sergeant is told in nonviolent prose. That *The Sun Also Rises* and *A Farewell to Arms* are emotionally and intellectually powerful has little to do with how Hemingway manages their inherent violence.

Somewhat ironically, given Hemingway's own rigorous stylistic demands on himself, he writes about violence with a reservation more like the Victorian stiff propriety he is credited with helping abrogate and less like the Edwardian skepticism and critical reexamination with which he is more commonly associated. He seems at times, even, to reveal a romantic infatuation with the topics of violence and suffering. That is, he hesitates to apply realistic or naturalistic criteria when depicting those topics. In short, there is an antiseptic quality to his depictions of violence that at best limits their artistic scope and at worst renders them unconvincing to the reader.

One might argue that such criticism of Hemingway's management of violence is problematic because we are viewing him from an end-of-century Age of Violence in which nothing shocks and little surprises. From a sociological viewpoint, the age in which he wrote is as ancient as pterodactyls and as emotionally remote. That argument has some probity, but is weakened by the fact Frank Norris, Faulkner, and others had written candidly about violence years before Hemingway wrote *For Whom the Bell Tolls*. It is hard to imagine, for instance, Hemingway ever writing the Grimm-Christmas castration scene or the scene in which McTeague bites Trina's fingers, "crunching and grinding them with his immense teeth" (236). Even Willa Cather's depiction of the horrors of trench warfare in *One of Ours* (1922), a novel that Hemingway disparaged, gives the stench of rotting flesh and the disgusting image of body parts more credibly than Hemingway. This hesitancy to write "truly" about violence might suggest that Hemingway suppressed the trauma of his own extraordinarily violent life more than even he realized and therefore could not bring himself to write with the blood and guts rhetoric that his topics seem to demand. Be that as it may, however, the fact remains that compared to other novelists who have chosen to write about violent topics, such as Faulkner, Toni Morrison and Cormac McCarthy, Hemingway's writing about violence is less than bold.

Further irony attaches to the fact that of the major novels, the least artistically realized of the three is the only one that qualifies as a novel of violence. *For Whom the Bell Tolls* is a significant work of fiction in spite of itself. It has problems with everything from point of view management to authorial insincerity. The point of view is shared by an unidentified narrator, just about every other character in the novel, then even by a horse. This awkwardness has long been recognized, but bears repeating because it implies a problem with narrative control that Hemingway consciously tried to solve, but by some critic's estimates didn't. As W. M Frohock recognized in his own discussion of *For Whom the Bell Tolls* as a novel of violence, "The technical problem involved is the one Stendhal discovered when he had to write about Waterloo: that while the individual sees little, understands less, and knows almost nothing of a battle, the only other alternative is to postulate a more or less omniscient observer, with all this implies in the way of calling in post facto and inevitably false-ringing history to complete the panorama" (188). Hemingway did not quite solve this technical dilemma as he had solved it in the early fiction, most often with his first-person persona.

Then too, some of the chapters simply disrupt the narrative flow, and are uninteresting. The entirety of chapter 18, dealing with the political and private intrigues at Gaylord's restaurant in Madrid, adds little to the plot. Adequate transition from chapter 17 is given at the beginning of chapter 19, and thus chapter 18 seems an appendage meant to prove that Hemingway was a concerned social writer capable of significant political commentary. He himself spent much time at Gaylord's and the Florida Hotel and perhaps felt compelled to record the experience. Some critics have even questioned the inclusion of Pilar's story about the beginning of the revolution (chapter 10). Frohock was perhaps the first to wonder "what all this is doing in the present story anyway, since it has nothing to do with Robert Jordan's story nor very much to do in revealing the character of Pilar." Moreover, he says, "the feeling grows that it is always Hemingway talking, rather than Pilar" (191). Frohock is correct in seeing that Pilar's is another of those awkwardly placed chapters and that the point of view management is suspect, but he fails to give the scene due credit as the most important scene of violence in the novel, as we shall see. (As a matter of fact, Frohock does not discuss any element of violence in *For Whom the Bell Tolls*.) J. N. Vaughan was more nearly correct early on when he recognized the "34 pages [that] tell of a massacre happening in a little Spanish town" are the only notable part of an otherwise "inferior" book (16). The rest of *For Whom the Bell Tolls* is hardly inferior, except perhaps when compared to other of Hemingway's fiction, but Vaughan is correct in stating that Pilar's story gives a "full portrayal of actual massacre" such as we never had before (16).

A flaw more serious than awkward chapters is the sentimentalism that taints the narrative—an unfortunate side effect, no doubt, of Hemingway's sincere devotion to primitivism and a common flaw of tough-guy American writers. As David Madden notes, "One of the striking correlative features of America toughness is sentimentality" (70). With a fine turn of phrase, Howard Mumford Jones in 1940 recognized Hemingway's sentimental journeys. *A Farewell to Arms*, Jones complained, "was a moving book, but it was also sentimental." *For Whom the Bell Tolls*, on the other hand, "is not a stunt and is not merely sentimental" (2.) Not merely sentimental, but recognizably so. This sentimentalism appears clearest in Hemingway's treatment of the sexual relationship between Robert Jordan and Maria. Even other characters in the narrative, such as Primitivo, try to put the affair into unsentimental perspective:

> Primitivo turned around and looked after [Maria].
> 'If she did not have her hair cut so short she would be a pretty girl,' he said.
> 'Yes,' Robert Jordan said. He was thinking of something else.
> 'How is she in the bed?' Primitivo asked.

> 'What?'
> 'In the bed.'
> 'Watch thy mouth.'
> 'One should not be offended when—'
> 'Leave it,' Robert Jordan said. . . .          (279)

Aside from being humorous, Primitivo's guileless question about Maria's sexual capabilities is more courtesy than prurient interest. He could just a easily ask Jordan how his morning coffee tasted. He knows that the relationship between Jordan and Maria is an ordinary, common occurrence—like the mating of the hares that Augustín kills in the snow. Such routine sexual contact has no great importance for Primitivo. We concur with Primitivo's commonsensical assessment. We too know that the great love affair is little more than a brief sexual fling, cast in the rhetoric of an adventurous romantic. Frankly, it is sophomoric both in intensity and description. Hemingway, however, forgets to listen to his own better judgment and insists on elevating the affair to seismic (literally) proportions. Thus the scenes in which he presents the four sexual encounters are overwrought and melodramatic. This excerpt from the fourth encounter speaks for itself:

> And she said, 'Nay, there is no pain.'
> 'Rabbit.'
> 'Nay, speak not.'
> 'My rabbit.'
> 'Speak no. Speak not.'
> Then they were together. . . .
> 'Oh, Maria, I love thee and I thank thee for this.'
> Maria said, 'Do not speak. It is better if we do not speak.'
> 'I must tell thee for it is a great thing.'
> 'Nay.'
> 'Rabbit—'
> But she held him tight and turned her head away and he asked, 'Is it pain, rabbit?'
> 'Nay,' she said. 'It is that I am thankful too to have been another time in *la gloria*.'          (379)

Though sex and violence are inextricably related, "*La gloria*" is not my concern here. I mention the sexual motif as prelude to a more important caveat I wish to offer about violence in *For Whom the Bell Tolls*. The sentimentalism that is so apparent in Hemingway's descriptions of the Jordan-Maria affair infiltrates the scenes of violence. The sentimentalism is muted there, but it nonetheless dilutes a novel that ostensibly is about the horrors of civil war specifically and the terrors of unleashed violence generally. Pablo Picasso (perhaps the name source for the pig-eyed betrayer of Robert Jordan's idealism) painted *Guernica* in 1937, the same year that Jordan blows his bridge. In its screaming graphic silence, totally void of sentimentalism, the massive painting depicts the violence of the Spanish War more eminently than Hemingway's long novel. Despite its weaknesses, however, *For Whom the Bell Tolls* does develop an articulated motif of violence and is informed by a clearly stated philosophy of violence.

Unlike Faulkner, who concentrates his violence in one central scene and attaches all other narrative elements to it, Hemingway diversifies his violence into three identifiable scenes and one predominant action. The predominant action is the Spanish Civil War and the doomed efforts of the Republican band to survive the fascist's efforts to eliminate it. This action gives the narrative historical credence. Any reader familiar with the Spanish Civil War or other similar guerrilla operations can immediately recreate the tension that such wars cause. This historicity grounds the tale on the solid rock of fact and makes credible events that would otherwise sound fabulous. The three scenes of violence, however, are what make the novel significant as a novel of violence.

The scenes as they appear in the text are: (1) Pilar's long story about the massacre at the village, (2) the unidentified narrator's account of the fascist's killing of El Sordo and his men, and (3) the blowing of the bridge. Pilar's tale is the crucial scene of violence in the text. While the other two scenes are important in the physical and dramatic organization of the narrative, as scenes of violence their primary function is to facilitate and enhance Pilar's tale. With these three scenes, Hemingway develops an interesting and important experiment in point of view management that probably accounts for some of the criticism we have previously noted. Insofar as violence is concerned, however, the technique works to force the reader to abandon the objective distancing that historical reality encourages and to participate more emotionally in the violence that is the true issue at hand. The technique might be called incremental reader involvement. That is, the scenes progressively increase the degree to which the reader bears direct witness to them. Pilar's story is presented totally in flashback, none of it being given to us in present action. It is by far the longest and most graphically violent of the three. We witness only the end of the El Sordo massacre but hear most of it from the distant hills, with Pablo's band. The blowing of the bridge is the only scene of violence to which we are direct witness from beginning to end.

This method of narrating the three scenes presents an ironic inversion compatible with the mountainous landscape that is the setting for the narrative. Just before making Jordan listen to her tale, Pilar refuses to accompany him any further up the mountain and tells him that in the mountains "there are only two directions," down and up (97). Transferring setting to narrative design, Hemingway does not build up to the most graphic and detailed scene of violence (like climbing a mountain) but reverses the expected order and gives us the Pilar episode first and then gradually descents (like descending a mountain). Though both El Sordo's battle and the bridge blowing are deadly and dramatic, neither approaches Pilar's tale in length or graphically described viciousness. Furthermore, the text gives us no reason to suspect the credibility of narration in the El Sordo and bridge scenes. We witness them either in their entirely or at least sufficiently to have no doubts that they occur and that what we see is authentic. This is not the case with Pilar's story. We see none of the events she details and no one else in the novel corroborates her version of how those events unfolded. In short, the credibility of narration is most in question in Pilar's story. Thus the longest and most violent of the three scenes is the one about which we should be most skeptical. Moreover, the sequential arrangement renders the other two scenes anticlimactic insofar as violence is concerned. This premeditated anticlimax and the varying degree of narrative credibility, along with its intrinsic complexity, make Pilar's tale perhaps the most peculiar approach to violence that we have in any American novel.

Pilar's tale balances on one of the fundamental narrative devices that help make *For Whom the Bell Tolls* dramatically successful: the contrast between violence and domesticity. The literary value of this thematic contrast is not so much that it argues that violence is a behavioral aberration that nullifies domesticity but that domesticity is a temporary stay against violence. That is, violence is the norm and tranquillity the exception. This paradox is seen both in the battles that occupy the textual forefront and in the numerous incidental allusions to other conflicts, such as Robert Jordan's several recollections of his grandfather's participation in the American Civil War and frontier Indian skirmishes. Two important allusions document the truth that violence is hereditary and as ancient as humankind, and not an aberration from civil behavior. In speaking of Gypsies Anselmo says "They only know now there is a war and people may kill again as in the olden times without a surety of punishment" (40). Later Robert Jordan thinks of Spanish peasants such as Augustín and how naturally they kill: "It is their extra sacrament. The old one that they had before the new religion came from the far end of the Mediterranean, the one they have never abandoned but only suppressed and hidden to bring it out again in wars and inquisitions" (286). In other words, violence is a mode of behavior much older than Christianity or any of the other institutions that developed to teach that humans are perfectible. Anselmo and Jordan's two allusions to primitive prehistoric violence make clear that violence is ancient as the granite mountains in which the rebels fight and that the superimposed codes of "civilization," though apparently strong and sustaining, are as flimsy as the bridge that Robert Jordan blows away.

Pilar's story is the most prominent illustration of this paradox of violence and domesticity because it operates on several levels. First, Pilar tells her intercalary tale as she, Robert Jordan, and Maria are relaxing in an idyllic setting—by a mountain stream, sitting in the heather. Second, Pilar's story itself uses the stark contrast between daily life in a Spanish village and a cataclysmic civil war that suddenly turns into mob violence. That the reader is also in some comfortable, nonviolent environment while reading her gruesome story brings a third degree of contrast to the tale. This series of contrasts between civil routine and civil war heightens the intensity of the wrenching descriptions that Pilar offers in her account and connects her tale of violence to the larger narrative design.

The tale itself is a fundamental paradigm of violence. Pilar catalogs almost every type of violence that one human can inflict on another: shooting beating, burning, hacking, flailing, and dropping, perhaps even drowning as the victims hit the river below. Only rape is missing, but is insinuated by Maria's being one of the listeners to Pilar's account. We already know that the Falangists have brutalized Maria, and later we get details of their torturing and raping her following a raid similar to the one Pilar describes. Pilar's is a long tale, and she likes to linger over the various forms of brutality. She details no fewer than four men being flailed and then tossed over the cliff into the river 300 feet below, then gives graphic accounts of incidents such as the drunken mob's breaking into the Ayuntamiento and hacking the priest to death. Moreover, though she retains a certain reticence about gory details, she includes enough rhetoric of violence to maker her tale typical as an account of human viciousness. This paragraph depicting the treatment of Don Ricardo Montalvo is representative. I have added italics to mark the specific instances of the rhetoric of violence.

> So they *clubbed* him to *death* very quickly because of the insult, *beating* him as soon as he reached the first of the men, *beating* him as he tried to walk with his head up, *beating* him until he *fell* and *chopping* at him with reaping hooks and the sickles, and many men bore him to the edge of the cliff to *throw* him over and there was *blood* now on their hands and on their clothing, and now began to be the feeling that those who came out with truly *enemies* and should be *killed*.
>
> (111)

Along with its wide-ranging and specific accounts of violence, what distinguishes Pilar's story is that Hemingway gives it to a female narrator. We have already raised the question of Pilar's credibility. Hemingway himself anticipated such questions about his assigning Pilar to the most violent scene in the novel, and perhaps the most violent in any of his fiction. "God," he has Robert Jordan avow, "How she could tell a story. She's better than Quevedo, he thought" (134). Hemingway satisfies the need to justify Pilar as the narrator by having Jordan vouch for her as a world-class story teller. Hemingway's assumption, apparently, is that because he is male we will not question Jordan's veracity. Though we have so far been eyewitness to nothing that Jordan has done, and know of his exploits only through his own stream of conscious recollections, we are nonetheless expected to sanction his evaluation of Pilar. Before condemning Hemingway's chauvinist assumptions, however, we must remember that Robert Jordan is an instructor of Spanish and has written a factual book about Spain. He is no fictionist, and his engineering expertise needed to blow bridges proves how much he is grounded in pragmatics. He does know, however, that Francisco Gómez de Quevedo was a vitriolic satirist who spent four years in prison for attacking the follies and vices of Spanish society. Therefore, when Jordan refers to Pilar's "story" and compares her to Quevedo, he is not necessarily verifying her credibility. Like the reader, he is simply amazed by how wonderfully Pilar paces the story, manages details, handles dialogue, and sustains dramatic intensity. "Story" to Jordan means fiction, and nothing in his comment suggests that he sees her tale as a historically accurate account. He is impressed, therefore, not so much by its authenticity as by its inherent condemnation of a society that permits such atrocities and of individuals who are willing to inflict them, even if their church and state approve such behavior. The ultimate irony of Jordan's appraisal, however, is that neither he nor Pilar seem to suspect that the village mob has reverted to the purest form of human conduct. The enamel of civilization has been stripped away; and for several hours at least, the true violent nature of the human animal has reigned unchecked.

Sufficient evidence exists, therefore, to defend Hemingway against accusations that giving Pilar this important narrative assignment was a point-of-view faux pas, as Frohock and others have suggested. More likely, it was an effort to realize a premeditated narrative design suitable for his motif of violence. We see signs of this design not only in the long tale itself but in ancillary passages that Pilar narrates. Collectively, these narrations and their associated consequences exert a tremendous influence on the narrative. To facilitate access to this design technique, Hemingway gives us such elements as Pilar's ugliness, a quality that she emphasizes as prelude to her "ugly" story of the massacre; her allusions to bullfighters, one of which is embedded in the long story; and Robert Jordan's unexpected decision to trust Pablo and not Pilar with Maria's welfare after his death. This decision too is in part the result of Pilar's primary and ancillary narrations.

Even before Pilar is introduced, Rafael characterizes her as being "of an unbelievable barbarousness" (28). Then when we see her, she is described as being "almost as wide as she was tall" and dressed in black (30). In an even more telling passage, important because of its implied androgyny, Pilar admits to Robert Jordan that "I would have made a good man, but I am all woman and all ugly" (97). Her behavior throughout the novel mirrors these traits. She is capable of great anger, has "a tongue that scalds and that bites like a bull whip" (28), is given to fits of jealousy, is motivated much by lust, and has irrational fears (as of the airplanes). These characteristics in turn greatly compromise her judgment, as when she first tells Robert Jordan he was wise not to kill Pablo and then reverses her opinion, and later when she allows Pablo to trick her so that he may steal the detonators (361). This compromised judgment partially explains why Jordan chooses Pablo as Maria's caretaker, a point we will revisit shortly.

Pilar's physical ugliness and the commensurate barbarous personality contrast sharply with Maria's physical beauty and gentle personality. Pilar is jealous of Maria because she too is sexually attracted to Robert Jordan and resents his interest in the girl. Ironically, Maria looks as androgynous as Pilar, though the physical attributes are different. Maria is short haired, small breasted, thin, and, according to Pilar, looks like Robert Jordan. The essential difference between the two women, however, is in their behavior. Whereas Pilar is irritable, self-willed, and cantankerous, Maria is amenable, compliant, and subservient. In other words, she is the stereotypical "Hemingway woman": beautiful, sexual, and obedient. Whether Maria is a cliché is hardly the point. What is important is that Robert Jordan so prefers Maria to Pilar that he is willing to jeopardize the success of his operation and even his life by loving Maria. Pilar's control of the band is nearly absolute. Without her approval, Jordan accomplishes nothing. Yet his flaunting of the affair heightens the possibility that Pilar will turn against him, just as Pablo does because he is jealous of the stranger who arrives and usurps his influence and his women. Actually, as the woman scorned, Pilar has as much cause as Pablo to betray Jordan. While Jordan and Maria are fornicating, practically before her eyes, she must sublimate her sexual desires into remembered liaisons with a matador lover appropriately named Finito because he is limited by tuberculosis, fear, and Pilar's imagination. That is, while Jordan is a handsome, dynamic young man, Finito is hardly the stuff dreams are made of. This dichotomy in turn suggests that Pilar may be exaggerating her romantic interludes with Finito specifically as proof to Robert Jordan that she too is a sexually desirable woman and more generally to cope with the erotic conflicts Jordan has brought her.

One particular scene captures the image that Jordan unconsciously applies to Pilar and shows how Maria is the polar opposite of that image. This epitomizing scene is Pilar's description of death, the ultimate resolution to all violence. Not only is

Pilar a fortune teller who foresees death, she also knows its smell. In trying to convey that odor to Jordan, Fernando, and Rafael, she establishes her affinity with death and reveals the subtextual role that she personifies in the novel. After trying a ship analogy that fails to convey the smell of death, Pilar tells Jordan:

> After that of the ship you must go down the hill in Madrid to the Puente de Toledo early in the morning to the *matadero* and stand there on the wet paving when there is a fog from the Manzanares and wait for the old women who go before daylight to drink the blood of the beasts that are slaughtered. When such an old woman comes out of the *matadero*, holding her shawl around her, with her face gray and her eyes hollow, and the whiskers of age on her chin, and on her cheeks, set in the waxen white of her face as the sprouts grow from the seed of a bean, not bristles, but pale sprouts in the death of her face; put your arms right around her, Ingles, and hold her to you and kiss her on the mouth and you will know the second part that odor [of death] is made of.        (255)

Perhaps the element of this description that strikes us most (after the initial blast of nausea) is that Pilar is parodying the romantic interludes that Jordan shares with Maria. In short, with this horrid image of death she is mocking the sexual encounters that Jordan has found so sweet but that have antagonized Pilar. This putrid kiss of Death, Pilar is saying, is the end to which your earth-shaking love will lead. She desires that Robert Jordan realize a harsh fact: the brave, violent man who has kissed the maiden of youthful dreams must now kiss the foul hag of death.

Equally important in relation to the death motif is how the passage connects Pilar to the old woman who drinks the blood of the slaughtered and who thereby becomes the personification of Death. A rather obvious verbal association develops when the other band members, especially Rafael, refer to Pilar as the "old woman" (28). More subtle, and significant, is Pilar's own rhetorical association with the death woman. In recalling the Valencia idyll, she remembers eating fish, shrimp, pastries, and other delicacies. "Then," she says, "we ate even smaller eels alone cooked in oil and as *tiny as been sprouts and curled in all directions*" (85). The added italics remind us that the hairs that grow on the stinking old woman's waxen face like "sprouts from the seed of a bean" distinguish her and make her repellent. As

Rafael says, about to vomit, "That of the sprouts was too much" (255).

This "sprout" association in turn takes us back to Pilar's description of the village slaughter. Farm allusions punctuate the entire narrative, such as the flails and pitchforks used to kill the fascists. The double lines that the peasants form as a gauntlet are also reminiscent of the chutes through which cattle are led to slaughter. Pilar is intimately associated with these images. She does not commit any of the atrocities, but she eagerly watches, and does nothing to prevent the slaughter. She vicariously drinks the blood of the slaughtered by encouraging the men who act so violently. Even should she be fabricating all or part of the tale, the psychological truth it reveals about her affinity with violence and death remains valid. Her death association also explains why Pilar so lovingly recounts that horrible day. Like the old blood-drinking woman with the sickening face spouts, Pilar is closely associated with death.

With her bullfight allusions, Pilar merges death and violence with sexuality. She constantly recalls her matadors and compares Pablo with them. To her the violence of the bullfights and the fear that the matadors must overcome to face that violence are aphrodisiacs. In one specific recollection, however, she precisely merges the sexual instinct with the violent. In recalling the Valencia tryst with Finito, she remembers making "love in the room with the strip wood blinds" while outside the firecrackers were "exploding with great noise and a jumping from pole to pole with a sharpness and a cracking of explosion you could not believe" (85). The image is a bit Hollywoodish in its Freudian symbolism, but it nonetheless serves well to connect Pilar's sexual memories, bullfighting, and the violence of war as symbolized by the firecrackers. Both in her own imagination and as a persona within the text itself, Pilar is the character who most directly establishes the violence-sex-death triad. This triad further reminds us that the violent instinct and the sexual instinct are inextricably combined.

As we see, then, Pilar's narrations subsume interlocking associations that ultimately bring us back to the violence motif that dominates the narrative. The associations also explain why Robert Jordan, facing death, entrusts Maria to Pablo rather than Pilar. All textual evidence argues that if Jordan is still thinking rationally, he should consider no one other than Pilar as the person to take care of Maria after his death. Pilar has mothered

Maria, instructed her in wifely duties, and has sublimated her own sexual desires so that the girl can enjoy her sexual interludes with Jordan. Furthermore, without Pilar's fiery personality, the girl would not have survived. One of the most brutal incidental scenes of violence in the narrative is Rafael's remembrance of Pilar's behavior when the band rescued Maria from the train:

> the old woman tied a rope to her and when the girl thought she could not go further, the old woman beat her with the end of the rope to make her go. Then when she could not really go further, the old woman carried her over her shoulder. When the old woman could not carry her, I carried her. . . . And when I could no longer carry her, Pablo carried her, but what the old woman had to say to us to make us do it!          (28)

Moreover, Pilar has overcome her jealousy to support Jordan against Pablo's drunken refusal to help blow the bridge. She rallies the other band members to his cause and leads him to Sordo's camp in search of additional men and horses. Physically and psychologically, Pilar is the single most important person who makes Jordan's affair with Maria and his bridge-blowing possible.

Nonetheless, though he marvels at her story-telling abilities and otherwise voices admiration for Pilar, Robert Jordan rejects her when in crisis. His leg is crushed and he knows he will soon die. Standing nearby, Pilar immediately tells how they can manage the emergency: "'We will bind it up,' Pilar said. 'Thou canst ride that.' She pointed to one of the horses that was packed.'" Pablo's nonverbal private message, however, is what Jordan heeds: "Robert Jordan saw Pablo shake his head and he nodded at him." He dismisses Pilar's offer to save him, and calls Pablo to his side. The man whom he twice almost shot now bends to him. Pablo is physically closer to Jordan than any other person in the text has been except Maria: "The sweat-streaked, bristly face bent down by him and Robert Jordan smelt the full smell of Pablo" (461). The scene is strangely intimate for two men who hours before were making sounds of deadly enmity.

We can offer a number of feasible explanations for Jordan's choosing Pablo. One explanation is that Robert Jordan and Pablo, so superficially unlike, share a number of traits, none particularly attractive in terms of conventional moral codes. Both have executed comrades (Jordan shoots Kashkin, Pablo shoots his five compadres at the bridge). Both admire and know

horseflesh. Both lust after Maria. Both drink to excess (one is already a drunkard, the other on his way). Thus, though they
dream of some placid, domestic future, both would be misfits in
a peace-time society, even should they survive the war un-
scathed. Also, Robert Jordan has known from the beginning that
dynamiting the bridge is futile because the republican cause is already doomed. Perhaps, therefore, he inwardly respects the
judgment that Pablo displays by stating frankly that the operation is pointless and will accomplish nothing other than endan-
ger his band (an evaluation that proves completely accurate).
Moreover, even though Pilar sides with him, Jordan does not
respect her humiliating a man with whom she has lived and
supposedly loved since the beginning of the revolution. As we
see in his relationship with his "little rabbit" and his intense hatred of his mother, Jordan neither likes nor respects autono-
mous females.

Then too, despite his overt friendship with Pilar, Robert
Jordan may well not trust her with Maria. Though he has no
qualms about bedding a girl who only a month ago had been
raped and brutalized so that "she would shiver like a wet dog" if
anyone touched her (28), Jordan is nonetheless prudish. Pilar,
Rafael, and the others make light of their own sexuality and try
to tease Jordan about his, but he persists in making his affair
with Maria a thing of utmost seriousness. He also swears to her
that he is a man of limited sexual experience. This puritanical
attitude toward eroticism makes him uncomfortable with Pilar's
freely confessed homoerotic interest in Maria, although the confession may be purposely aimed at mocking Jordan's repressed
sexual attitudes.

All of chapter 12 concerns Pilar's jealousy and her overtly
admitted love for Maria. The three stop to rest under a pine tree
as they return from El Sordo's camp. Pilar insists that Maria lie
in her lap and then precipitates a conversation that is so clearly
homoerotic that even the naive Maria perceives immediately
what Pilar means. When Maria protests that "It was then explained to me there was nothing like that between us," Pilar
replies "There is always something like that" (154). Jordan
silently, and dourly, watches this exchange. When Pilar goads
him by asking what he thinks about what she has said, he curtly
replies "Not much" (156). Though Pilar insists that "I do not
make perversions" (155), her argument is hardly convincing to
Jordan and Maria. The chapter ends with Maria claiming that

Pilar is "Gross" and demanding that Robert Jordan not stay to assist Pilar. "Let her go," the humiliated Maria demands. "Let her go!" (157). This is the only time in the narrative that Maria shows any disobedience to Jordan or makes the slightest effort to have her own wishes obeyed. Her fear of "perversions" overcomes her fear of offending the man she loves. Jordan must keep his silence now because he does not want to agitate Maria or risk Pilar's loyalty. Later when he must ignore Maria's feelings and Pilar's loyalty no longer matters, he remembers the incident and decides Maria is safer with the pig-eyed traitor Pablo than with Pilar.

Finally, Robert Jordan may unconsciously associate Pablo with the two men who personify the two extremes that violence occupies in his psyche: his grandfather and his father. Jordan admires his grandfather almost to the point of obsession and disdains his father as a hopeless coward. One rises almost to myth because of a pistol; the other sinks to contempt because of that same pistol. One represents the violence of gallantry while the other represents the violence of self destruction. Superficially there seems no kinship between Grandfather Jordan and the drunken Pablo. Essentially, however, they are similar. Both are soldiers in wars of rebellion and both are cavalry men. Grandfather Jordan is a revered warrior of the Civil War and frontier Indian wars. He in turn admired John Mosby (who fought for the southern rebels) as the "finest cavalry leader that ever lived" (339). The bows and arrows, arrowheads, saber, and guns that his grandfather kept as souvenirs from his warring days are icons to the young Robert Jordan (336). Until very recently, Pablo too was a revered guerrilla leader and cavalry man. "Pablo was brave in the beginning," Anselmo, explains to Robert Jordan. "He killed more people than the cholera," Rafael adds admiringly (26). Now, however, Pablo is "very much afraid to die" (26).

This fear is what connects Pablo to Jordan's father. Jordan sees in Pablo's fear the cowardice that he attributes to a father who used Grandfather Jordan's .32 caliber Smith and Wesson pistol to shoot himself in the head. Because of that suicide, Jordan has to throw the gun away, thereby breaking a tie with his grandfather and tarnishing his memory. Moreover, Jordan has discussed suicide with Golz and has otherwise contemplated it, especially because he has had to shoot Kashkin to prevent his being tortured. Jordan knows that suicide is a very real possibility for him. This is why the ending of the novel presents such un-relieved tension. If Captain Berrendo and his troops do not kill Jordan after he fires upon them, will he try to kill himself to prevent capture? Ironically, how he will end his life is the most crucial decision in his life, and we do not know how he will handle it. His grandfather's heroic violence and his father's cowardly violence stand as the two poles by which Robert Jordan gauges his life, and by which he must determine his death.

This conflicting emotional melange is personified for Jordan in the ambiguous personality of Pablo. In many important particulars, Pablo is the apotheosis of all Jordan's doubts and fears and of his finest bravery. Because Jordan senses much of his own life in the old guerrilla, his choosing Pablo over Pilar is therefore consistent with his other decisions. As incongruous as it may seem, in the penultimate scene we have two warriors who in the face of death let all jealousies over women and politics dissolve. Violence bonds men as no other factor can.

One final ironic element of Pilar's narrative helps clarify Hemingway's philosophy of violence. The irony arises when Pilar says just before she begins her long tale of bloodlust that "I like to talk. It is the only civilized thing we have" (98). This statement associates the tale with the theme of domesticity versus violence that we have already noted. However, its greater importance is in the paradox that arises when Pilar uses "the only civilized thing we have" as a vehicle for conveying a graphic example of the most uncivilized thing we have. What Pilar seems to mean by her statement is that speech and the subsequent ability to fabricate immensely complex expressions of human actions and motivations are one of only two characteristics that separate Homo Sapiens from other animals. The other distinctly human characteristic, as we have noted, is that humans kill each other for no reason other than the apparent joy of the slaughter. (Pablo's shooting of the *guardia civiles* epitomizes this gratuitous killing, though the entire episode reflects it.) Therefore, Pilar's tale weaves a complex series of ironies relative to those three elements (speech, gratuitous violence and violence generally). She uses the one thing that makes us unique as communicators (speech and language) to reveal an example of the one thing that makes us unique as violent animals (gratuitous violence), while keeping both in the larger context of generic animal violence. What her tale ultimately reveals apropos violence is that because we have language we are the only creatures that can celebrate and perpetuate our viciousness. We bequeath oral and written histories of our gory deeds. *For Whom the Bell Tolls* is precisely such a record. Realizing this shadowy example of metafiction, we thus glimpse another example of how Pilar's tale stands as the violent paradigm of a violent novel.

What I have said so far may suggest that Hemingway created a mass of interrelated but murky ideas about violence. Certainly others have argued that possibility concerning various elements in his fiction. To his credit, however, Hemingway made an effort to articulate a philosophy of violence. What he actually states is more a rationale for violent male behavior than a philosophy that explains violence per se. Yet we cannot fault him on that basis. No one to date, whether he be biologist, theologian, or fictionist, has articulated a meaningful philosophy of violence. That is, violence is simply part of the genetic and instinctual human constitution and cannot be explained beyond that fact. One might as well philosophize about why Homo Sapiens has ten toes rather than twelve. Like poetry, violence doesn't mean; it just is. Most novelists, in fact, use violence as motif and motivation without making any effect to state clearly what rationale underlies their appropriation of the subject. Given the impossibility of creating a philosophy of violence, then, Hemingway actually excels in trying to state his philosophy succinctly without drifting into preachments—a trait he would not tolerate and which would have disrupted the narrative even more than some of the intercalary chapters that we have already noted.

Hemingway saves his statement of purpose till late in the novel. Whatever other faults Jordan may have, he is a man of conscience who thinks deeply about his actions and what motivates them. Thus it is appropriate that Jordan, inside one of his many interior monologues, voices the philosophy that drives men to such violence as the novel celebrates. Feeling contrite for having had to shoot the young Spanish cavalryman who happens upon him and Maria, Jordan tries to fashion some sort of philosophy to explain his violence. He tries first to comfort himself by rationalizing that he has "avoided killing those who are unarmed." His logic, however, invalidates such quaint thinking. Instead, he tells himself that "you have no right to do the things you do." Rationalizing that truth regarding his killing, he then fashions a philosophy of violence based on a clearly stated principle: "no man has a right to take another man's life unless it is to prevent something worse happening to other people" (304).

The question immediately arises, however, as to what Jordan means by something "worse." Does he mean worse than the taking of life or worse than the general situation he has witnessed with the loyalists in Spain? Or something else again? The context in which the philosophy is stated suggests that Hemingway means something worse than the taking of life. In other words, some "things" are worse than murder and therefore give one the "right" to kill. The text of the novel itself has already given us numerous examples of what that worse "something" might be: keeping segments of a population in poverty and ignorance; censuring political and religious thought; terrorizing citizens with threats of military reprisals; driving families from their homes. Things such as these, and other idealistic formulations, are what Jordan has in mind when he refers to something worse than killing. Thus, if there is a man whose actions work to cause any such enslaving circumstances for others, then Jordan is justified in killing that individual, no matter how good or innocent he may otherwise appear to be. The young cavalryman with the red Sacred Heart of Jesus may be a Christian youth from a loving family, but his service to promote fascism is cause enough for Jordan to kill him. This is true because his single death is overshadowed by the large number of "other people" who benefit from it. That Jordan's colleagues and the cause for which they struggle fail does not alter the concept that Jordan voices. The ideals of equality and freedom are promoted, even if they are not institutionalized as a direct result of the violent actions used to oppose their antitheses.

We might better understand Hemingway's idea if we recall that Faulkner promotes a similar philosophy of violence in *Light in August*. Though Faulkner does not state his idea so succinctly, it is visible in the Joe Christmas-Percy Grimm confrontation. Faulkner admires certain traits possessed by Percy Grimm. Ironically, some of those traits are shared by Robert Jordan, or at least Grimm attempts to rationalize his pursuit of Christmas with ideas that Christmas and his kind are a threat to freedom, young girls, and community service. He is deluding himself, of course, and the reader. Faulkner does not disagree with the ideas and idealism that Grimm espouses, but he severely condemns the methodology. Faulkner rejects Grimm because he does not personify a philosophy of violence that transcends his own unilateral, vicious actions. Grimm's warrior response in shooting and castrating Joe Christmas is not sanctioned by a greater good. The citizens of Jefferson are not saved from any horror by Grimm's actions, and no ideal of liberty is promoted. Though Faulkner and Hemingway are dissimilar in most essentials, they nonetheless agree on this one important facet of violence: to be justified as the act of a reasonable being, violence must benefit the species, not simply gratify the violent individual.

# Truman Capote's

## *In Cold Blood*

Mostly because of Truman Capote's publicity blitz, *In Cold Blood* significantly blurred the distinctions between "fiction" and "nonfiction" when it was published in 1965. C. Hugh Holman says wisely that the "best definition" of the novel "is ultimately the history of what it has been" (299). Now after all the critical and popular hoopla has long since subsided, we know that *In Cold Blood* is a notable part of what the novel has been. Not because of any media hype or authorial idiosyncrasies, but because of its enduring artistic integrity, it has modestly redefined "novel." For that reason, and because questions still arise about its genre, I need first to explain the presence of Capote's "nonfiction novel" in a study devoted to the *novel* of violence.

Capote, as Gerald Clarke reports, "had long maintained that nonfiction could be both as artful and as compelling as fiction" (356-357). By "treating a real event with fictional techniques" he felt that it was possible to make a synthesis between factual journalistic story telling and the novelistic technique of taking the reader "deeper and deeper into characters and events." Thus, when he wrote *In Cold Blood*, he repeated "the themes, images, and leitmotifs that permeate his novels and short stories." As a result, "his true-life chronicle is the culmination of his fiction" (357). Anita Loos called it "a Homeric poem" (quoted in Clarke, 361).

As participants in the investigation of the Clutter murders have attested, Capote's "true-life chronicle" is not as factual as it may first seem, or as Capote claimed. Kansas Bureau of Investigation agent Harold Nye, for instance, records that he was upset when he read the galleys of *In Cold Blood*. "I was under the impression that the book was going to be factual, "Nye claims, "and it was not, it was a fiction book" (quoted in Plimpton, 64-65). Nye's complaints may be based on relatively minor deviations from factual events, but they do suggest that Capote was not at any time during the writing of the book restricted by an allegiance to fact. Somewhat ironically, the one scene in which Capote admittedly deviates from fact and turns to fiction weakens the entire narrative. Wanting to affix a positive ending to an otherwise dark and pessimistic parable of the American heartland, Capote fabricated the scene between Alvin Dewey and Susan Kidwell that closes the novel. As Clarke notes, summing up general critical response, "that nostalgic meeting in the graveyard verges on the trite and sentimental" (359). Nonetheless, that one artistic faux pas hardly detracts from what Jimmy Breslin referred to as Capote's "flat, objective, terrible realism" (quoted by Clarke, 365).

Ultimately, however, we do not require extra-textual reassurances to convince us that *In Cold Blood* is novelistic. Capote's text itself demonstrates the traditional elements of fiction that he set out to master. The under-populated Kansas prairie offers a significant and appropriate stage for the conflict between protagonistic forces of good and antagonistic forces of evil that are played out upon it. The ironic contrast between the desolate landscape and the intimate nature of the murders creates a subconscious apprehension that no setting in New York, Paris, or any other of Capote's urban haunts could duplicate. Murder in the cosmopolitan world is frequent and usually anonymous. Murder in villages such as Holcomb, Kansas, is infrequent and very personal. Furthermore, when Capote moves the action from the desolate plains into the dark Clutter home, he creates a startling shift from agoraphobia to claustrophobia. This emotional alternation is an effective, dramatic use of setting. Traditionally, especially for an Easterner such as Capote, the empty plains are what terrify. In such geographic vastness, the home is supposed to be sweet sanctuary. Here, however, the home becomes a trap more appalling than the void.

Moreover, Capote elaborates characters who are psychologically and personally compelling. The killers and their victims are not mere figures passing across a historical backdrop. We get to know them well if not intimately. Consequently, we understand the conflict that their personal histories and social environments have set into motion. Through meticulous plotting, Capote brings the victims, killers, and lawmen inevitably into contact. Their interactions, however, do not conform to history or chronology. Capote rearranges and juxtaposes events for their dramatic impact, not for their factual accuracy. He manipulates historiotemporal reality to attain drama as intense as any classic tragedy. This dramatic rather than literal adherence to chronology is especially noticeable in the flashbacks that are a distinctly imaginative or fictional element of the narrative. As no nonfiction reportage could do, the flashbacks permit us to step inside the mind of Perry Smith to visit his childhood and to glimpse the fantasies that churn his imagination. That imagination, ironically, is what dissociates him from "reality" and permits him to kill four fellow humans as if he himself has become a stage actor. As he says, killing the Clutters "was like I wasn't part of it. More as though I was reading a story" (272). Perry's comment works as a metafictional observation by Capote, meant to sustain the fiction-nonfiction mode and to emphasize the razor thin division between fact and fantasy. When Capote's imagination encountered reality, a significant work of art resulted from the merger. When Perry Smith's imagination encountered reality, violence and death resulted. Ironically, by those polar opposite responses, both men were assured a place in the "factuality" of American history.

We can strengthen our argument by noting that *In Cold Blood* compares favorably to other texts that critics unequivocally accept as "novels." Several of these texts appear in this study—Kurt Vonnegut's *Slaughterhouse-Five* and E. L. Doctorow's *Billy Bathgate*, for example. These novels, too, are as much history as fiction. In *Billy Bathgate*, Doctorow encapsulates a fictional narrator with Dutch Schultz's biography and 1930s history. He extensively uses newspaper accounts and Schultz's dying proclamation, and except for Billy himself the major characters are "real" people. In fact, little fictionalizing appears in the narrative. How Doctorow presents facts is what makes the text a novel rather than biography, history, or some other hybrid genre. The same may be argued for *Slaughterhouse-Five*. Chapter one is especially difficult to distinguish as biography or fiction. It is not unlike Hawthorne's "Custom House" section of *The Scarlet Letter*, introducing the author and distancing himself from the lies that follow. In his first sentence, Vonnegut announces that "All this happened, more or less" (7), and we believe him more or less. We know Dresden was bombed. We know that approximately 130,000 citizens were incinerated. We know that the real person Kurt Vonnegut, Jr. was in Dresden (just as Truman Capote was in Holcomb, Kansas). We know that Harry Truman was President and ordered the bombing of Hiroshima. We know that John F. Kennedy and his brother Robert were assassinated. That is, we know history when we hear it, and history is fact. Yet, we also know that *Slaughterhouse-Five* is a novel even before we complete the pseudo-biography of chapter one and meet the fabulous Tralfamadorians that lie beyond history, fact, and credibility.

We do not doubt that either *Billy Bathgate* or *Slaughterhouse-Five* is fiction. Their purpose is not simply to record history but to take the reader, as Capote says, "deeper and deeper into characters and events." Authorial intent and the management of the material distinguish fiction from factual or historical reportage. As experienced readers, we easily recognize these distinctions. Doctorow is not interested in recording for the umpteenth time the violent history of Dutch Schultz and the New York gangs in the 1930s. Vonnegut is not interested in giving another factual, dispassionate account of the firebombing of Dresden, Germany, on February 13, 1945. Neither is Truman Capote interested in giving a factual, dispassionate account of the murder of the Herbert Clutter family in Holcomb, Kansas, on November 15, 1959. The bloody crimes of Schultz, his own violent death, and the firebombing of Dresden are incidental to Doctorow's and Vonnegut's intentions. So too is the shot-gunning of the Clutter family incidental to Capote's intentions. As Gerald Clarke notes, "What excited his curiosity was not the murders, but their effect on that small and isolated community" (319). Though the murders form the narrative core and violent center of focus, they do not serve as the essence of the book. Thus, Jack De Bellis is certainly correct when he notes that "Capote failed in his intention to write a 'nonfiction novel'" (524). He in fact wrote a novel.

To some degree, however, the entire argument concerning the genre issue is mute, more so now perhaps than when Capote raised the question in the mid-1960s. More important issues are at stake. As we will see, Capote started out to write one kind of book but ended up writing quite another kind. Capote's subtle but stunning redirecting of his original literary goals had both personal and cultural repercussions. The demand for aesthetic and ontological redefinition made *In Cold Blood* eminently appealing in an era when assassinations, war, and political lies had caused thinkers to begin a fundamental reassessment of traditional values. As Nelson Vieira says of Doctorow's *Billy Bathgate*, published twenty-four years and a cultural lifetime later, *In Cold Blood* challenges "our traditional views of aesthetic beauty and ethical goodness, obliging us to reposition and reconsider the comforting optic of our daily lives" (356). It was this reconsideration, moreover, that contributed significantly to Capote's personal disintegration after writing *In Cold Blood*. As John Knowles says, "I think he lost a grip on himself after [the success of *In Cold Blood*]. He had been tremendously disciplined up to that time, one of the most disciplined writers I've ever met. But he couldn't sustain it after that. A lot of his motivation was lost. That's when he began to unravel" (quoted in Plimpton, 57). Gerald Clarke recognizes that Capote "had mined his subject, but his subject had also mined him, exhausting his nerves, his reservoir of patience, and his powers of concentration; depleting, in short, his capital as both a man and a writer" (397-398). Exhausted too was Capote's moral, aesthetic equilibrium. Writing *In Cold Blood* forced a debilitating reappraisal from which he never recovered; but it also placed him in the forefront of a cultural reevaluation that continues today.

At this juncture, we need to address more specifically the element of violence in Capote's redefining narrative. What he intends and what he achieves with violence are much more subtle (some might say insidious) than any defense we might raise about the "nonfiction novel." Using fact and history but manipulating them with imagination and passion, Capote celebrates homicide. What is more important, he persuades us to join the celebration. Ultimately we have as much or more sympathy for the killers as for the victims. Almost against our will, Capote makes us analyze our preconceived notions about crime and punishment. As we read *In Cold Blood* we alter the way in which we view our culture. The care and artistry with which he manages this feat form the single most important factor in making *In Cold Blood* a significant "novel" of violence and a substantial literary accomplishment.

Capote's technical manipulation of violence sets the tone and direction of the narrative. The action begins in a nondescript Kansas prairie town that few Americans have ever heard of. We soon hear, however, "four shotgun blasts" (15) that will memorialize Holcomb. These ominous blasts echo throughout the remainder of the text, forming an effective auditory image that unifies the narrative. To complement this auditory image, Capote inserts a horrific reiterated visual image: hair splattered on bloody walls. Dick Hickock asks his cohort Perry Smith, "Ain't that what I promised you, honey—plenty of hair on them—those walls?" (50). The "them—those" is Dick correcting his usage for Perry, who is a strict grammarian. It is also Capote's subtle reminder of how important are rhetorical devices. Dick repeats this hair-on-the-walls promise. Later Susan Kidwell varies the image when Nancy Ewalt insists hysterically that Nancy Clutter is not dead. Susan demands that Nancy rethink what she has seen: "There's too much blood. There's blood on the walls. You didn't really look" (76). Then Larry Hendricks, the Ernest Hemingway manqué who is one of the first on the murder scene, reports that Nancy Clutter has "been shot in the back of the head with a shotgun held maybe two inches away . . . and the wall was covered with blood" (78). Capote gives a final gaudy variation of the blood-on-the-wall image when he reports Susan Kidwell's and Bobby Rupp's visit to the funeral home. Though their judgment tells them not to go, they cannot overcome their human desire for violence. Susan Kidwell describes the murder victims: "the head of each was completely encased in cotton, a swollen cocoon twice the size of an ordinary blow-up balloon, and the cotton, . . . twinkled like Christmas-tree snow" (113). Her words are an apt closure for the "hair" motif and a poignant example of the incongruities of middle-America values that energize the narrative. In trying to disguise violence, we merely exaggerate its consequences.

Other instances of the rhetoric of violence could easily be recorded, but these examples make the point that Capote's text is replete with such rhetoric. He uses it to set the tone of horror and impending doom that compels audience attention and allows him to realize his artistic intentions.

From this mass of images and allusions, three dominant violent elements emerge to dominate the text and subtext of the narrative. Two are obvious, but nonetheless compelling. The third is subliminal and is born out of the previous two. Capote establishes the first two elements with utmost care so that he might insinuate the third past our unconscious desire to deny our own violent instincts. The first violent element is the murder itself. The second is the pheasant hunting that parallels the murder. The third is the sublimated violence that dictates the

Clutter family's life and that is subsumed by the greater tension between domestic tranquillity and chaos. For the ease of discussion, I will refer to this third type of violence as Clutter violence. Thus we have the violent triad upon which the narrative stands: the murder, the hunting motif, and Clutter violence.

The murders themselves are incidental to Capote's artistic intent. They are, however, the central focus of violence and the frame to which all else is attached. Capote teases us with the murders. First we hear the four shotgun blasts announcing that the murders have occurred. Perturbed that we are not permitted to witness this violence, we wait rather impatiently for an explanation. Approximately 50 pages elapse before Nancy Ewalt and Susan Kidwell return to the Clutter home. Then we learn what the shotgun blasts were all about (731). Yet the two girls do not detail what they saw. Several more pages elapse before Larry Hendricks, the English teacher, gives our first look inside the death rooms. He is a careful observer and an accurate recorder. He reports that Nancy Clutter had "been shot in the back of the head with a shotgun held maybe two inches away . . . and the wall was covered with blood" (78). Mrs. Clutter was shot "point-blank in the side of the head, and the blast—the impact—had ripped the tape loose" from her mouth. "Her eyes were open. Wide open" (79). Herb Clutter's throat has been cut, too. A bloodstained footprint is on the mattress box where Clutter lay.

Though Hendrick's report satisfies much of our curiosity about the carnage (though not all), we still do not know who murdered the Clutter's or why. We still are missing our eyewitness account. That final accounting will not come for another 180 pages or so, when on the drive back from Las Vegas Perry Smith watches "carcasses of shot-gunned coyotes festooning ranch fences" (263). Serving as an epiphany that activates the Catholic guilt he cannot escape, these carcasses initiate Perry's confessing what happened inside the Clutter home on the night of the murders. This confession covers sixteen pages, adds intimate details to Hendrick's version, and concludes essentially when Perry tells how he blew Herb Clutter's head off: "Then I aimed the gun. The room just exploded. Went blue. Just blazed up. Jesus, I'll never understand why they didn't hear the noise twenty miles around" (276). Like agent Al Dewey, who never feels "a design justly completed" (382) about the murders, we are not totally satisfied even with Perry's account. At least, however, we are content that it is the best we will ever get. Having heard his eyewitness version of his own psychic explosion and the shotgun blasts that reify it, we have experienced some dramatic purgation.

The pheasant hunting motif that parallels the murders is perhaps one of the reasons that we feel that the design of crime and punishment is never "justly completed." What the hunting does is keep us constantly aware that the instinct to violence is omnipresent and that strangers with deadly weapons are daily in our fields and passing through our villages. It is worth noting, perhaps, that pheasants are not a native American bird. They were introduced from Asia to supply American hunters with a relatively large, slow-flying, attractive bird to kill. Though edible, they are more often used as trophy birds. In other words, pheasant hunters pursue a semi-domesticated bird primarily for the thrill of destroying it. This information brings the hunting motif much closer to the Clutter murders than would otherwise be the case. The images of the pheasant and the men who kill it symbolically juxtapose the violent instinct with the culturally imposed domesticity that it meant to protect against such violence. The birds live in Herb Clutter's fields and fruit orchard. They, therefore, literally attract men with shotguns to his home. Year after year, violence and death have been as close as his back yard, and he cheerfully condones it.

Our first encounter with the pheasant hunters is when Herb Clutter comes across them one morning in his orchard (24). Clutter loves the orchard. Moreover, Capote makes sure we relate it to the Garden of Eden by giving the "Eden on Earth" and "raise Cain" allusions in the passage. Herb Clutter has recently sued an unfortunate pilot for crashing a plane into this Eden. Consequently, we at first expect Clutter to be angry at the "five pheasant hunters from Oklahoma" (24) who are invading his paradise. Instead, however, Clutter welcomes the hunters. A touch of hubris underlies Clutter's unexpected graciousness. He takes great pride in his land and in being so wealthy that he does not charge for hunting rights. This hubris is interpreted by his local culture as power and influence. Yet, when it is distorted by prison gossip among petty criminals such as Dick Hickock and his cell mate, the hubris leads to Clutter's death. Capote wants to emphasize that Herb Clutter is unconsciously welcoming the source of his imminent death. Thus he ends the pheasant-hunter paragraph with this ominous farewell: "Then, touching the brim of his cap [to the hunters], he headed for home and the day's work unaware that it would be his last" (24). He does not run out to meet death, but he does acquiesce in its arrival.

Soon after Herb Clutter's portentous meeting with the pheasant hunters, Dick Hickock arrives to keep his rendezvous with Perry Smith. In the back seat of his 1949 Chevrolet is a 12-gauge pump-action shotgun, with "pheasants in flight etched along the stock" (33). This distinctive, artistically enhanced weapons becomes a sub-motif in the novel when at the home of Hickock's parents agent Harold Nye sees "a .12-gauge Savage shotgun, Model 300; a delicately etched scene of pheasants in flight ornamented the handle" (196). This discovery lets the agents know for certain that they are after the right killers. However, more important than serving as an effective plot device and agent of narrative unity, this decorated stock conveys a subtle irony. Showing the live, free birds in their natural habitat on the instrument that will soon kill them in sadistic, indicating the conflicted motives of the hunter who fires  the weapon. What psychology underlies the desire to beautify a weapon of death? Why would one intent on killing wish to have the victim immortalized artistically as something eternally alive?

Capote obviously does not miss the irony of a weapon that brings art and violence so intimately together. Both Dick Hickock and Perry Smith are intelligent men with considerable artistic talent as painters and musicians. Smith especially is sympathetic and compassionate. Yet he is the one who uses the ornamented gun to blow the heads off the Clutter's, after taking care to see to their comfort. In that dichotomy we glimpse again the convoluted ironies and motives that the gun symbolizes. The most destructive human instinct meets with and proves superior to the instinct to create beauty and thus immortalize human transience. The pheasant gun may not resonate with the same subtlety as Keats' Grecian urn or Yeats' hammered gold artifices of Byzantium, but it serves well to show that violence and beauty can get appallingly confused in the American heartland.

The sublimated Clutter violence is presaged by several overt signs. One we have already seen in Herb Clutter's passively condoning the killing of pheasants on his land. Another sign is the actions of the Clutter son, Kenyon. Outwardly a "sensitive and reticent boy" (52), Kenyon barely conceals his violent instincts. He has an old truck that he calls the "Coyote Wagon" from which he chases coyotes over the Sand Hills (51). He also shoots dozens of rabbits and sells them to the "rabbit factory" in Garden City (52), which in turn ships them as food to mink growers. He takes pride in delivering wild ducks to the family dinner table, his subtle connection to the pheasant hunters. These activities can be explained as mere teenage fun or normal midwestern male rights of passage. More difficult to explain, however, is why Kenyon one day rides his pet horse Skeeter so hard that he drops dead under him (54). Any farm boy with the least knowledge of horses knows their limitations. To ride one to death has to be a conscious and unpardonable act of malicious violence—an act that indicates sublimated anger and aggression. In other words, it hints at a repressed "psychopathic rage," the term that agent Dewey uses to characterize the individuals who "commit such a crime" as the Clutter murders (99).

The Clutter females personify the diametrical opposite of this male violence. However, they nonetheless reflect its influence. Bonnie Fox Clutter is the antithesis of violence. A "defenseless" woman who spends most of her time in bed, she is so little a threat that she causes others to relax around her (36). She is a fossilized child who collects "Lilliputian gewgaws" and has a set of "doll-house teacups" her daddy gave her. "I had a lovely childhood," (37) she tells Jolene Katz wistfully. A sexually repressed, hysterical woman, Bonnie Clutter reminds us very much of Katherine Anne Porter's Ellie Thompson in *Noon Wine*. She is bound to a domineering, not very sensitive man, in a culture that empowers him and diminishes her. She turns to chronic illness and her darkened bedroom for sanctuary. Bonnie's daughter Nancy is a gifted over-achiever. Unlike her brother Kenyon, she loves her old horse Babe and treats him compassionately. Nancy is the All-American girl: "a straight-A student, the president of her class, a leader in the 4-H program and the Young Methodists League, a skilled rider, an excellent musician (piano, clarinet), an annual winner at the county fair (pastry, preserves, needlework, flower arrangement)" (29). Facing death, she talks kindly of her attacker and listens to the "tearjerker" life story that Hickock gives her (274). "I really liked her," Perry admits (274). We as readers also like her, and her death is more haunting than any of the other five in the novel.

Nancy's pacifistic response in the face of such violence is not surprising, given her age, naiveté, and the incredible circumstances. Nor is her mother's passivity out of character if indeed she has suffered the postnatal depression brought on by four births. Yet such reaction suggests also that both Nancy and Bonnie Clutter have learned such survival tactics in a family that is not as perfect as its sterling image first indicates.

The Clutter family epitomizes the tyranny of perfection. The ropes with which their killers tie them are no tighter than the Bible Belt that has confined them. Herb Clutter is so much a product of "that gospel-haunted strip of American territory" (46) that he cannot easily be separated from it. As Gerald Clarke says, "Alone with his many good qualities, Herb Clutter is rigid and self-righteous" (356). We might add that he is also pious, intolerant, and domineering. His son's repressed violence erupts in his running a horse to death, but his wife and daughter's repressed emotions manifest themselves in more subtle forms. We need look no further than Herb Clutter to discover a major cause of his wife's sexual hysteria and of his daughter having fingernails that are chewed "to the quick" (31). His demands for purity, in direct conflict with the sexual demands he has made on a wife who suffers visibly because of them, testify to a Calvinistic inflexibility and hypocrisy that have dominated the females closest to him. If the psychological assessment is that Perry Smith is killing his father when he murders Herb Clutter (as Dr. W. Mitchell Jones' analysis suggests), an equally valid assessment of Nancy Clutter is that she is trying to pacify an angry father when she strives to live a perfect life, cajoles Dick Hickock, and smiles sweetly at Perry Smith minutes before she dies.

In Gerald Clarke's biography of Truman Capote, between pages 312 and 313, is a photograph of the Clutter family, taken apparently five or six years before the murders. It appears to be a photograph posed for a Christmas card. All four children are included. The family is gathered round an unlit fireplace, with Christmas stockings hung above it and with a manger scene arranged on the mantle. In the background is a piano. The furniture is crowded, and is typical 1950s conventional style. All family members are smiling, obviously on cue from the photographer. Mrs. Clutter draws the viewer's attention most. She is seated, with a book held stiffly in her hands, and looks frail and uncertain. A tall, big man, Herb Clutter stands behind his family, his hand resting possessively on the back of his wife's chair. He looks slightly smug, and is obviously proud to be patriarch of such a clan. The photograph could be an advertisement for the All-American Family of the Eisenhower era. However, in its posed, artificial serenity and the false security it projects, it is a terrifying document. The photograph graphically reminds us of something that Gerald Clarke notes as one of the leitmotifs of the narrative: "Going about its peaceful pursuits in Holcomb is one America—prosperous, secure, and a little smug. . . . Speeding across the plains is the other America—poor, rootless and misbegotten" (356). When those two Americas meet, "victims and killers are America in microcosm—light and dark, goodness and evil" (356). The problem, however, is that we can no longer easily distinguish which is which.

A disturbing irony attaches to Herb Clutter and his patriarchal pride. He is a pious, God-fearing, overtly peaceful man done in by what Alvin Dewey calls a "psychological accident," a violent psychic explosion that no logic can explain (277). Herb Clutter is big and strong, so protective of his wife and offspring that he has repressed them with over-protective concern and holy sureness. Yet he lets his wife and two youngest children, and himself, die without protest and with no effort to save them. He acquiesces in death with a passivity that surprises all who know him. Of the many things about the case that perplex Dewey, Herb Clutter's failure to resist is one of the most disturbing. "Herb, his friend Alvin Dewey felt certain, would have fought to the death defending Bonnie's life and the lives of his children" (271). He did not, however, fight at all.

Herb Clutter's cloistered virtue kills him and his. He is betrayed by his own failure to acknowledge violence, though the warning signs of its presence and potential deadliness are all about him. Excessively bound by his piety and the certainty that his little world is safe from attack, he has no defense against violence when it appears. As Capote says, "Herb was handsome, he was pious, he was strong-willed" (38); but in the ultimate confrontation he cannot defend himself and his family from two existential, absurdist drifters who have been cut loose from society's guy wires. Perry Smith's sister Barbara knows from childhood that her family "shared a doom against which virtue was no defense" (212). It is a dreadful lesson that Herb Clutter never learns, or at least learns only in the final seconds of life after Perry Smith has slit his throat.

Many types of violence mark the narrative. Hunting: we have already noted the pheasant hunting. War: Perry Smith serves in the Korean War. Rape: Perry is raped by his shipmates. Child abuse: the nuns beat Perry for wetting the bed; his father threatens to kill him. Sexual abuse: Perry's mother is brutalized

by her husband and sexual partners; Dick Hickock assaults pre-
teen girls. Suicide: Perry's brother and sister-in-law shoot themselves. Execution: Dick and Perry are hanged. And of course,
murder. This violence is perpetrated with knives, tire chains,
flashlights, fists, automobiles, ropes, and shotguns. It surrounds
the artificial haven of the Clutters like a dark cocoon. Yet, the
Clutters too are part of the violence. They simply repress it and
refuse to recognize its existence. This refusal leads to Herb Clutter's deadly passivity in the face of imminent danger. What the
Clutters, and their fellow villages do not acknowledge is the
"primitive violence, born out of previous, and now unconscious, traumatic experiences" (335) that Capote draws to our attention by quoting extensively from Dr. Joseph Satten's essay in
*The American Journal of Psychiatry.* This primitive instinct to
violence erupts to the surface in psychic drifters such as Hickock
and Smith, but it is no less a part of the Clutters and of all Homo
Sapiens. By erecting polar opposite choices, Capote wants us to
reevaluate the moral and cultural dimensions of such violence.
One pole is stated by Don Cullivan. Perry's Catholic friend assures him (and us) that "God made you as well as me and He
loves you just as He loves me" (294). The other pole is stated by
James Latham, the convicted serial killer who shares death row
with Hickock and Smith. "It's a rotten world. . . . There's no answer to it but meanness" (362). Thanks to Capote's narrative, we
are no longer sure which of those is the righteous argument.

    Given the horror of the Clutter's deaths, the most dread-
ful irony of *In Cold Blood* is the one that Capote inserts most
subtly. He reverses the traditional killer-victim role vis-à-vis
the audience's response to them. Even a recent novel such as
*Billy Bathgate*, though it resonates with postmodernist implications, leaves no doubts that we are meant to detest the brutal,
murderous Dutch Schultz. Our confused loyalties come in our
response to Billy, because here we have to reconcile our sympathies for a boy who is himself gentle but who nonetheless facilitates felonies and murders. Schultz, however, is a cold-blooded
killer for whom conventional disapprobation immediately and
consistently applies. Though Dick Hickock and Perry Smith are
as cold-blooded and murderous as Schultz, we nonetheless finish *In Cold Blood* with as much sympathy for them (or at least
for Perry Smith) as we do for the Clutters.

    Breaking the mold of such strong moral conventions in
the reader is no easy task, though Capote makes it seem so. He

makes the change less difficult for us by having the most influential or informed characters in the story set the precedence of
sympathy. We thus, ironically, have the comforting support of
traditional authority for our unconventional shift in sympathies. Agent Al Dewey, the most authoritative voice in the narrative, and the man most likely to condemn the murderers, is
the first to express his sympathies for Perry Smith. Dewey
knows that the Clutters "had experienced prolonged terror, they
had suffered." Yet he cannot repress his "measure of sympathy"
for Perry (277). Later, when he must watch Hickock and Smith
hang, Dewey reiterates this sympathy. Perry "possessed a quality,
the aura of an exiled animal" (381) that impresses Dewey.
Josephine Meier, the jailer's wife, is immediately drawn to Perry
when he is placed in her "ladies" cell. She talks with him, cooks
his favorite meals, and thinks of him as a gentle man who can
tame a squirrel in his cell. A "direct and practical woman" (283),
she says in typical understatement that "he wasn't the worst
man I ever saw" (285). Don Cullivan, the ex-army acquaintance
from Massachusetts, devotes much of his time and money to
consoling Smith during his years on death row. A truly devout
Catholic, Cullivan assures Perry that God loves him (294). (This
is ironic, because one of the things that Perry has rebelled against
is his treatment by the Catholic nuns.) Finally, even Nancy Clutter seems to have some sympathy for the man who will in a few
minutes murder her.

Through this displaced sympathy we sense that Capote
himself has considerable sympathy for the killers. Perry Smith is
clearly his doppelganger, the violent self that lurked in a mild,
effeminate individual. Jack De Bellis is correct in concluding
that Capote identified with Perry (531). In Smith's own mind,
there was a "close relation . . . between violence and his intellectual insecurity" (524). Capote recognized this peculiarity in
Perry's psyche, and thus "saw in Smith's life and death a parable
about the serious artist in America" (536). It may be going too far
to say that Kansas replaces the hated "South" in Capote's psyche,
as De Bellis contends, but it is certainly valid to recognize that
Capote closely identified with the condemned mass killer.
"From the beginning," as Gerald Clarke says, "theirs was a confused, uneasy, but unremittingly intense relationship" (327).
KBI agent Harold Nye contends that Capote and Smith "had become lovers in the penitentiary" (quoted in Plimpton, 70).
Though Nye's conclusion is based on circumstantial evidence at

best, there is no doubt that Capote passed his intense sympathy for Smith on to his readers. That transmission is the power source of his narrative.

When Capote first read about the Clutter murders in *The New York Times* on November 16, 1959, his goal was to write a traditional, factual account of good versus evil in a small rural American village. Instead, he ended up writing a far more complex postmodernist parable, not unlike a longer variation of Shirley Jackson's "The Lottery." The very meanings of good and evil are challenged, rearranged, blurred and ultimately negated. He gives us no one with whom we can clearly identify and no one with whom we can unequivocally sympathize. We become, therefore, part victim and part criminal, with no distinct guidelines for determining which part is which. If we enter the text still possessing any traditional values, and if we read the text attuned to its moral, legal, historical, and economic nuances, we leave it with none of those old values intact. Capote makes us redefine the comforting dogmas of our mundane lives. Once those fundamental values are destroyed, the distinctions among literary genres are rendered inane. If the essential guides to "reality" are destroyed, then the superficial debate over what is fact and what is fiction hardly matters.

# Kurt Vonnegut's
# *Slaughterhouse-Five*

It is sobering, for some at least, how quickly topicality becomes historicity. Kurt Vonnegut's *Slaughterhouse-Five* is as
much a satire of the 1960s decade in which it was written as it is
of World War II and the bombing of Dresden. As William Allen
correctly observes, "A major reason *Slaughterhouse-Five* had
the enormous impact it did was because it was published at the
height of the conflict in Vietnam, and so delivered its antiwar
message to a most receptive audience"( 92). At century's end,
however, Vonnegut's novel seems torn from another epoch—
back before MTV, video records, TV disks, PCs (Personal Computers *and* Political Correctness), Calvin Cline, and the Internet.
Back there in primitive times. The historicity of *Slaughterhouse-Five* encompasses time from the children's crusades of
1213 to the reign of Richard Nixon. It derives its power, however, from the contemporary history of the violent decade that
shaped its composition—a history that proved, if nothing else,
that as a culture we had learned little from Hiroshima, Dresden,
and what Dwight Eisenhower superciliously termed our Crusade
in Europe.

    *Slaughterhouse-Five*'s durability as a satiric masterpiece is
explained by two factors. First, the 1960s loom more and more as
a definitive era as we move further away from them. This is
true because in that decade, with the help of television, domestic
violence and martial violence merged for the first time in the
cultural imagination. The Cuban Missile Crisis, Vietnam, student riots, racial battles, political assassinations, and our usual
glut of homicides, rapes, and assaults became the design of the
national fabric. Second, Vonnegut's satire is the best from the
era and the most acerbic commentary on the era. He unifies as

no other author the aforementioned cultural violence and the resultant blasé (some would say cynical) attitude that developed in response to the violence. In short, *Slaughterhouse-Five* is a topical novel that has become part of the history that it excoriates.

The single most important element that makes *Slaughterhouse-Five* a classic satire is Vonnegut's narrative control of violence. As his subtitle informs us, a fundamental cliché controls narrative design in *Slaughterhouse-Five*. Simply stated, Vonnegut does something conventional and something unusual with the venerable maxim that we are all in "A Duty Dance with Death" and owe God a dying.

The conventional element is that he packages his violence as a war novel. Using war as a metaphor for the genocidal violence of Homo Sapiens is itself a venerable literary practice. Its prototypes in western culture go back at least to the Pentateuch. As Erich Maria Remarque's *All Quite on the Western Front*, Dalton Trumbo's *Johnny Got His Gun*, and countless other modernist war novels have shown, the genre is also a common platform for anti-violence messages, which is what *Slaughterhouse-Five* claims to be. Furthermore, the war-as-protest novel is a futile convention. As the movie maker Harrison Starr reminds the "Vonnegut" narrator of *Slaughterhouse-Five*, "there would always be wars" and "they were as easy to stop as glaciers" (9). Poor old Edgar Derby reads *The Red Badge of Courage* (91), but nonetheless is doomed to die by firing squad for picking up a teapot. The shortcomings of the war genre, therefore, are well known to Vonnegut and irrelevant to his design. He uses the genre only for the convention of violence that it automatically evokes.

We see how little he cares about the conventional war novel in the way that he handles the firebombing of Dresden. This central violent episode around which his narrative revolves is one of the most horrendous examples of unmitigated violence in history. As such it offers an opportunity for graphic depictions of violence. Vonnegut, however, refuses to exploit that potential. Although the Dresden Affair gives an otherwise chaotic narrative a degree of focus, it is not—as Wayne D. McGinnis claims—"the source of its great originality" (114). Instead of trying to dramatize the absurdity of modern warfare that Dresden epitomizes, Vonnegut sublimates the event and his experience of it. By way of layered points of view, we are forced outside *Slaughterhouse-Five* to get "the frightful picture of the civilians killed at Dresden," a massacre that Ira C. Eaker and Sir Robert Saundby so staunchly defend (166). In Vonnegut's text we hear about the corpse factory to which Dresden is reduced and know that it reeks of mustard gas and roses, but we are not eyewitnesses or participants. We do not actually see men, women, children, animals dying or hear their screams or watch as they are incinerated.

Even the incidental scenes of violence are peculiarly distanced. Private Eddie Slovik and poor old Edgar Derby are executed by firing squad, but we are not present. We hear about the events only after the fact, and not from a firsthand observer. Compared to Pilar's gory retelling of the village massacre in *For Whom the Bell Tolls*, Vonnegut's direct account of violence and its consequences is pristine. *Slaughterhouse-Five* is a "war" novel, but it reports a war as if from a distant promontory. As Edward Hoagland says accusingly but correctly, Vonnegut "quickly ducks into the incongruous sci-fi world of Tralfamadore whenever fright at the scenery of World War II overtakes him" (33). Thus, *Slaughterhouse-Five* borrows the convention of the war novel, but does nothing new with the genre. Like most war novels, it talks about violence but not violently.

The true source of great originality in *Slaughterhouse-Five* is how Vonnegut transforms the war paradigm into an excremental vision that effectively captures the instinctual and definitive violence of the human animal. Vonnegut's exact term is "excrement festival." Though he develops the concept throughout the narrative, the specific rhetorical identifier occurs in one of the defining episodes of the narrative, when the English prisoners see the diarrheic Americans fouling their "tidy" latrine:

> Billy looked inside the latrine. The wailing was coming from in there. The place was crammed with Americans who had taken their pants down. The welcome feast had made them as sick as volcanoes. The buckets were full or had been kicked over. . . . Billy reeled away from his vision of Hell. He passed three Englishmen who were watching the excrement festival from a distance. They were catatonic with disgust.
>
> (113-114)

Vonnegut uses "excrement festival" as rhetorical shorthand for a fundamental horror that lies beyond the capabilities of conventional language. The deductive schema for which "excrement festival" is substituted might be stated thus: War is the most massive expression of human violence. Modern warfare has become so horrific that rhetoric fails to describe it. What, therefore, is the only other fundamental and universal human action that might replace war and serve as a literary metaphor for violence? Vonnegut's answer, as seen in the "excrement festival" epithet, is bodily functions. They are, ironically the great democratic constant. "Festival" and the joy the term connotes shows that Vonnegut is not taking himself or the process very seriously. Like Walt Whitman, he celebrates the bodily functions; but he does so with an absurd humor that the nineteenth-century romantic would hardly appreciate, or recognize.

At this juncture, with talk of excremental visions, we need to acknowledge Vonnegut's debt to Jonathan Swift. The textual similarities between *Slaughterhouse-Five* and *Gulliver's Travels* range from the voyages of Lemuel Gulliver and Billy Pilgrim to the satiric diagrams that decorate the text. Moreover, both Pilgrim and Gulliver come to distrust and distance themselves from their fellow humans. We are not surprised to learn, as Edward Hoagland reports in reviewing *Palm Sunday*, that Vonnegut once wrote a "foreword to the Book-of-the-Month Club's edition of Jonathan Swift" (3). Although the foreword was never published because it was so badly written, it does prove Vonnegut's awareness and appreciation of Swift. The essential debt is that Vonnegut borrows Swift's excremental vision, a seminal motif recognized years ago by Norman O. Brown and others. Vonnegut applies the vision consciously, whereas Swift probably developed it unaware. The point remains, however, that both Swift and Vonnegut realize that excreta more than reason symbolizes Homo Sapiens.

There is a significant difference between the two, however. Swift's excremental vision is limited almost exclusively to feces and anality. These two topics in turn lead to a psychological uproar about all sorts of sublimated doubts and fears—genital failure and vaginal abhorrence, to name but two. The Freudian conclusions drawn from Swift's fixation with anality may be valid or specious, but to argue this is not now my point. Norman O. Brown put a cap to the issue by observing sardonically that psychoanalysts have a "capacity for finding the anus in the most unlikely places" (36). The fact remains, nonetheless, that in the context of Vonnegut's excremental vision apropos Swift's, the borrowed term issued in its broader capacities. For Vonnegut "excrement" means all the waste matter discharged from the body, including semen. Perhaps "orificial vision" would be a more appropriate designation for Vonnegut's satire, since the term covers all the bodily apertures through which Vonnegut sees waste oozing or exploding. However, "excrement festival" is Vonnegut's own term, used with full awareness of its Swiftian and Freudian connotations. It is thus the more appropriate phrase to use in discussing Vonnegut's motif.

Vonnegut's recognizing these fundamental associations among war, excrement, and the ideas by which America identifies itself is at once simple and ingenious. Using various techniques, Vonnegut artfully correlates the associations. The simplest narrative device he uses to correlate the three elements is the conventional rhetorical connectors that unite excrement, war, and American values. For example, Roland Weary, the rabid defender of democracy, threatens to beat the "living shit" out of Pilgrim. Valencia Merble and the callous girl at the Chicago City News Bureau both eat Three Musketeers bars, thereby connecting themselves to Weary's idiotic identification with Dumas's fabulous martial quartet (there were actually four musketeers, though Weary would not know that). Such connectors effectively anticipate the more subtle digestion motif identified as the "excrement festival."

With the digestion motif, Vonnegut unifies all other significant elements of the text apropos war and waste production. Lest we forget, digestion is the process of enzymes relentlessly attacking food inside the body. This essential life process in turn produces feces, urine, sweat, phlegm, and other waste materials that make up Vonnegut's "excrement festival." Therefore, the human body is both a very efficient waste producer and a macrocosmic battle ground of unrelenting violence. Like the collective human body called society, the individual human body is in a constant duty dance with death. The body will ultimately dance its last and become waste that in turn becomes food for other microbes that carry on the same eternal battle. So it goes. Others have used the war-biology metaphor before, as Hemingway does in *A Farewell to Arms*, where he develops the "biological trap" concept. Only Vonnegut, however, develops this attack-and-destroy cycle of the digestive processes into the linchpin association between war and excrement. Once developed, it works on levels ranging from the absolutely farcical and juvenile to the totally tragic and extra-linguistic.

In *Slaughterhouse-Five*, the rhetoric of violence is the seemingly endless obscenities used to describe the excrement festival. Vonnegut's references to "filth" are so abundant that wardens of the national virtue have often tried to ban *Slaughterhouse-Five*. Vonnegut himself refers in *Palm Sunday* to his battles with book-burners in North Dakota; and *the Christian Science Monitor* reports that a circuit court judge in Oakland County, Michigan ordered that *Slaughterhouse-Five* be removed from the schools. It is, the judge declared, a "'degradation of the person of Christ' and full of 'repetitious obscenity and immorality'" (681). To enumerate all the references to bodily functions that make up this "repetitious obscenity" would require that we separate the implied or metaphorical allusions from the overt. That in turn would cause us to risk imitating Brown's psychoanalysts by finding anuses or excreta where none was meant to be. The simple fact is that excremental allusions ranging from basic Anglo-Saxon profanities to sophomoric double entendres to complex metaphors dominate the text of *Slaughterhouse-Five*. From the mass, I have arbitrarily chosen four substantive examples to illustrate the development of Vonnegut's satiric, excremental vision: the description of the Tralfamadorian, the prison boxcar scene, the backward move, and the photograph of the girl and pony. For the ease of discussion, I refer to them as summary passages.

Billy Pilgrim's description of his alien kidnapers is the indispensable summary passage in the narrative design. It pictorializes the creatures who form the core of Vonnegut's satire and who determine Pilgrim's peculiar philosophy. In a letter to the Ilium *News Leader*, he describes the Tralfamadorians:

> The letter said they were two feet high, and green, and shaped like plumber's friends. Their suction cups were on the ground, and their shafts, which were extremely flexible, usually pointed to the sky. At the top of each shaft was a little hand with a green eye in its palm.
>
> (28)

The initial point to make about the Tralfamadorians is that because they have no concept of death they also have no concept of pain or suffering. Thus they personify pure violence. With a shrug, and dismissing the act with their usual "So it goes," they blow the universe to bits without qualms or regrets. Also, these are "second generation" or "second stage" Tralfamadorians. In *The Sirens of Titan* the Tralfamadorians are not peculiarly shaped and emotionless machines. They are very much like humans. Feeling superior, they invent a machine to do all their low purpose tasks. When the machine reports to them that they have no purpose at all, they therefore start killing each other because they hate things that have no purpose. This irrational, violent demise foreshadows the fate that awaits Earthlings.

The two features most striking about the Tralfamadorian are: (1) its likeness to the common household gadget used to unclog toilets, and (2) its exaggerated optic capacity. These are the two characteristics that Vonnegut uses to establish the connection between mundane, ordinary domestic life and imminent violence. Despite this spastic world view, Pilgrim is the typical American. He is an innocuous drudge from a dysfunctional family who does his military duty, goes to school, marries the ugly daughter of a wealthy man, fills a respectable job, and dreams of escape from the Capitalist rut. When in psychological crisis, therefore, it is fitting that Pilgrim turns not to the crucified Christ whose picture hangs above his bed but to the supermundane American values that have caused his crisis. He envisions his savior in the image of an ordinary household device used for loosening excrement and accumulated filth from sewage pipes.

Symbolically, this is the same function that the Tralfamadorians perform for Pilgrim: they cleanse the pipes of his perception, unclog his vision by disabusing him of historical, sociological fixations. The parallax view of this function is that Pilgrim himself is also excrement. He cannot willfully inflict pain upon another human being. Consequently, no matter how benevolent his intentions or how financially successful he becomes, he remains a scrap of human waste sticking in the cultural pipes. Pilgrim cannot alter the social predicament, but thanks to a brain trauma and the Tralfamadorians, he transfers his dilemma to a second dimension. He comes "unstuck in time" (26), thereby unclogging his own perceptions so that he realizes "the negligibility of death, and the true nature of time" (169). To realize the true nature of time simply means to quit trying to understand time. That is, by acquiescing in his own status as waste, he frees himself from spatio-temporal reality. He lets go of all intellectual pretense and philosophical biases and drifts into a psychic state where he is untethered to any moral or political codes. He is freed from cultural gravity.

What we are meant to realize about Pilgrim's revelations about time and history is the same truth that Chief Bromden, the "insane" narrator of Ken Kesey's *One Flew Over the Cuckoo's Nest*, warns us about: It's all true, even if it didn't happen. Cabined, cribbed, and confined as we are by our pet dogmas and rules, however, our perceptions remain clogged. Consequently we see Pilgrim at worst as a raving lunatic or at best as a postwar Walter Mitty who enters a daydream and cannot find the exit back to an exclusionist reality that we carefully define. If we could see ourselves as the Tralfamadorians see us, we would realize that we too are scraps of waste clogging the cosmological pipes. Unfortunately we do not have that clear vision. Our own perceptions have been obstructed by history, philosophy, psychology, anthropology, fairy tales, literature, theology, and an endless list of similar obstructions. They form a matrix of lies so dense that the sharpest of truths cannot penetrate. More befitting Vonnegut's terminology, our pipes are so clogged with half-digested and indigestible claptrap that nothing can purge them. Our vision, of all kinds, is severely limited.

The Tralfamadorian eye, on top of the phallic shaft like a periscope and seeing "in four dimensions" (28-29), mocks all forms of human vision. Ironically, Pilgrim himself is an optometrist who tries but usually fails to improve the way in which his fellow Homo Sapiens sees. As his own vision is progressively cleared by his experiences with the spacemen, as he realizes the fallacies of history and earth time, Pilgrim is less able to function as an eye doctor. He begins to fall asleep during exams, to weep, or to take one of his spastic time jumps. Finally he is forced to abandon his efforts to repair human sight. Pilgrim is "rich as Croesus" (59), but is also a postmodernist, spastic Tiresias. He is taught by supernatural powers not only how to see into the past, the present, and the future but how to visit as well. However, unlike the Greek seer, Pilgrim can never convey his vision to others.

Vonnegut's sight parody also encompasses the myth of poetic vision—a myth accepted and propagated by writers such as Ralph Waldo Emerson and Walt Whitman who announce that they possess all-seeing eyes that can gaze into the essence of nature's purpose. Vonnegut denigrates such romantic self-delusion. He realizes that human insight is limited and offers at best a distorted view. The artist has no more perspicacity than the fool. In fact, they are occasionally the same, as Kilgore Trout proves. Vonnegut's own poetic vision produces only "this lousy little book" (8). From the Children's Crusade to the bombing of

Hiroshima, from the "Iron Maiden of Nuremberg" to the corpse mines of Dresden, humankind has failed to "see" its violent instinct. It has chosen instead to construct elaborate disguises. In the context of this historical reality, poetic vision is farcical. Vonnegut makes no claim to it and has no faith in it. His narrator self observes wryly that "Among the things Billy could not change were the past, the present, and the future" (58). Though Pilgrim is truly a seer, unlike the idealistic poets, he fails to convince the populace that he is anything other than a madman.

This "sight" metaphor carries over to the second summary passage: Vonnegut's description of the American prisoners in the German boxcars:

> To the guards who walked up and down outside, each car became a single organism which ate and drank and excreted through its ventilators. It talked or sometimes yelled through its ventilators, too. In went water and loaves of blackbread and sausage and cheese, and out came shit and piss and language.     (66-678)

The boxcar scene shows how our pipes get so clogged. Everything entering the human body or mind—food, language, history—emerges as waste. To an objective observer, in this case the indifferent Germans and later the Tralfamadorians, the excreta are all that can be seen. The "shit and piss and language" are the ultimate product of all human endeavors. In the microcosmic confines of the prison car, the men are reduced to their basic biological form: they are consumers and excreters, a collective singular waste-producing organism. They see the world only through occasional cracks in the boxcar door or through the ventilators, a condition paralleling the human tunnel vision that the Tralfamadorians later ridicule. Moreover, the boxcar further shows how human vision is impaired by human waste. The prisoners view the universe through the same apertures that have just been fouled by their own excrement.

The direct connection between the boxcar and the beautiful, doomed city is that the "sausage" eaten by the American prisoners probably comes from the Dresden slaughterhouse. The black bread too later shows up in the kitchen of Schlachthof-fünf, cooked for the Americans by an impatient German war widow (142). In this way the Dresden slaughterhouse produces the excrement that comes out through the boxcar apertures. Dresden epitomizes urban civilization. There the genius of man produced a viable monument to architecture, music, and art, as

described by Mary Endell in 1908 (21). That same genius produces the prison trains and the bombs that destroy Dresden.
That incineration reduces Dresden's inhabitants to "tons of human bone meal" (7), a metaphor that returns us to the waste-
producing paradigm from which we began. The narrative cycle
encompassing Dresden and the prison boxcar symbolizes the
conflict between the human instinct to violence and the conscious awareness that such violence must be controlled lest the
species disappear. It is a lesson, obviously, that humans have
not learned.

The boxcar scene also symbolizes *Slaughterhouse-Five* per
se. The book itself is part of Vonnegut's excrement festival.
Vonnegut has consumed hunks and fragments of history, the
most indigestible being his experiences in Dresden. He says that
he "thought it would be easy for me to write about the destruction of Dresden" (8), but discovers that he suffers from a creative
constipation that remains unrelieved for twenty-three years. In
trying to purge Dresden from his memory he recalls a limerick
that concludes: "And now you won't pee you old fool" (8). By
tragicomically associating his own inability to write with the inability to urinate, and by expressing his frustration in a bawdy
limerick, Vonnegut shows that his novel is the ultimate example of the excremental motif that sustains it. *Slaughterhouse-
Five* is, in short, the waste product of Vonnegut's purgation of
the imagination. Language, whether written or oral, is merely
part of the excrement that passes through the mental ventilators.

Finally, and perhaps most sobering, is how the boxcar
scene evokes and subsumes the Holocaust. The concentration
camps are a horror that Vonnegut avoids in his catalog of allu-
sive violence. They lurk, however, in the subtext of *Slaughterhouse-Five* like a parallel guilty conscience. Frederick J. Hoffman's study of war violence, *The Mortal No: Death and the
Modern Imagination*, was published less than five years before
*Slaughterhouse-Five* and serves as an informative philosophical
adjunct to Vonnegut's thinking. Hoffman discusses at length
the phenomenon of the concentration camps. He evokes a boxcar image and implies a waste metaphor very similar to Vonnegut's: "Hundreds of persons crowded into one car or one
'block' are no longer hundreds of identifiable persons but a mass
of undifferentiated human matter" (270). This boxcar with its
depiction of the loss of individual identity is a microcosm of the
concentration camp phenomenon. At some point in the ordeal,

"the succession of brutalities dulls the sensibility" of victim, assailant, and observer so severely that death itself becomes undeniable. Analysis of the phenomenon itself becomes impossible
(268) and beyond a certain stage "no kind of human emotion is
relevant" (269).

Further, if concentration camp inmates survived for any
length of time, they "developed the dispositions of the 'concentrationary'" and "might gleefully torture others or with a sick
sense of machoistic pleasure improve upon their status as victims of torture" (277). Such absolute dehumanization is "the
end result of modern violence" because it "all but destroys any
meaningful relationship between assailant and victim" (268). As
Hoffman sees it, this lost relationship between the killer and the
killed is the horror of horrors. The reason for this, Hoffman
concludes, is that the concentrationary experience utterly destroyed human intellect and spirituality. The Holocaust proved
that "Man as a thinking animal had disappeared; motives for
trusting in God's ultimate benevolence vanished" (281).

Some of the parallels between Hoffman's analysis and
Vonnegut's satire are self-evident. As we have seen, the soldiers
in the cars, and the German guards who oversee them, are no
longer individual humans. They are a collective "mass" of biological processes. Intellect and spirituality are as far removed
from their world as Pilgrim's Tralfamadorians are from our own
conventional reality. Compassion is nonexistent. Religion is as
putrid as the filth that exits the ventilators. The image extends
to the Dresden slaughterhouse and the melted mass of
humanity that remains after the British and American bombers
fly away. Indeed, Dresden is the end result of modern, technological violence. Though the mechanics of the paradigm are
important, Hoffman's placement of blame is especially pertinent
to Vonnegut's text. Hoffman fixes responsibility for the concen-
trationaries' suffering not on the victim and not on the assailants who themselves are dehumanized, but upon the citizens who closed their eyes to what was happening. Hoffman
concludes that "the ultimate moral causes of concentration camp
abuse existed outside of it" (280). In other words, he puts the
blame on an indifferent and cynical citizenry. With the boxcar
analogy, the sight motif, and the Dresden imagery, that is precisely where Vonnegut implies that blame for such horrors as
the Holocaust should rest.

The chasm that modern technological warfare creates between the victim and the assailant is a profound issue in Vonnegut's satire. The men that we meet—and the few women too, for that matter—are ignorant, arrogant inept, foolish, stupid, misinformed, mentally disturbed, sociopathic, and pathetic. Even the spurious Vonnegut narrator admits he is nothing more than smoke and flatulence. Billy Pilgrim, Roland Weary, Wild Bob, Bertram C. Rumfoord—we meet them, listen to them, and learn what pathetic, comic creatures they are. Who could possibly take them seriously? They seem to be harmless, misdirected specimens in the human zoo. How can men so inept as these manage devastation so absolute as Dresden or Hiroshima?

The question puzzles Vonnegut, even though he does not clearly answer it. The answer seems to lie in a peculiar distortion of the individualism that marks the American Dream and that men such as Rumfoord worship. The machine that is symbolized by the bomber and other war engines and that is personified in the Tralfamadorians has become too complicated for any one individual to comprehend. Thus, specialization results. Each person, man or woman, becomes responsible for a precise, solitary, and isolating task. One individual creates or advances the war technology so that en masse killing from greater and greater distances is possible. One individual builds the bombs, one individual flies the plane, one individual releases the bombs, and so forth. The degrees of specialization are actually much more detailed and precise than this list suggests, but the point remains that even though each individual is crucial in the war-making process, no single person is accountable. No one individual stands eye to eye with an enemy, club or lance in hand, and makes the conscious decision to kill him. Modern weaponry makes it easy to kill with no blood on our hands.

This is why, for instance, Roland Weary's obsession with medieval knights and highly personalized death has such a quaint, humorous ring. The individualized experience of killing and the subsequent individualized experience of having to cope spiritually or psychologically with that act are as antiquated as chain mail. Technology has guaranteed that the collective consequences of each action are fragmented and dispersed. The apparently harmless citizen we pass on the street may be the same bombardier who loosed the first bomb on Dresden. How are we to judge him, however? No one person can be censured for incinerating 130,000 fellow humans. Even one so mild and seemingly harmless as Pilgrim is desensitized by the machine: "Billy found the afternoon stingingly exciting. There was so much to see—dragon's teeth, killing machines, corpses with bare feet that were blue and ivory. So it goes" (62). It is this loss of responsibility for the violent act per se and our subsequent inability to distinguish the criminal from the victim that worries Vonnegut. It too closely parallels the concentrationary mentality that Hoffman details.

The third summary passage exemplifies the war technology implied in the boxcar episode. The scene in which Pilgrim imagines viewing a war movie backward, perhaps more overtly than any other in the novel, shows how closely violence is linked with every trait of the human animal:

> American planes, full of holes and wounded men and corpses took off backwards from an airfield in England. Over France, a few German fighter planes flew at them backwards, sucked bullets and shell fragments from some of the planes and crewmen. They did the same for wrecked American bombers on the ground, and those planes flew up backwards to join the formation. . . . When the bombers got back to their base, the steel cylinders were taken from the racks and shipped back to the United States of America, where factories were operating night and day, dismantling the cylinders, separating the dangerous contents into minerals. Touchingly, it was mainly women who did the work. . . . The American fliers turned in their uniforms, became high school kids. And Hitler turned into a baby, Billy Pilgrim supposed. That wasn't in the movie. Billy was extrapolating. Everybody turned into a baby, and all humanity, without exception, conspired biologically to produce two perfect people named Adam and Eve, he supposed.                                    (69-70)

Vonnegut was not the first to exploit the similarity of bomber and defecation. In John Hersey's *The War Lover* (1959), narrator Charley Bowman co-pilots a B-17 nicknamed *The Body*. He refers to the bomber's dropping their bombs as "their function" and says that some of them shake as if they are guilty about their public "defecations" (16). Bowman concludes that "War equaled s-----, and peace equaled s----" (17). Vonnegut, however, greatly extends the convenient Freudian metaphor. To the bomber's defecation he adds the fighter planes' spewing bullets in steel ejaculation. Like Freud, whom he satirizes, Vonnegut associates defecation and ejaculation with destructiveness: war, in one way or another, is the collective human response to sexuality and poor toilet training. His bomber-fighter plane scenario resonates with the comment by Freud in *Civilization and Its Discontents* that "Excremental things are all too intimately and inseparably bound up with sexual things" (quoted by Brown, 39).

In Pilgrim's idealistic dream world, however, evil and brutality are removed from the excremental-sexual processes. Pilgrim imagines that the indefinite reversal of the biological functions will terminate in the re-perfection of Adam and Eve, the original apple-eaters, fornicators, and waste producers. Appropriately, Pilgrim the naïf sees Eve's modern counterparts as the ones who eliminate the "dangerous contents" from the cylinders that suggests both the phallic and the fecal. Pilgrim characteristically misses the point that Eve is the archetypal mother of evil and that the contemporary women who now disarm the bombs also produced the soldiers and bombardiers who use the munitions to kill the sons and daughters of other mothers. In Pilgrim's defense, however, we have to remember that when he envisions the comforting reversal depicted in the backward movie, he has not yet been re-educated by the Tralfamadorians. The spacemen soon come to flush such romantic sentimentalism (shit, Vonnegut would say) from his mind. They eliminate the myths, old wives' tales, and historical-psychological sewage from his thinking. Conventional wisdom judges him insane, but the psychic flushing is nonetheless what frees Pilgrim from his mother, his wife Valencia, his officious daughter Barbara, and other daughters of Eve. Once freed, he replaces them with his ideal posmodernist Eve: Montana Wildhack, a porn queen whore.

The fourth summary passage is not so much a scene as a recurring emblem. Vonnegut, like Swift with his maps and charts, has a penchant for graphics. Therefore this fourth instance is another graphic, though one that does not appear literally in the novel but only in the reader's salacious imagination. It is the "dirty picture of a woman attempting sexual intercourse with a Shetland pony" (40). This is the first pornographic photograph in history, having been made in 1841 by André Le Fève, an assistant to Louis Daguerre. Like a bawdy cue card, the photo pops up throughout history and Vonnegut's narrative. Le Fève defends it as representing mythological couplings. Despite this artistic effort, he is condemned as a pornographer and dies in prison. Roland Weary, in World War II, carries a copy as part of his survival kit. The Germans who capture him steal it. Pilgrim stumbles across another copy in 1968 while investigating a New York porn shop that is appropriately adorned with "fly shit" on the windows (177).

Not only is the photograph a graphic example of sodomy and a mocking reminder of what Eve's sin has led her daughters to, but it is another link in Vonnegut's thematic satire of artistic creation. John Keats' urn, for instance, is an "unravished bride of quietness" and a "Sylvan historian" that also depicts a scene of seduction from Greek myth. Like the doomed original photographer of the woman-and-pony tableau, Keats' ode claims to make a statement about truth and beauty. Vonnegut's reoccurring photograph of a willing whore about to be ravished by a horse, however, is a reminder that throughout history love has been the catalytic converter in a waste producing machine. One of the cruelest aspects of the joke implied by the photograph is about poets such as Keats who attempt to understand and transcribe the follies of humankind. Love, fornication, art, and the general human predicament are not expressed in pretty sonnets or irregular odes, but in profane doggerel such as that sung by the barbershop quartet for Pilgrims' father. One obscene limerick encapsulates the excrement, the violence, the sexuality, the failed artistic idealism, and the racism that marked World War II, and all of human history:

> In my prison cell I sit,
> With my britches full of shit,
> And my balls are bouncing gently on the floor.
> And I see the bloody snag
> When she bit me in the bag.
> Oh, I'll never fuck a Polack any more.          (134)

If Swift's excremental vision is revealingly unpremeditated and unconscious, Vonnegut's on the other hand is very much premeditated and conscious. Vonnegut, no doubt, would find nothing more absurdly humorous than for a commentator to draw Freudian, psychological conclusions from the numerous excremental allusion he puts into *Slaughterhouse-Five*. As his spurious self notes, it is a novel that has "almost no characters" and "almost no dramatic confrontations, because most of the people  in it are so sick and so much the listless playthings of enormous forces" (145). Against such odds, Homo Sapiens plays in the face of almost certain defeat. Vonnegut's view, therefore, is called an excremental *festival*, not a vision, and people are meant to laugh at festivals. Thus, with sardonic joy, Vonnegut uses defecation, urination, ejaculation, and related functions not necessary to suggest the psyche of Billy Pilgrim or Kurt Vonnegut but to show that each such process is part of the biological production of waste. In Vonnegut's scatology the world is coming from and tending back to waste. All aspects of that world are ridiculous and all efforts to discover fine patterns of meaning are doubly ridiculous. If, as Vonnegut shows, history is a morass of lies and biased reporting; if the poet's vision culminates only in lousy books and obscene limericks; and if psychology is a pointless game of correlation in which one meaningless thing is substituted for several other meaningless things, then what might literary criticism be?

The ultimate irony underlying the excremental vision is that humans have developed some truly beautiful, inspiring myths and ideas (the Garden of Eden, Heaven, Nirvana, Love, Art). The powerful instinct to violence, however, with all its resultant horrors, has distorted such visions beyond recognition. Little in Vonnegut argues for optimism, but deep in the black mass of his absurdist talent flickers a minute candle of possibility. He still hopes that through the modicum of reason and compassion that has survived the devastation, we can somehow learn to recognize our innate viciousness and the lies by which we disguise it. Otherwise, we will be blasted into subatomic particles. Violence per se is not the threat. The failure to recognize and control it is.

# E. L. Doctorow's
# *Billy Bathgate*

In discussing James M. Cain and *The Postman Always Rings Twice*, we raised the question about the worth of what Joyce Carol Oates called the "sleazy" and "vulgar" (110) fiction of a novelist who was "an entertainer with an uncanny knowledge of the perversities of his audience, the great range of their vulgarity" (114). Few would automatically connect Cain and E. L. Doctorow, certainly not to the extreme of accusing Doctorow of sleaze and vulgarity. Yet, the same questions that Oates and others raised about *Postman* could legitimately be asked of *Billy Bathgate* (1989). Both are pulp fiction. Both are popular crime stories based on real people and actual cases. Both are set in the Depression. One might even argue, with considerable logic, that given its violent sex and gore *Billy Bathgate* is also aimed at the perversity and vulgarity of the reading public. However, the most significant trait shared by Cain's masterpiece and Doctorow's foray into crime fiction is that both are pulp potboilers redeemed from insignificance by how they manage violence. Evidence of how essential violence is to the *Billy Bathgate* is suggested by the mediocre film Walt Disney made from it. As Robert Haas says of that movie, Disney eliminated the sex and violence. Consequently, movie goers "rejected this sanitized produce as meaningless and uninteresting" (74). In short, without the violence, there is no story worth noticing.

Aside from its violence, *Billy Bathgate* is so deep in the American tradition that it flirts with triteness. Alfred Kazin, who years earlier had accused *Postman* of "pandering to the same taste which enjoyed the synthetic violence of the murder mystery and drugstore treatises on lesbianism" (303), immediately recognized that *Billy Bathgate* was just a Bronx Huck Finn.

Indeed, Doctorow's novel owes just about everything to Twain. The rest it owes to Sigmund Freud as formulated in pop psychology. It is a picaresque, Bildungsroman story told by a little-educated but street-wise juvenile who has one parent missing altogether and the other prone to sociopathy. As a Bildungsroman, it is one of the oldest types of fiction; and the search for the lost father was commonplace even before Freud elevated it to a mythic cliché. However, nothing Billy Bathgate says or does is in the same league with either Twain's linguistic genius or Huck's moral decision to risk Hell for his beloved Jim. For that matter, even Holden Caulfield's poignant psychological dilemmas (themselves noticeably Freudian and set in New York) are more convincing than Billy's and more likely to evoke empathy.

Likewise, we are not certain what compels Billy's confession, or, more correctly, his braggadocio. Just who is supposed to be listening to his tale is equally vague. (It is a psychiatrist, priest, his bastard son?) His lapses into unpunctuated run-on sentences are unexplained, or unexplainable. By the time we hear him, Billy is supposed to be a graduate of an Ivy League university, and, we would assume, is ordinarily articulate and grammatical. The lost syntactical control parallels no psychic traumas or guilt Billy may suffer, unless as I suggest later, he has lost contact with his characteristic reason. Till the end of his narrative, he is distinctly amoral and without conscience. Unlike Huck Finn (also poor until providence rewards him and as sexually pure as spring rain on the Mississippi), Billy copulates with a child (Rebecca), steals all the money he can glom on to, and participates in numerous other serious crimes. Moreover, the baby who arrives at the conclusion of the novel to delight Billy and his eccentric mother does not derive logically from previous narrative design. Aside from compromising the rest of the narrative, the baby seems to have the wrong sexual partner as its mother. If Doctorow wants to unite everybody as one big happy family, the infant should come from Rebecca, the poor orphan child whom Billy has bedded and abandoned. In that scenario, Billy, Rebecca, baby, and grandma could live together in wealth and comfort, the epitome of the nuclear family.

Suggesting such possibilities is of course beside the point. Yet Douglas Fowler is correct in complaining that the plot of *Billy Bathgate* is as "essentially unreal as a James Bond novel," the style suffers from "Faulknerian excess," and "we are never *involved* in it as we are with Doctorow's best work" (150).

Speaking more generally of Doctorow's fiction, and more harshly, Carol Iannone concludes that "it is ironic that a writer who has forgone most of the demands of character and plot should speak, as Doctorow does, of the 'salvation available in the witness and moral assignment' of the aesthetic art." On the contrary, she says, his work is "spurious" (56). Iannone's assessment is too severe, but *Billy Bathgate* does indeed demonstrate certain qualities that are difficult to justify on an aesthetic or even entertainment basis.

However, one significant quality of Doctorow's novel saves it from being just another piece of hack work: *Billy Bathgate* is among the very few pulp fiction novels in American literature to be elevated to artistic integrity solely by violence. Violence forms the core of the plot, incidental scenes of violence energize the action, and the rhetoric of violence permeates every narrative element. Ultimately, this unrelenting violence constitutes a disturbing parable of American life and serves as a treatise on the art of fiction.

The dominant scene of violence opens the novel and continues as the narrative center to which all subsequent action adheres. The long scene detailing Dutch Schultz's preparations for the drowning of his former associate Bo Weinberg is, as Fowler terms it, "a comic-book opening, a pulp-thriller opening, the best moment in the novel" (146). Doctorow knows the dramatic potential of violence, and he uses this scene adroitly. All of chapter 1 is devoted to describing the circumstances and preparations surrounding Weinberg's impending murder. He is abducted, hauled to the pier in an ominous black Packard, taken to sea, bound to a chair, and then required to place "one foot at a time in the laundry tub in front of him that was filled with wet cement" (9). Thus situated, Weinberg and the reader wait. Not until chapter 11 do we learn precisely how Weinberg died and how he reacted as he awaited his horrible fate. In great detail, Billy explains how Weinberg sat waiting for the cement around his feet to dry, how he sang "Bye Bye Blackbird" to keep up his courage and retain his dignity, and how he was finally dumped into the black sea. Billy tells that he "quickly and accurately" helped "roll Bo on the dolly quite easily with the sea's help to the open hatch." Then "I see the back of his head moving and his shoulders and his head is up facing into this world of inexplicable terror and though I can't hear it for the wind I know he is singing" (162). Ironically, Billy is blithely describing this horror to Weinberg's lover, Drew Preston, ostensibly to comfort her. This triangular relationship among tale, reporter, and listener intensifies the horror of Bo Weinberg's ordeal.

The Weinberg scene per se is not expressly violent. In fact, it is grimly humorous. However, as he leisurely describes the preparations for Weinberg's death, Doctorow uses flashbacks to introduce other scenes that are explicitly violent. The most prevalent of these intercalary scenes of violence shows how Dutch Schultz "stove in the skill of the fire safety inspector" (3). The episode is alluded to immediately in the text and is repeated with incremental details. Unlike the strangely unemotional killing of Bo Weinberg, the fire inspector scene is stunningly violent:

> . . . he sort of jumped forward screaming with his arms raised and brought his whole weight of assault on the poor fuck, and carried him down in a kind of smothering tackle, landing on top of him with a crash that probably broke his back, who knows? and then with his knees pinning down the outstretched arms, simply grabbing the throat and pressing the balls of his thumbs down on the windpipe, and when the tongue came out and the eyes rolled up walloping the head two three times on the floor like it was a coconut he wanted to crack open.                                        (5)

With such interpolated scenes, Doctorow compounds the horror of the primary scene and lets us know that Schultz's past performances guarantee that no deux ex machina is going to save Bo Weinberg. Thus we await the details of his death with increasing unease, and impatience.

This past murder of the fire inspector connects Bo Weinberg's murder, which occurs in present time, to the other incidental scenes of violence that collectively dictate the entire narrative design. These scenes occur both in past and present time and serve as chronological connectors for Billy's nonsequential thoughts. Though many such organizational scenes appear in the text, three standout: the murder of the two window washers, the murder of Julie Martin, and the breaking of Billy's nose. These scenes are the objective correlatives of how Doctorow uses violence to organize the text. These correlation scenes warrant scrutiny because they calibrate the various types and intensities of violence, thereby permitting the audience to measure its own experiential relationship with the fictive violence.

The death of the sabotaged window washers is an espe-

cially disturbing scene of violence because it indicates the impersonal, random nature of Schultz's malevolence. For some reason that Billy does not at first understand, Abbadabba Berman
tells him to go to a certain spot on Broadway and watch. Billy
silently obeys and eventually spots two window washers on the
fifth or sixth floor of an office building. He knows instinctively
that these doomed workmen are what Berman wanted him to
observe:

> And it was this scaffold with the two men and their
> sponges and pails and rags which suddenly lurched, the
> rope on one side snapping up into the air like a whip,
> and the two men flinging their arms back and spilling
> down the scaffold. One of them came down the side of
> the building wheeling. . . . Then the body at a point of
> flat and horizontal extension hit the roof of a car
> parked in front of the building and the sound it made
> was as a cannon going off, a terrible explosion of the
> force of bone and flesh, and what made me gasp was
> that he moved, the guy moved in that concavity of
> metal he had made, a sinuosity of bone-smashed inch-
> ing, as if it was a worm there curling for a moment on
> the hot metal before even that degree of incredible life
> trembled out through his fingers.             (71)

From such experiences, Billy learns that he must obediently accept the mob's mindless violence and how the mob uses violence to enforce its will on unions and other uncooperative
groups. Moreover, the scene emphasizes how any individual is
vulnerable to the intricate maze of corruption and violence that
Schultz and his kind construct. It is a naturalistic epiphany for
the reader.

The violence demonstrated by the sabotaging of the window washer's scaffold is premeditated and purposeful. An irrational and perhaps more terrifying form of violence is seen in
the mindless explosions of Dutch Schultz's temper. Such behavior so frightens the other mob bosses that they have Schultz assassinated. The most telling scene depicting this type of instinctive and unreasonable violence is the Julie Martin episode. The
incident occurs in a quiet hotel in the "country" town of
Onondaga, New York. Ostensibly because he thinks Martin has
stolen money from him but actually because he does not like
Martin's looks, Schultz "Takes out his gun in the middle of a
sentence and shoots into the man's mouth" (198). Billy arrives
on the scene immediately after the shooting:

> The furnishings were awry, the chairs were pushed
> back, this Julie Martin lay in his bulk across the coffee
> table in the living room, he was not yet dead but lay
> gasping on his stomach with his head turned sideways
> and a rolled-up hotel towel under his cheek and an-
> other towel rolled up neatly behind his head to take
> the blood, and both towels were reddening quickly, and
> he was gasping, and blood was trickling out of his
> mouth and nose and his arms hanging over the table
> were trying to find something to hold on to and his
> knees were on the floor and he was pushing back. . . .
> (197)

Rather than being sickened or horrified by the ghastly scene,
Billy calmly crawls around on the floor to find the spent shell
casing under the couch. With such callous acts he ingratiates
himself with Schultz and gives the audience information by
which to judge the narrator's moral perspective.

Though Billy himself is not expressly violent, and is characteristically nonchalant, his own violent instinct is revealed
when he is suddenly made the victim of Schultz's self-serving
viciousness. So that Julie Martin's blood on the hotel carpet
may be explained, Schultz directs Lulu Rosenkrantz to break Billy's nose so that it bleeds. The attack is savage and unexpected:

> . . . a blinding pain struck me dumb, my knees buckled,
> and a starlike flash exploded in my eyes, just the way
> prizefighters say it does, and an instant later I was
> crouched over, groaning and dribbling in my shock,
> holding both my hands over my poor nose, my best fea-
> ture, bleeding profusely now through my fingers to the
> stained rug. . . .                                    (202)

For the first time, Billy realizes his own potential for violence: "I
remember what that whack across the face did to the passage of
time, in the instant I felt it, it became an old injury and the rage
it engendered in me was an ancient resolve to somehow pay
them back, to get even" (202). We know that Billy subsequently
serves in the military and that he steals the gang's money, thus
implying that violence and revenge are in his future when he
makes this resolution. Moreover, his statement implies that violence other than that sanctioned by his country may be a part of
the unrecorded years between his initiation into the gang and
the time when he recounts his adolescence to us. "Ancient" violence is a human trait that Billy will not escape, no matter how
nonchalantly he responds to it or how hard he tries to distance
himself from it by carefully editing his memory.

As noted, these correlative scenes organize the text. Their secondary contribution is that they also energize the story. When violence wanes, the novel is boring and fails in what Fowler terms its "attempt to elevate crime-thriller subliterature into art" (146). The interlude in Saratoga with Drew Preston, for instance, is too long and essentially trite. When scenes of violence attain their potential, however, the overt and graphic violence interfuses every facet of the narrative.

Doctorow uses the conventional rhetoric of violence rather extensively, as the above passages readily illustrate. However, he takes the rhetoric of violence into a dimension not typical of crime fiction. He is able to make this elevation partially because of his own artistry but more so because he is freed from linguistic restrictions that inhibited earlier novelists. We see this new dimension in two specific instances: Bo Weinberg's obscenity-laced damnation of Dutch Schultz and Billy Bathgate's striking description of his primitive sexual encounter with Drew Preston. The violence of both passages, especially Weinberg's epic curses, is intensified by a grim humor that is typical of the entire narrative. The scene in which Bo Weinberg sits with his feet encased in a tub of cement, awaiting death by drowning, is a comic book cliché. There is no more hackneyed account of how mobsters dispose of their enemies. "Wearing cement shoes" is a euphemism for a victim of mob violence. Yet Doctorow adds a crucial postmodernist element to the cliché. Bound tightly and wearing his cement slippers, Weinberg has nothing left with which to fight Schultz except his tongue and language. He uses this final weapon with obscene effectiveness:

> I don't know what stinking womb of pus and shit and ape scum you came out of. 'Cause you're an ape, Dutch. Hunker down and scratch your ass, Dutch.    (14)

> May you fuck your mother flying through the air, . . . May your father lick the shit of horses off the street. May your baby be served to you boiled on a platter with an apple in its mouth.    (18)

Such obscenities are the verbal equivalents of gunfire and knife attacks. They are foreign to the usual aesthetic criteria we have developed for language, both as a tool for communication and as a cultural identifier. Even the much-maligned *Slaughterhouse-Five* fails to challenge our traditional linguistic sensibilities so strongly. Weinberg's outbursts are the superlative (but certainly not only) examples in the novel of how language is a

disguise for the fundamental violence that dictates human behavior. That is why his vile outbursts are so startling. Most literature, including many of the novels discussed in this study,
repress the violence that underlies language. Such repression
stems either from the authors' own volition or, more likely,
from the pressures of publishers and editors. Whatever the
causes, we as readers seldom hear language used so viciously as
the weapon of last resort.

Weinberg's verbal attacks may be seen as an example of
what Nancy Armstrong and Leonard Tennenhouse refer to as
"the violence of representation." Writing, they note, "is not so
much about violence as a form of violence in its own right" (2).
I would not go so far as to remove all distinctions between words
describing violence and violence per se, as Armstrong and Tennenhouse do. I agree, however, that words used as Weinberg
uses them and in the circumstances under which he uses them,
are a surrogate for actual violence that has been repressed. We
see this correlation between language and violence confirmed by
the inverse rhetorical situation of Dutch Schultz. Unlike Weinberg, Schultz can activate the violence that drives him. His own
verbal response, therefore, remains uncharacteristically calm in
face of Weinberg's vicious insults: "'But look, Bo,' he said. 'I'm
standing here and you're sitting there and you're all finished
and who would you rather be at this moment, Mr. class-act Bo
Weinberg?" (18). This Weinberg-Schultz exchange clearly defines the close ties between the language of violence and violence per se. Moreover, it illustrates how carefully Doctorow
manages the cliché-ridden verbal domain of the pulp fiction
genre.

While Billy's description of Drew Preston in the throes of
passion does not at first seem related to Weinberg's obscene outburst, the two scenes are actually closely connected. As in Weinberg's curse, Billy's description relates to fornication ("fuck"), the
copulation occurs in the muck ("scum" and "shit"), and a baby
results from their literally brutish or apish union:

> . . . I found the primeval voice in her, like a death rat-
> tle, a shrill sexless bark, over and over again as I
> jammed into her, and it became tremulous a terrible cry-
> ing despair, and then she screamed so shriekingly I
> thought something was wrong and reared to look at her,
> her lips were pulled back over her teeth and her green
> eyes dimmed as I looked in them, they had lost sight,
> gone flat as if her mind had collapsed, as if time had

> turned in her and she had passed back into infancy and
> reverted through birth into nothingness. . . .     (217-218)

Unlike Bo Weinberg, who personifies the violent gentleman, Drew Preston personifies the nonviolent lady. Outwardly,
she is perhaps he least aggressive and most passive character in
the novel (except for Billy's saintly and slightly deranged
mother). Drew demonstrates not only her self-preservation instincts but her nonviolence when she acquiesces in Schultz's
sexual overtures even as her lover Weinberg awaits execution in
a nearby cabin. Under stress, she epitomizes tranquillity and
cool reasonableness, if not loyalty. Yet, when her facade of urbane nonviolence is removed and her sexual instincts prevail,
we see the irrational violence that defines even the most placid
of individuals. The savagery that Billy displays as he fornicates
with Drew (his "jamming" her), is characteristic of male violence and therefore not surprising. Her reversion to primordial,
animalistic violence, however, is quite another matter. Our
stereotypes and traditional values do not adequately prepare us
for her response.

Aside from its value as pulp fiction and apart from its
erotic attraction, therefore, Billy's description of Drew's primordial violence subsumes an important narrative irony. Her
sexual frenzy proves that just below the smooth white skin and
beyond the control of even the most urbane and imperturbable
individual, the animal genes of Homo Sapiens dominate.
To the public, she is the epitome of the cultured lady. Only
in the secret and caddish revelations of Billy's confession do
we discover that she too has just arrived from the primordial
slime. With her wealth, beauty, sophistication, and expedient
morals she personifies those values that we endorse as a society.
That image and those values remain valid only so long as
our contact with her is superficial, fleeting. When we enter
the slime with her and witness her violent, primitive self, we
are painfully reminded of the superficiality of our cultural and
personal values. If one who personifies the best that our
modern culture has to offer can be driven to such primitive
outbursts, Doctorow makes us ask, then what hope is there for
civilization?

Billy's description of his affair with her also clarifies why
Drew Preston so instantly bonds with Dutch Schultz and joins
him in a hotel room for "two whole full days without coming
up for air" (121). Drew Preston's sexuality and Dutch Schultz's

violence stem from the same instinctive behavior. At one point Billy even associates Schultz's animalistic killing sounds with those of sexual passion (82). Biologically, beauty and beast are ultimately synonymous. However, Schultz, the vicious killer, is a more honest portrayal of Homo Sapiens than the sophisticated society lady. In his raw violence and cunning, Schultz is a throwback to a much earlier time in human evolution. His predatory nature is overt while hers is concealed by literal and psychological cosmetics. Her portrait may be more palliative to our torn sensibility, but the raw picture that Doctorow gives of Schultz is a more honest rendering of our species.

Doctorow makes no commensurately overt demonstration that this innate violence by which Schultz, Drew Preston, and the others define their lives transfers into the insensate world. His rhetoric, however, subtly insists that violence pervades the animate and inanimate realms of existence. The chain-wheel drives on the old World War I Mack trucks used in Schultz's bootleg operation sound like "bones being ground up" (24). The elevated train "came along thundering overhead" and "the streetcars rang their gongs" (106). Returning to New York from Onondaga, Billy describes the city as a war zone: "all I could smell was burning cinder, my eyes smarted and the clamor was deafening. Everything was broken down and falling apart, the tenements looked worn out by history, the empty lots were rubble" (247). The Jersey shore looks infernal with its "ranks of coral barges lying at anchor and brick factories spewing smoke and the whole western horizon filled with the pipes and tanks and catwalks of hellish refineries" (285). The point is that the human violence is so historic and pervasive that it has interfused the machinery and matrix of the post-industrial city. We do not know, of course, which route the violent transference has taken. Is human violence environmentally derived or did human violence corrupt a once pristine or neutral environment? Doctorow does not attempt to answer that conundrum, but he does show that violence is endemic. Violence is not merely something that humans *are*. It is existence itself.

To emphasize this rather somber point, Doctorow shows that no American cultural institution has been an effective counter agent to violence. It is in part to emphasize this lesson that Doctorow puts his faith in a narrator who is clever and "capable" but ultimately naive. Sometimes totally unaware, at other times blinded by sentiment and neuroses, Billy Bathgate guilelessly limns the failure of education, politics, religion, and family.

The most visible education in the text is that taking place on the streets. Dutch Schultz, himself an honor graduate of the gutter, frets that Billy has not graduated from a street gang. "Well how you expect to get anywhere, how you expect to learn anything?" Schultz worries. "That's the training ground" (68). Traditional schooling is conspicuously absent, but we do know that Billy is no devoted scholar. He brags that from a very early age he "could smell the truant officer before he even came around the corner" (23). This disinterest in formal education is why Billy's claims of a sudden return to school and subsequent graduation from an Ivy League college are suspect, a point we will return to later. We never see Billy in school, but we do see him learning to shoot a pistol and contemplating other lessons learned from the gang. Like Huck Finn, his schooling is pragmatic and of the hard-knocks variety. Unlike Huck's learning, however, Billy's does not culminate in any moral awakening. Quite the contrary, it seems to put him into a moral coma.

Politics in *Billy Bathgate* indicate the consequence of such ineffectual public education. From the lowest to the highest echelon in Doctorow's world, politicians represent moral and economic decay. Whether it be the greedy fire inspector whose head Schultz smashes or Thomas E. Dewey himself, politicians are self-serving and corrupt. James J. Hines, the "Tammany man" fixes the police and city officials for Schultz, until Dewey's political ambition starts to make things too hot. The entire town of Onondaga is easily corrupted by Schultz's influence peddling. A jury subsequently renders a notoriously bad verdict of innocent at his tax evasion trial. Even Dewey himself, the man who would be President, ends up making deals with the mob. In 1942, as governor of the state, he pardons the man with "bad skin" who assassinated Schultz, ostensibly because he helped against the Nazi in New York. That Dewey announced his candidacy for the 1944 Presidential race about this time suggests that other motives may have also been involved, though Doctorow does not have his young narrator address such issues.

While clearly distrustful of politics and politicians, Doctorow saves his most scathing irony for religion and its representatives. Two notable name changes—Flegenheimer to Schultz and Behan to Bathgate—imply how far removed Billy and Schultz have become from their Jewish and Catholic heritage.

Also, when Bo Weinberg is facing certain death and has ample time to contemplate his sins and eternal destination, he calls not upon God but sings instead to a black bird. These instances are only implicit attacks upon religion, but Doctorow offers more explicit examples. When Billy inadvertently carries a Bible with him to one of the gang's Onondaga business meetings, the faux pas shows Schultz how to use religion to cover his criminal activities. He first enrolls Billy in a Bible study class, but then carries the sham much further. He mocks his own Jewish heritage and corrupts the Catholic church by "converting" to Catholicism. Father Montaine tells Schultz that the move "From the Jewish to the Holy Church is a great revolution" (173). It will take at least five years "to purify yourself and prepare for election" (172). With money, Schultz persuades Father Montaine to accomplish the conversion by next Sunday. Afterward, Schultz and the father "drank from a bottle of Canadian whiskey on the table and smoked cigars" and "both of them [were] stolid and neckless and sloppy with their ashes" (174). Showing how well he has learned the mobster's ways, Billy grasps what the wily Schultz has done: "he'd appropriated speakeasies, beer companies unions, numbers games, nightclubs, me, Miss Drew, and now he was appropriating Catholicism. That was all" (176). Billy's naive understatement here is a devastating criticism of Judaism, Catholicism, and religion generally. Even if the church is not itself flagrantly corrupt, it has let itself open to appropriation by callous secularism. Such sins of omission as those personified by Father Montaine seem worse in Doctorow's view than the overt sins of commission embodied by Schultz and his kind. At least, our traditional moral standards make the hard-drinking expedient Father Montaine appear more reprehensible than the psychopathic Schultz.

The dysfunctional family has been a staple in American literature since before Matthew Maule cursed the Pyncheon clan. So Doctorow is hardly breaking new literary ground with the motif of failed marriages and families. He does effectively use the motif, however, as a clue to how we should interpret narrative closure. The series of doomed marriages lead directly to Billy's peculiar ideas of family that close *Billy Bathgate*. Billy's best childhood friends are orphans, the cultural garbage left by decayed relationships and then dumped into the Max and Dora Diamond Home for Children. (We do not know what happened to Max and Dora.) Drew Preston is casually adulterous, moving

from Weinberg to Schultz to Bathgate. Her husband is a homosexual, and their union mocks traditional ideas of marriage and
family. Furthermore, she gives her child away, apparently with
no qualms and without regrets. The Behan marriage has also
failed, and textual evidence suggests that the separation was
hardly amicable. Billy's mother X's her husband from the photograph and nails his suit to the floor. Though Billy reveres his
mother, the same violence that is overt in Schultz lurks just beneath the surface of mother Behan's benign countenance and eccentric behavior. Though the gangsters have families somewhere—even Schultz—we never see those families in operation. The mob is the only "family" visible, and it is a violent,
deadly clan that proves that blood and violence are much
stronger bonds than love, honor, and obedience. Moreover, the
most horrific violence is often juxtaposed with conventional
domestic situations or described in terms of domesticity. We
have already noted the scene in which window washing precipitates a horrible death. Then too, Schultz recounts the assassination of Vincent Coll in terms of sewing and cooking: "my guy,
he *stitches* the rounds up one side of the phone booth and down
the other, . . . and that was how we did in the Mick, may his *giz-
zards boil* in hell till the end of time" (265) [emphasis added].
This persistent anti-domestic motif must be reconciled with
Billy's sentimental closure, where he suddenly presents the idea
of family to us as if it is justification for and salvation from the
dreadful lives he has just described.

    Before such reconciliation can occur, however, we must
ask the most important question about a first-person narrator: is
he credible? The answer for Billy, as for most first-person narrators, is yes he is and no he isn't. He is reliable insofar as reportage. He tells what he sees and he reports it thoroughly and
factually. He observes the most vicious events and relates them
without hysteria or exaggeration. His objective tone and the casual indifference it conveys give the events the grim tone that
accounts for much of the novel's success. Therefore, insofar as
good reporting is concerned, Billy is indeed a "capable boy." As
his double-jointedness and his juggling imply, however, he is
ambiguous. When Billy is called upon as an educated, thoughtful adult to show that he understand the pragmatic lessons
learned from his youthful days with Schultz and his gang, he
fails.

    As we have seen, each cultural institution with which

Billy comes into contact attests to the corruption and moral decay that Billy describes and personifies. Nothing in his experience justifies his naive belief in the bliss of domesticity with which the novel closes. Billy ends up living with his other "in a top-floor five-room apartment with a southern exposure overlooking the beautiful trees and paths and lawns and playgrounds of Claremont Park" (322). It is an idyllic arrangement for a boy who loves his mother so, and it is perfected when the chauffeur delivers Billy's bastard son. Here the narrative loses its credible, objective voice and deteriorates into sentimentalism. We can accept and probably even applaud that crime does indeed pay. Little in our postmodernist, technological culture can be used to prove otherwise. However, Billy's version of the American Dream purchased by such booty does not reasonably evolve out of the events that Billy describes. His is the Dream as it appears through a Freudian cloud: a poor boy who has never held an honest job, who steals a fortune, who is symbolically married to his mother, and who suddenly gets a wee son to rear in his own image. It is a ridiculous Horatio Alger fantasy appended to a naturalistic chronicle. By the end of the 1980s, when *Billy Bathgate* was published, we were far too jaded as a culture to validate such folly.

The bastard child does suggest, however, the infantilism and the permanent naiveté that mark Billy's intellect. We do not know what becomes of this unexpected son because in many respects Billy himself personifies the child. His mother's dressing the doll in Billy's old baby clothes foreshadows this infantilism. Though his experience with the gang and subsequent stints in college and the military suggest a cosmopolitan personality, Billy is happiest at home with mother and child. Such a situation is in many ways his own self resurrection into a life that is literally high above the Bathgate Street existence that helped form him. Such cloistered mentality compromises all else that Billy has said and done. Whereas Huck Finn closes his narrative vowing that he has had enough of mother figures and is heading for the literal and psychological openness of the wild west, Billy gladly seeks sanctuary in an apartment overlooking Claremont Park. Such an act hardly suggests independence of mind or of action. Moreover, we know that no high-rise apartment in New York is tall enough to allow escape from the terror that still dominates the streets below.

The text supports two feasible explanations for Billy's closing scenario. One is that Billy, like his mother, is out of touch with reality and thus slightly delusional. The overblown rhetoric of his last several pages differs significantly from the previous tone. This tonal change indicates that Billy has become slightly hysterical in trying to convince us of his truthfulness. His claims to wealth and renown, and his insistence that his whereabouts must remain "secret" may sound feasible, but they also ring with a note of paranoia. He insists that "I have told the truth of what I have told in the words and the truth of what I have not told which resides in the words" (321). We might note that Billy's words here reflect Doctorow's own words about the novel: "Words have no physical existence. Books are events in the mind. You don't know as time passes if what was in your mind as you wrote is really what's on the page" (Tokarczyk 321). It is a warning that we must abide as we try to figure out where "truth" lives in Billy's words. Their tone is obviously messianic, enigmatic. Billy is guilt stricken about events from his earlier life, probably mostly from events to which we are not privy. If we look for the truth "I have not told" in his words, we can only conclude that his closing statement suggests that somewhere during those years we do not hear about, the clever, capable young man has become an old man touched with delusions of grandeur and prophecy. He is, in short, slightly daft. He is indeed his mother's son, and the tyranny of genetics has won again.

We could argue too, with equal feasibility, that Billy's retreat to childhood with the trappings of sweet domesticity is his response to the violence he has witnessed. We recall how indifferent he is to Bo Weinberg's situation at the beginning of the novel. He complains about sea sickness, but has no real qualms about helping "roll Bo on the dolly quite easily with the sea's help to the open hatch" and dumping him into the black sea to face "inexplicable terror" (162). Billy will do anything to ingratiate himself with "Mr. Schultz." Moreover, there are indications that Billy may have witnessed or participated in events even more horrible than those he reports. How, for instance, does he know what "bones being ground up" (24) sounds like when he uses that phrase to describe the noise of truck gears? Billy's retrospective, casual reporting of Bo Weinberg's death and all the other violent incidents may be a manifestation of his repressed emotional responses. That repression could be the untold truth we are supposed to find in Billy's word. Becoming inured to excessive violence and retreating into a self-preserving callousness is a common phenomenon. We recall, for instance, Frederick J. Hoffman's *The Mortal No: Death and the Modern Imagination,* in which he discusses how victims of the Holocaust reached a point at which their moral and social systems shut down. At some point "the succession of brutalities dulls the sensibility" of victim, assailant, and observer so severely that any analysis of the phenomenon itself becomes impossible (268). Beyond that point "no kind of human emotion is relevant" (269). In his objectively, essentially emotionless reportage, therefore, we glimpse how thoroughly Billy has suppressed the horrific violence that has dictated his life. Only in his final guilt-driven outburst do we glimpse the truth that words cannot reveal.

Finally, we certainly cannot deny that Billy's life has been successful as defined by the Capitalistic American Dream. Even if only a modicum of what he tells us about finding Schultz's millions and his subsequent life is true, he has been immensely successful. He is Horatio Alger with mob connections. His success is precisely the ultimate horror of the novel because it blinds Billy to the violence and horror that his own experiences once taught him. In his first novel, *Welcome To Hard Times,* Doctorow gives us another autobiographical scribbler. Blue, trapped in the violence and desolation of the nineteenth-century Dakota frontier, yearns for social structure, stability, economic success, and a loving family. He sacrifices everything, including his own manhood and ultimately his life, to attain his American Dream. However, looming over the landscape like the Black Hills is the Bad Man from Bodie. He is the personification of mythic evil, and no one escapes him. The Bad Man is very real because he is our own primordial self come to disabuse us of the comforting lives with which we camouflage our violent nature. Like Blue, who is blinded by his own naive sentimental idealism but yet feels compelled to transcribe it for posterity, Billy Bathgate seems on the verge of reencountering the Bad Man. That impending clash makes us very uneasy.

Though I personally remain uneasy with the overly facile application of the term "postmodernism," Nelson H. Vieira is correct when he argues that *Billy Bathgate* exhibits a kind of postmodern heroics and is one of those recent novels that "challenge our traditional views of aesthetic beauty and ethical goodness, obliging us to reposition and reconsider the comforting optic of our daily lives" (356).

# Cormac McCarthy's
## *Blood Meridian*

Cormac McCarthy's *Blood Meridian* (1985) is the alpha and omega of the novel of violence. It is not a novel about violence. It is not a novel in which violence is incidental. It is not a novel in which violence is central. It is violence, period. Remove violence from the narrative mix, and *Blood Meridian* decoheres. It may not be the first novel to imply that violence is the nucleus around which all our genetic atoms revolve (Faulkner's *Light in August* probably holds that distinction), but it is the first to promote that theory quite so convincingly. McCarthy himself has stated the philosophy underlying his fiction:

> There's no such thing as life without bloodshed, . . . I think the notion that the species can be improved in some way, that everyone could live in harmony, is a really dangerous idea. Those who are afflicted with this notion are the first ones to give up their souls, their freedom. Your desire that it be that way will enslave you and make your life vacuous.
>
> (quoted in Woodward, 36)

Let us begin with three random passages that suggest how thoroughly McCarthy transposes his philosophy of violence to the text of *Blood Meridian*:

> The murdered lay in a great pool of their communal blood. It had set up into a sort of pudding crossed everywhere with the tracks of wolves or dogs and along the edges it had dried and cracked into a burgundy ceramic. Blood lay in dark tongues on the floor and blood grouted the flagstones and ran in the vestibule where the stones were cupped from the feet of the faithful and their fathers before them and it had threaded its way down the steps and dripped from the stones among the dark

red tracks of the scavengers.                    (60)

. . . The White man looked up drunkenly and the black
stepped forward and with a single stroke swapt off his
head.
     Two thin ropes of dark blood and two slender rose
like snakes from the stump of his neck and arched hiss-
ing into the fire. The head rolled to the left and came
to rest at the ex-priest's feet where it lay with eyes
aghast. Tobin jerked his foot away and rose and
stepped back. The fire steamed and blackened and a
gray cloud of smoke rose and the columnar arches of
blood slowly subsided until just the neck bubbled gently
like a stew and then that too was stilled. He was sat
as before save headless, drenched in blood, the cigar-
illo still between his fingers, leaning toward the dark
and smoking grotto in the flames where his life had
gone.                                          (107)

They found the lost scouts hanging head downward
from the limbs of a fire-blacked paloverde tree. They
were skewered through the cords of their heels with
sharpened shuttles of green wood and they hung gray
and naked above the dead ashes of the coals where
they'd been roasted until their heads had charred and
the brains bubbled in the skulls and steam sang from
their nose-holes. Their tongues were drawn out and
held with sharpened sticks thrust through them and
they had been docked of their ears and their torsos
were sliced open with flints until their entrails hung
down on their chests.                          (227)

Similar depictions of violence appear in every chapter and on
almost any page. In no other novel can we find a rhetoric of violence so lovingly applied. As Steven Shaviro rightly notes,
"*Blood Meridian* sings hymns of violence, is gorgeous language
commemorating slaughter in all it sumptuousness and splen-
dor" (111).
     This gorgeous language works in ironic contrast to the
death trade it celebrates. McCarthy is an aesthetic vivisectionist
who refuses to accommodate romantic illusions about Homo
Sapiens and the place he occupies in nature. At the same time
McCarthy sends his scalphunters off to ravage the Southwestern
borderlands, Walt Whitman was in New York singing that "If
anything is sacred the human body is sacred." The human body,
McCarthy counters, is about as sanctified as disposable waste.
When the kid arrives in Bexar (San Antonio), the first thing he

sees is a "deadcart bound out with a load of corpses" (22). Stripped naked, these recent victims of pestilence and violence are unidentified and unmourned. Though they do glow with the eerie phosphorescence of quick lime, nothing sacred attends them. They will fertilize the grass or nourish the little prairie wolves that haunt the narrative; but such recycling implies no great cosmic unity. It is merely nature's way of handling waste.

These bodies are an appropriate initiating emblem of McCarthy's philosophy and a subtle reminder that such idealism as Whitman's is ludicrous when compared to the horrific violence seen in the passages quoted above. Indeed, we must divest ourselves of romantic, transcendental nonsense if we are to come to terms with what Vereen M. Bell terms McCarthy's metaphysics of violence. *Blood Meridian*, Bell notes, "presses the psychology of the frontier theory to its logical, appalling extreme. It is not a story for the squeamish, least of all for the philosophically squeamish. But it compels us to call forth from ourselves a capacity for understanding evil that the various meanings of our lives otherwise cause to be suppressed" (The Achievement 199).

Bell is correct in his assessment of the special demands that *Blood Meridian* places upon its readers. Because it is sui generis regarding violence, we must accept McCarthy's philosophy of violence in order to articulate an intelligent response to the text. To understand its violence, we need to set aside the niceties of our reading chairs, central air conditioning, and satiated appetites, plus whatever illusions of peace and tranquillity we may still foster. We must live intimately with rape, genocide, infanticide, disemboweling, torture, and general savageness. This vicarious life requires that we become as bestial as the scalphunter and as callous as Judge Holden (who is all brain and no soul). Some readers may be unwilling to commit to such a devilish compact, choosing instead to see a theodicy secreted in the novel's hellish weave. Nevertheless, there is no mystical communication at work in *Blood Meridian*. Quite the contrary, its weltanschauung is grounded in the meanest of reality. Its lessons rest solidly on a text that in every particular substantiates McCarthy's premise that humans are violent animals who deny their genetic heritage. What McCarthy says of the kid as an infant speaks for all Homo Sapiens: ". . . in him broods already a taste for mindless violence." And, McCarthy adds, the child is father of the man (3).

My interpretations are shaped by this philosophy of violence imposed by the narrative. What follows, therefore, is an analysis of three revelatory elements of *Blood Meridian*: (1) the humor that is an integral part of the violence; (2) McCarthy's ironic use of history to substantiate his philosophy of violence; and (3) the specific, deadly relationship between the kid and Judge Holden.

\* \* \* \* \*

In analyzing McCarthy's humor we need first to emphasize that it is humor and not wit that we mean. With the probable exception of Judge Holden, the dramatis personae of *Blood Meridian* are incapable of the verbal repartee, skillful phraseology, and intellectual riffs that define "wit." Their actions and words make us laugh, or at least smile uncomfortably, but the characters themselves are unaware of the comedy they provide. For that matter, they are equally incapable of perceiving humor, but they are "humorous" to us. Most often, the men are quite literally a deadly serious bunch, unaware that their actions and words are often comic. In fact, as we will see, this dramatic irony that puts us in possession of knowledge that the scalphunters do not possess is one of the methods by which McCarthy brings us to a painful self-awareness vis-à-vis his legion of horribles.

The humor begins when we first meet the judge, at the Reverend Green's tent revival in Nagodoches, Texas. Green's sermon is gibberish, but it greatly impresses the gullible townspeople. It also immediately lets us enjoy a feeling of moral and intellectual superiority over such rustics:

> Neighbors, said the reverend, he couldnt stay out of these here hell, hell, hellholes right here in Nacogdoches. I said to him, said: you goin to take the son of God in there with ye? And he said: Oh no. No I aint. And I said: Dont you know that he said I will foller ye always even unto the end of the road?
>
> Well, he said, I aint askin nobody to go nowheres. And I said: Neighbor, you dont need to ask. He's a going to be there with ye ever step of the way whether ye ask it or ye dont. I said: Neighbor, you caint get shed of him. Now. Are you going to drag him, *him*, into that hellhole yonder? (6)

At this junction, the judge enters the tent. Holden is as physically comic as Green is intellectually comic:

> An enormous man dressed in an oilcloth slicker. . . . He
> was bald as a stone and he had no trace of beard and he
> had no brows to his eyes nor lashes to them. He was
> close on to seven feet in height. . . . His face was serene
> and strangely childlike. His hands were small.    (6)

Bored by the incessant rain, and inherently opposed to any theology, the judge immediately proclaims that the Reverend
Green is an impostor: "In truth, the gentleman standing here before you posing as a minister of the Lord is not only totally illiterate but is also wanted by the law in the States of Tennessee,
Kentucky, Mississippi, and Arkansas" (7). He further accuses
Green of being a child molester. We are promptly in league with
the judge (an alliance we regret once we learn more about him)
because we too have already ascertained that Green is illiterate
and because we are offended by his moronic garbling of scripture.
Learning of his pederasty seals our disapproval. We can therefore laugh guiltlessly at the predicament into which the judge's
accusations plunge the wicked reverend:

> Let's hang the turd, called an ugly thug from the
> gallery to the rear.
> Not three weeks before this [the judge continues] he
> was run out of Fort Smith, Arkansas for having congress
> with a goat. Yes lady, that is what I said. Goat.
> Well damn my eyes if I wont shoot the son of a
> bitch, said a man rising at the far side of the tent, and
> drawing a pistol from his boot he leveled it and fired.
>                                          (7)

In a turmoil of shots, screams, and curses, the tent collapses.
Green flees, pursued by a posse of morally outraged yokels who
minutes before had revered the holy man. Only later in the
saloon is the culminating humor of the scene revealed: the
judge has never been in Fort Smith and has never heard of or
laid eyes on Green before today. His practical joke is destructive
and underlaid by violence, but like the saloon patrons, we laugh
at his revelation because we lack sympathy for Green and his
backwoods theology. The episode echoes Mark Twain, especially
in his depiction of the rivertown bumpkins, the King of Duke's
flimflam, and their ridiculous soliloquies. In fact, coming so
early in the text, the Reverend Green episode could mislead us
into thinking that the yarn to follow may well be a modernist
rendition of Huck and Tom out West. The social and moral
implications of McCarthy's journey, however, prove to be
noticeably darker than Twain was willing to risk. The Reverend

Green episode is the first step McCarthy takes toward making us disconnect from traditional values and institutions and align ourselves with a violence that soon overwhelms all pretense of civil behavior. We have begun our psychological journey toward joining the truly damned human race.

Other enlightening humorous passages fill the narrative. Immediately after the Reverend Green episode, the kid engages in a vicious, deadly battle with a stranger in the mud. The kid's battle is as unmotivated as the fight the judge picks with Green: one will not step aside and let the other pass on the plank walkway to the jakes. Toadvine, the antagonist, is also a grotesquely comic figure. He wears a "primitive coiffure," has lost his ears, and—in a parody of Hester Prynne—has the letter "F" branded on his forehead (11). The two battle with fists, broken bottle, and knives till someone prevents their death by clubbing them over the heads. They later awaken in the slime. "Is my neck broke?" the kid asks. "Can you get up?" Toadvine replies:

> I dont know. I aint tried.
> I never meant to break your neck.
> No.
> I meant to kill you.                                                    (10)

With such callous non sequitur their camaraderie is established. They immediately go to the dramhouse, viciously attack a man named Sidney for no discernible reason, then burn the building. The muddy slime, the outhouse, the childlike viciousness, the incoherent thinking, the truncated vocabularies, the fate of poor unidentified Sidney—all combine to form a scene so adroitly humorous that its mindless violence is overshadowed. The juxtaposed episodes of Reverend Green and Toadvine show that the humor-violence associations are growing increasingly hard to distinguish.

The text is also replete with one-liners that sustain the humorous tone and link the larger comic episodes. Hayward prays for rain: "Lord we are dried to jerky down here" (47). Sproule drolely assesses the Indian "legion of horribles" who have just mortally wounded him: "Damn if they aint about a caution to the christians" (56). Ironically, Sproule came West to cure his tuberculosis. Black Jackson drunkenly vows "to Shoot the ass off Jesus Christ, the long-legged white son of a bitch" (171). The old vet in prison tells the kid about the bullmeat they are fed: "You best keep chewin. Dont let if feel ye to weaken" (77).

The culminating humor is the episode in Griffin, Texas, where "you can get clapped a day's ride out when the wind is right" (319). The episode closes out the narrative and is too long to quote in its entirety. It is bawdy, raucous, burlesque. It is full of huge whores in "green stockings and melon-colored drawers" (332), a dark little dwarf whore, a dancing bear dressed in crinoline, old men, soldiers, little girls. It is loud with music, drunken songs, and gunshots. Men urinate in the mud, discuss the wisdom of entering outhouses, and drink themselves into stupors. Appropriately, the kid will confront the judge in the muddy jakes behind the bordello, uniting the motific ribaldry, filth, and violence in parodic finale. The episode is Rabelaisian and Goyaesque in its depiction of the disasters that are life's war. By this point in the narrative any division between humor and violence has disappeared. The two elements have blended like blood in creek water.

We might first assume that this humor is traditional comic relief because it provides a respite for the otherwise depressing human conditions. That is only incidentally correct, however. Instead of interspersing humor to relieve the relentless pressure of living with such violence, McCarthy makes humor an integral part of it. Humor, therefore, exponentially intensifies rather than alleviates the impact of the violence. It is progressive rather than sporadic, evolving from relatively harmless affiliations with violence, as in the Reverend Green episode, to increasingly deadly associations. The result of this progression is that early in the narrative we cross a border beyond which the violence ceases to shock. At yet another juncture, it ceases to disturb. And at yet another we commence to anticipate what new horror we might next encounter. We are titilated by the comic potential of violence. Eventually we commence to see humor in such actions as the kid casually braining a child with a stone (71), white Jackson getting his head "swapt" off (quoted above), and in the bacchanalian scene in the Griffin whore house.

When we realize that the humor and violence have merged, we must also realize that a rather intriguing bit of knowledge has developed from the dramatic irony. That is, once more we know something that the funny men of the text do not know: humor is the catalyst that merges us with them. Having been so distracted by the violence, we have forgotten the fundamental biological truth that even more so than violence, humor defines us as Homo Sapiens. We share our violent natures to some degree with all other animals, but only humans see mirth in the darkest subjects and express that strange joy in peculiar vocalization. Being reminded of this truism, we must then ponder a corollary question: why, in our agonizingly slow change from unicellular amoeboids to our present selves, did we develop the ability to discern the essential absurdity of the creative process? What in our genetic construct made us need to laugh? In short, assuming there is purpose to anything, what is the purpose of humor? Obviously the question is as moot as why did we evolve as violent rather than peaceful animals. Perhaps, however, our ability to perceive humor and to laugh evolved to counterbalance the simultaneous evolution of yet another unique human phenomenon: conscience. Some evolutionary trickery made us violent but wanted us to suspect that violence was not in our best interest. Perhaps humor evolved, consequently, so that we could tolerate the terrifying conflict between right and wrong. As Pudd'nhead Wilson wisely observed, "The secret source of humor itself is not joy but sorrow." It is both this paradox of a violent animal questioning the rightness of that violence and our futile pondering of the paradox that McCarthy satirizes with his humor.

He knows that we are laughing, violent, and curious creatures. He trusts, therefore, that at some point these three traits will interact to make us realize that we are in league with the scalphunters. Like they, we are comic, violent creatures, whether we are intellectually aware or unaware, whether laughing at or being laughed at. Therefore, when we cross the border where humor and violence become indistinguishable, we have also crossed the border that separates savagery from civilization. McCarthy hopes that somewhere on the far side of that crossing we will have a moment of enlightenment, when we realize that like the scalphunters we too are violent brutes. McCarthy's ability to merge violence and humor facilitates this progression toward such an agonizing reappraisal. As others have shown, McCarthy locates his tale in American history. John Emil Sepich, for instance, offers a convenient summary of this history in *Notes on Blood Meridian*, while his essay "The Dance of History in Cormac McCarthy's *Blood Meridian*" more specifically addresses the origins of Holden and other characters. The action occurs in the American southwest and northern Mexico, during the years from approximately 1849 to 1878. Moreover, the events and characters are based in part on factual journals, diaries, and other accounts of men who shaped the era. Captain Glanton, Judge Holden, Mangas, and numerous other of the minor characters are drawn from actual personalities. However, the most important character in the novel, the anonymous "kid," has no apparent historical prototype. The purely fictional kid allows McCarthy to escape the magnetic demands of historical factuality and superimpose on the narrative a kind of aesthetic centrifugation. Important as historicity is, it does not hold the narrative to a limiting central axis. We will discuss the kid shortly, but at this juncture we need to understand why McCarthy grounds his fiction in historic fact. He does so for several important reasons relative to violence.

Our first impulse is to assume that by painting his characters with historical colorings, McCarthy validates their stories or lends credence to a fiction-making process that might otherwise be distrusted. To some degree, this validation theory is credible. Authorial dissimulation is certainly a venerable practice in the American novel. Nathaniel Hawthorne fixed the standard when in "The Custom House" he set forth the historic subtext upon which he grounded his fabulous romance of sin and redemption. No one since has synchronized the transition from fact to fiction so smoothly or convincingly. Nor, for that matter, has any fictionist since so cleverly used historical camouflage to circumvent his audience's biases against scribblers of fiction. That the opening action of *Blood Meridian* coincides with the publication of *The Scarlet Letter* is probably mere coincidence, but it is a propitious correlation that suggests what McCarthy had in mind with his retrospective point of view. By disguising his brutes as historic personae, he strengthens their credibility and thereby makes it more difficult for us to dismiss them as the mad illusions of an eccentric myth-maker. To reject Glanton, Holden, ex-priest Tobin, Toadvine, the kid, and the other scalphunters as mere fictional aberrations is to risk dismissing American history. As a nation, we may distort our past, but we do not reject it. If history's aura can convince us that a teenage adulteress and her love child transformed the hardened hearts and benighted souls of an entire Calvinist enclave, then history's aura can convince us that a feral kid and his cohorts might teach us humility. Like Hawthorne, McCarthy plays on his countryman's weakness for history. He wants to inform us that our heritage is one of violence, and associating his characters with historic fact strengthens his cause.

Typical of the complexity of McCarthy's text and style, however, his use of history is paradoxical and contradictory. Despite its clever allusions that resonate with metafictional possibilities and its effective reminder of our ferocious national heritage, McCarthy uses the historical validation schematic only with some notable reservations. He realizes, like Henry Ford, that much of history is bunk. Rather than advocating that history is verifiable facts that serve as benchmarks for present and future actions, McCarthy instead admonishes that history is a miscellany of vagaries. It is much too open to the caprice of yesterday's interpretation and today's reinterpretation. McCarthy humorously satirizes the instability of historical interpretation in the convoluted episode of the harness-maker who kills the traveling stranger then confesses to a son who himself becomes a killer of men. The judge relates this lengthy version of Freud's Oedipal theory to the scalphunters. They listen attentively till the judge finishes?

> Here the judge looked up and smiled. There was a silence, then all began to shout at once with every kind of disclaimer.
> He was no harnessmaker he was a shoemaker and he was cleared of them charges, called one.
> And another: He never lived in no wilderness place, he had a shop dead in the center of Cumberland Maryland.
> They never knew where them bones come from. The old woman was crazy, known to be so.
> That was my brother in that casket and he was a minstrel dancer out of Cincinnati Ohio was shot to death over a woman.          (145)

Illiterate, unschooled, and responsive only to life's most fundamental demands, each listener nonetheless has his own version of history and is adamant about its correctness. Ironically, one preposterous version is as creditable as another, for we as audience have no criteria by which to evaluate. We are at the mercy of the teller of the tale.

The judge's tale proves an incongruity that we must transfer to our own awareness of history. Our evaluation of the Western frontier and its dominant personalities, for instance, was once determined by dime novels and celluloid fantasies. More recently it has been determined by pop-psychology and academic trendiness. Native Americans, once bloody savages to be annihilated, are now noble primitives to be emulated. Women, once prostitutes or virgin school marms, are now the civilizing force that tamed the wild masculine West. That wild masculine West itself is now an apologist's embarrassment. (Larry McMurtry, in *Lonesome Dove* but especially in his post-1985 fiction, is particularly enamored of the proto-feminist, emasculated version of Western history.) McCarthy knows that violence is primordial, constant, and unchanging. It is our genetic pole star. Its harsh realities cannot be altered to suit the latest claptrap. History, on the other hand, is a recent phenomenon. It has been around only so long as the language that records it and is only as reliable as the prejudices of its transcriber. Like the scalphunters' versions of the judge's tale, one version of past events is about as reliable as the other. That is, not reliable at all. History, in other words, simply is not a worthy criterion by which to measure violence.

In yet another ironic twist, McCarthy seems to satirize the very process that he employs: using history to promote one's own philosophical biases. We see hints of this self satire in some clichés and stereotypes that we have already mentioned. As with history, however, what appears to be is not necessarily what is. What seems to be flagrant self-satire is in fact satire directed at the era in which McCarthy found himself writing *Blood Meridian*. We must preface on explanation of this social satire with a reminder that violence is a male phenomenon. Indeed, females can express "aggressive behavior," especially what Luigi Valzelli calls "Maternal Protective Aggression." As Valzelli explains, this type of aggression is "characteristic of female animals for purposes of defending the newborn against any potentially or actually threatening agent" (82). Violence as I have defined the term for the purposes of this study, differs significantly from this type of "aggression." Women seldom exhibit "violence." Almost exclusively it is the male of the species, in Valzelli's words, who "alone fights destructively, with cruelty and malice, and is capable of becoming a mass murderer . . ." (62). Even Toni Morrison's Sethe of *Beloved* does not contradict this male prerogative. As we will see, Sethe's violence is a transmuted form of Maternal Protective Aggression and an immensely complex example of feminine violence. Sethe is, however, the exception that proves the rule of male violence. As Robert Wright says, writing on the biology of violence in *The New Yorker*, "the leading cause of violence is maleness" (72). Evolutionary biology encourages male violence, crime statistics substantiate it, and scientific studies of violence presume it. Violent females are the rare aberration, not the norm. The point is that McCarthy advantages this unique male characteristic. He takes the one undeniable male prerogative and enforces its edicts so emphatically on the text that no one can challenge it. Thus, in the 1980s, when male chauvinism had become a curse word and the term "dominant male" was safely used only in studies of wolves, McCarthy champions dominant and chauvinistic males by exaggerating violence to the point of incredulity.

A comparison will help make the point. In the same year that McCarthy published *Blood Meridian*, Larry McMurtry published *Lonesome Dove*. Both are Westerns, set in Texas and Mexico, and both occur in the latter half of the nineteenth century. Both might safely be termed epics. *Lonesome Dove* was (and is) immensely popular. It won the Pulitzer Prize, has been read by millions, and was made into a very successful TV series. By comparison, *Blood Meridian* received practically no recognition and remains a novel that few Americans have ever heard of and fewer still have read. One of the major differences accounting for the huge popular success of *Lonesome Dove* and the relative obscurity of *Blood Meridian* is that McMurtry capitalizes on the trends of the day by depicting numerous female characters, both minor and major. They range from the clichéd good-hearted whore (Lorena Wood) to the tough, smart dominant wife, nurse, lover, and business woman (Clara Allen), beautiful as an orchid and tough as saddle leather. How much McMurtry wants to show such women dominating selfish, essentially stupid males is symbolized by Clara's husband Bob. His foolish accident with a horse has reduced him to a helpless infant whose diapers Clara must change regularly. In *Streets of Laredo*, the sequel to *Lonesome Dove*, McMurtry exaggerates this female dominance till the men are little more than knavish fools, severely punished with psychological and physical dismemberment. In contrast, no women of note appear in *Blood Meridian*. The Virgin Mary is, ironically, the only major feminine presence, implied in town names, churches, and topographical features. All the other females are whores, victims of the rampant violence, or helpless onlookers. Even women who occupy critical (albeit minor) roles in the narrative are unnamed, as the good Samaritan in New Orleans who nurses the kid back to health after he has been shot (4). McCarthy deviates from this nameless practice only once, and then to emphasize how anonymous the other women have been: late in the narrative he tells us that the woman who washes the excrement off the idiot James Robert Bell is named Sarah Borginnis (256). The novel is otherwise totally dominated by males, and the most minor of them is distinctly named to imply their superiority over the females. (Cloyse Bell, for instance, is the idiot's brother.)

McCarthy makes absolutely no compromises to his version of history or to his art by inserting anachronistic modern women and pusillanimous males for them to dominate. Other than as casual victims of rape and murder, no living women have any direct bearing on the actions of any man in the text. (Glanton does miss his wife, whose murder galvanizes his homicidal hatred of Indians.) None of the violence is directed at preserving, acquiring, or impressing a female. Brutes the scalphunters may be, but their motives are pure: unmitigated love of violence, camaraderie, and money. Moreover, McCarthy neither passes moral judgments against these men nor stigmatizes them as social misfits. Like lizards and snakes, they are adapted to the harsh environment they inhabit and suited to the social tasks they must perform. They are hired to rid the borderlands of marauding Indians so that the Mexican settlers can live in peace and prosper. McCarthy describes a troop of Indians that characterize the enemy:

> . . . a pack of viciouslooking humans mounted on unshod Indian ponies . . . , the trappings of their horses fashioned out of human skin and their bridles woven up from human hair and decorated with human teeth and the riders wearing scapulars of necklaces of dried and blackened human ears . . . half-necked savages reeling in the saddle, dangerous, filthy, brutal, the whole like a visitation from some heathen land where they and others like them fed on human flesh.     (78)

That the men hired to confront such adversaries go from heroes to villains in the estimate of the Mexicans results from the degree to which they do their jobs, not from any change in the moral codes that might be used to evaluate them. Only when the scalphunters commence to apply their brutal extermination tactics to the Mexicans themselves do Glanton and his gang change from Christian crusaders to Satanic lunatics.

The narrative tone conveys grudging respect for these men. They suffer incredible pain and hardships without flinching, kill and are killed without a whimper. They give no quarter and expect none. For example, Grimley, who has been stabbed in a cantina brawl, dies silently, expecting neither sympathy nor attention from his departing comrades: "Grimley sat slumped sideways against the mud wall of the building. He did not look up. He was holding his pistol in his lap and looking off down the street and they turned and rode out along the north side of the plaza and disappeared" (180). From the retrospective of 150 years it is tempting to condemn such men and deplore such barbarity. McCarthy's text, however, does not support such air-conditioned-and-automatic-transmission morality. As brutal and harsh as his men are, modern American civilization rests on their bones. To pretend otherwise because the truth does not salve our delicate modern sensibilities is both pretentious and dangerously naive.

A feasible rebuttal to McCarthy's demand that we recognize our violent natures might be that the nineteenth century frontier environment dictated that men who inhabited it be brutal. We of the modern era, however, are free from such restraints and thus have risen to a higher moral order. Again, however, the text of *Blood Meridian* refuses to support such an argument. Despite the fact that landscape and weather are important components of the narrative design, environment plays a limited role in dictating the dispositions and responses of such violent personalities. These men are appropriate to the physical environment, but they are not predominantly shaped by it. As we have seen, the kid's "mindless violence" (3) is in place when he is an infant and long before he ventures into the harsh, arid lands of the Southwest. The judge, as we have also seen in the introductory Reverend Green episode, is innately vicious and would be violent no matter where or when we might encounter him—whether in Harvard Yard of a Mexican whorehouse. The limited impact of environment on temperament is conveyed throughout the text, but it is best personified in the kid and Judge Holden.

They are polar opposites. The kid is semi-literate, inarticulate, and uninformed. He is as close to a dumb brute as one can get and still be recognized as human. The judge, on the other hand is pragmatic, inventive, able to discourse articulately on any subject, multi-lingual, musical, and authoritative. He is well educated, cosmopolitan, and urbane. That his discourses are occasionally little more than double-talk only serves to prove how sophisticated and politic he is. In fact, Judge Holden is the ideal American gentleman. He and the kid seem to have nothing in common.

Yet, in terms of violence, no other two men in the narrative are as closely united. Both are capable of instantaneous and unrestrained violence. The kid will fight with knife, gun, broken bottle, and bare fist in total disregard for his physical well being. Ironically, he is willing to die in order to survive. When Toadvine tells him after their vicious battle in the mud that he meant to kill him, the kid's laconic reply is "They aint nobody done it yet" (10). That could be his motto, for many try to kill him, but none succeeds (except possibly the judge, as we will discuss later). The judge, in ironic contrast to his gentlemanly demeanor that would be much admired in the modern coffee-shop or faculty meeting hall, is equally fearless. He is assured of his immorality, and responds to the world accordingly. He drowns puppies, crushes skulls with his bare hands, scalps Indians, and rapes children. He is absolutely fearless and without remorse. There is little wonder that he is immediately drawn to the kid and smiles each time he sees him. So unlike superficially, they are essentially connected. They alone survive the brutal life that carries them together through the most crucial years in the formation of the American nation.

Their union is why they are at odds with each other. McCarthy wants to bring them together in one violent, final confrontation in the Griffin, Texas, "shit house." After carefully detailing each previous instance of violence, McCarthy gives us no details in this closing scene. We do not know what happens in the jakes, nor even if the kid is dead. Our imaginations are left to ponder this final enigmatic episode, thereby keeping the question of violence alive long after the narrative has concluded. This "jakes" scene is crucial to understanding the kid-judge relationship and the specific type of violence that drives it:

> . . . Then he [the kid] opened the rough board door
> of the jakes and stepped in.
> The judge was seated upon the closet. He was
> naked and he rose up smiling and gathered him in his
> arms against his immense and terrible flesh and shot
> the wooden barlatch home behind him.
> In the saloon two men who wanted to buy the hide
> were looking for the owner of the bear. The bear lay on
> the stage in an immense pool of blood. All the candles
> had gone out save one and it gutted uneasily in its
> grease like a votive lamp. In the dancehall a young
> man had joined the fiddler and he kept the measure of

> the music with a pair of spoons which he clapped be-
> tween his knees. The whores sashayed half naked,
> some with their breasts exposed. In the muddie dog
> yard behind the premises two men went down the
> boards toward the jakes. A third man was standing
> there urinating into the mud.
>> Is someone in there?
>> I wouldn't go in.
> He hitched himself up and buttoned his trousers
> and stepped past them and went up the walk toward
> the lights. The first man watched him go and then
> opened the door of the jakes.
>> Good God almighty, he said.
>> What is it?
> He didn't answer. He stepped past the other and
> went back up the walk. The other man stood looking
> after him. Then he opened the door and looked in.
>
> (333-334)

The narrative focus then shifts from the jakes, and the episode closes with two paragraphs, one describing an immense seminude prostitute and the other Judge Holden dancing naked and gloating that he will never die.

The prevailing interpretation of this enigmatic scene is that Holden simply murders the unsuspecting kid. In *The Achievement of Cormac McCarthy*, Vereen M. Bell concludes that the judge is a "murderer of innocents—of a Mexican boy, of an Indian girl, of a mere puppy, and of the kid . . ." (134). In "Fate and Free Will on the American Frontier: Cormac McCarthy's Western Fiction," Tom Pilkington states that the kid's death "is presided over by Judge Holden, a bloated angel of war and death" (317). John Emil Sepich in "The Dance of History in Cormac McCarthy's *Blood Meridian*" states that the kid "meets death in an outhouse in Griffin, Texas, in 1878 at the hands of a former compatriot named Judge Holden" (16) and predicates his thesis upon the "motive behind the murder" (18). Other critics who have confronted McCarthy's blood epic, though not directly mentioning the kid's death, seem implicitly to agree that Holden kills the anonymous kid in the Griffin "jakes."

While these critics offer insights into other elements of McCarthy's complex novel, to conclude that the judge simply kills the kid overlooks several crucial issues that interfuse the narrative and that McCarthy wants to articulate in the jakes episode. The text convincingly supports the hypothesis that the kid's death is not the crucial issue and that the judge's essential motivation is to assault the kid sexually. Some noteworthy psychoerotic motifs in the narrative are clarified as a result of an act which for the kid is an intolerable form of violence. In fact, as we have seen, the kid will do anything to survive. Yet he had rather not survive what happens to him in the jakes.

Here in the closing jakes scene, a type of violence is introduced so subtly that it stands in notable contrast to the graphic, numbing violence we have already discussed. In chapter 4 the "legion of horribles" attacks the filibusters (52). The description of the Comanches' bloody assault takes more than three pages, with characteristic bloody exactitude. However, as the scene fades, the narrator adds in afterthought that some of the Indians "fell upon the dying and sodomized them with loud cries to their fellows" (54). The inconspicuous allusion to the Comanches' uninhibited sexuality introduces male-to-male sexual assault to the androcentric, super-masculine frontier culture of *Blood Meridian*.

This masculinity was not only an attitude but a geopolitical and demographic reality. Henry Nash Smith has shown that beyond the first agricultural line of settlement the frontier was void of females other than prostitutes (*Virgin Island: The American West as Symbol and Myth*, Cambridge: Harvard UP, 1970). The androcentrism of the western frontier is commonplace in both the fiction and history of the trans-Mississippi area. The contemporary journals from which McCarthy borrows for *Blood Meridian*, such as James O. Pattie's *The Personal Narrative* (1831) and Samuel Chamberlain's *My Confession* (c. 1860; pub. 1956), glorify masculine camaraderie and adventure. Blake Allmendinger, in *The Cowboy: Representations of Labor in an American World Culture* (New York: Oxford UP, 1992), analyzes at length how the western cowboy's image as a sex-starved predator of women ironically developed form a bachelor culture methodically purged of feminine influence. A we shall see, this particular form of sexual violence acts in conjunction with the other types of violence, characterizes Judge Holden, and is a crucial element in constructing a plausible interpretation for the kid's ultimate encounter with the judge.

Drawing from this context of violence, we discover several arguments to support the premise that simply murdering the kid is not the judge's intent. The most apparent is that during the months the scalphunters ride together, the judge has numerous opportunities to kill the kid if mere killing were his goal. Like black Jackson dispatching white Jackson the judge could have surprised the kid in the night and swapt off his head with a Bowie knife. None of their comrades would have interfered. Like the reader, however, the perceptive judge discerns that killing the kid is no routine matter. The kid's first vicious meeting with Toadvine reveals a violent instinct that converts to action viper fast and that makes the kid afraid of no man or consequences. We see this in the bloody fight scene with Toadvine, which foreshadows the muddy jakes scene at Griffin. Subsequent to the Toadvine fight, the kid survives thirty years on the Texas frontier, where life was a short-lived phenomenon. In fact, just before arriving in Griffin the kid (now middle aged) has easily killed the young would-be assassin Elrod. Unlike Sproule, Glanton, Toadvine, Brown and the rest of his filibustering, scalp-hunting companions of old, the kid is still alert, quick and adept at self-preserving homicide. It is problematic that even the wily, murderous judge could surprise and kill the kid so easily that he could then celebrate by dancing naked without a mark of combat on his white, hairless body (as the closing paragraphs show the judge doing).

Moreover, even if he could easily kill the kid, the judge would receive no satisfaction from simple murder. Such straightforward acts are neither conducive to the attainment of his goals nor compatible with his personality as previously established in the text. The Reverend Green episode that introduces him shows that insofar as adults are concerned, the judge derives more satisfaction from tormenting than from eliminating. He expresses no concern whether Green lives or dies but seems pleased to have destroyed his reputation and livelihood with a preposterous lie. The Green episode indicates that the judge had rather humiliate than murder those whom he chooses as adversaries, because he enjoys the satisfaction he drives from that particular form of violence. This punishment via humiliation is especially true insofar as the kid is concerned, for the judge sees the kid as having reserved in his soul "some corner of clemency for the heathen" (299). The judge cannot tolerate this quality of mercy. As Vereen Bell notes, "by the perverse logic that rules the judge's system of values, even this breach of faith is impermissible" (130). With such a hint of "clemency," the kid commits heresy that the merciless judge wishes to punish in the most humiliating and devastating way.

As a glance at the closing text will show, witnesses at the Griffin jakes also do not attest to a simple killing, regardless of how bloody. In a town synonymous with murder, an everyday strangulation, knifing, or shooting in an outhouse would not account for the surprised response of the hardened trio of brothel habitués. The urinating man has been the first to witness what has happened in the jakes. The scene does not traumatize him so much that he forgoes his bodily functions, but he has been sufficiently disturbed to deem the outhouse actions inappropriate for two other adult males to witness. Accordingly, he advises them not to enter the privy. The first of these two men ignores the advice and looks into the outhouse. His exclamatory "Good God almighty" in a text where violence is pandemic but blasphemy scarce suggests that he is notably more shocked by what he sees than was the urinating man. Made curious by his companion's exclamation, the third man looks into the outhouse and is shocked to silence. Clearly, the men have seen something which experience and their androcentric culture has taught them to abhor.

Finally, the most compelling and persuasive evidence against the simple-killing scenario is the narrative itself. Such a deus ex machine conclusion as implied by having the judge dispatch the kid is not compatible with a text that in the wise evaluation of Vereen M. Bell is so complex that "what it may be said to mean in conventional discourse is beyond claiming" (128). A telling example of our being warned against drawing simple conclusions about the judge-kid relationship occurs when Tobin the ex-priest tries to convince the kid that Holden wants him dead. Upset by the accusation, the judge argues his case to the kid with a sardonic denial of Tobin's charges: "You think I've killed Brown and Toadvine? They are alive as you and me. . . . Ask the priest. The priest knows. The priest does not lie" (300). As we learn, Brown and Toadvine are indeed alive, destined to hang in California. The kid's subsequent actions demonstrate that he rejects the ex-priest's evaluation of Holden. In the "sand wallow" as the kid and Tobin are fleeing the judge and his imbecile companion (298), the kid still has four rounds in his pistol. He is recognized as an expert marksman and has demonstrated strong survival instincts. Despite Tobin's urging, however, he does not fire upon the judge. His decision not to be goaded into quick judgments is a quiet reminder that (1) McCarthy is saving the final encounter between the judge and the kid for a more dramatic conclusion, and (2) that we as readers also should not jump to hasty conclusions about the Holden-kid relationship.

What, then, does happen in the Griffin jakes? McCarthy offers no explicit answer to this question, but he gives strong circumstantial evidence to support the premise that the ultimate encounter between the kid and the judge is sexual.

The most consequential evidence is the judge's identification with pedophilia. His first association with pedophilia occurs when the scalphunters find a half-breed boy in the ruined presidio at Santa Rida del Cobre. He is "maybe twelve years old. He was naked save for a pair of old calzones and makeshift sandals of uncured hide" (116). The judge is immediately interested in him, asking "Who's this child?" The others "shrugged," having no regard for the boy or (perhaps more likely) suspecting that noticing a naked boy might be misinterpreted by their peers. When next we see the boy during the violent nocturnal rainstorm, he "watched them with his dark eyes" (117). Then someone "reported the judge naked atop the walls, immense and pale in the revelations of lightning, striding the perimeter up here and declaiming in the old epic mode" (118). In the dawn, the men discover the boy dead. "His neck had been broken and his head hung straight down and it flopped over strangely when they let him onto the ground" (119).

We can only suspect the judge of having violated and then murdering this particular boy, but McCarthy soon gives another piece of compelling evidence to strengthen the charge that Holden is a violent pedophile and child killer. In the cantina at Nacori, during one of the several gratuitous brawls in which the scalphunters involve themselves, a Mexican confronts the judge and tries to cut him:

> But the judge was like a cat and he sidestepped the man and seized his arm and broke it and picked the man up by his head. He put him against the wall and smiled at him but the man had begun to bleed from the ears and blood was running down between the judge's fingers and over his hands and when the judge turned him loose there was something wrong with his head and he slid to the floor and did not get up.        (179)

The casual ease with which the judge single-handedly hoists the man and crushes his skull demonstrates his immense strength and his tendency to kill by inflicting head injury. To further reinforce conclusions about the judge's pedophilia, McCarthy later replicates the dark-eyed boy scene with a captured Apache boy, whom the judge dandles on his knees, then scalps (164). Furthermore, hints of pedophilia conclude the judge's seemingly compassionate relationship with the idiot child James Robert. During the Yuma revolt, the Indians break into the judge's quarters, where they find "the idiot and a girl of perhaps twelve years cowering naked in the floor. Behind them also naked stood the judge" (275).

Though McCarthy omits the characteristic gory details from the scenes involving the judge and children, he constructs a sequence of events that gives us ample information to visualize how Holden molests a child, then silences him with violence. As in Attic tragedy, McCarthy makes us imagine the details. Even in a text otherwise replete with the rhetoric of carnage, such acts are horrible beyond words. We, therefore, settle for this palatable scenario explaining the judge's contact with the half-breed boy: the judge sexually abuses the child, breaks his neck, then does a celebratory satyr's dance atop the wall in the storm. Though Denis Donoghue concludes that "There is no merit in looking for a reason" for such scenes (5), the judge's pedophilia explains them quite reasonably. Moreover, the inversion is consistent with Erich Fromm and John Paul Sartre's definition of violence. As Tony Stigliano notes, Sartre argues that aberrations such as sadism, masochism, and even striving for love arise from existential needs and are characteristic of the human animal (52f).

Along with textual evidence, the historicity that we have previously examined substantiates the argument that McCarthy intentionally emphasizes the judge's sexual aberration. Samuel Chamberlain's *My Confession*, the only historic record of Holden, sketches the same odious personality that we find in *Blood Meridian*. However, McCarthy deviates from Chamberlain's factual account in one important feature. Chamberlain states that Holden's "desires was [sic] blood and women" and cites one specific incident in which the judge is suspected of having "foully violated and murdered" a girl of ten (271). In McCarthy's version of the judge's pedophilia, the gender of the victim is changed from female to male. Like the historic Holden, McCarthy's fictive judge is suspected of "foully" using and then murdering children—but in *Blood Meridian* the dead victims are exclusively male. That significant modification of detail is compelling evidence that McCarthy intends to stress the male-to-male nature of the judge's sexuality, to inculcate it into his personality, and to announce it as a key to other textual cruxes.

The pedophilia becomes acutely meaningful to interpreting the jakes episode when the judge transfers his sadism to the kid. The first sign of this transference appears after the scalphunters return to United States territory from their depredations south of the border. In the San Diego jail, which also is made of "mud" to anticipate the imminent jakes scene, the kid is awaiting execution, apparently for his part in the scalphunters' plundering. If the judge wishes only to kill the kid, here he has the ideal opportunity. Brandishing a "small silver-mounted derringer" (305), Holden stands unmonitored outside the bars and tries to intimidate the kid, mimicking the death threat that Tobin has earlier supposed. Though still a youth and defenseless—truly a child—the kid makes no concessions and vows again that "I ain't afraid of you" (307). In this instance, the bravado is understandably ambiguous, because on one level it is true while on another it is bluster. The kid does not fear that the judge will cold-bloodedly shoot him with the derringer. If the judge were so openly murderous, he too would be awaiting execution with the kid and his other scalphunting companions. The judge's ability to disguise his violence keeps him free and dangerous. Besides, the kid believes he is soon to be hanged, so quick death by gunfire is not an especially frightening alternative.

What the kid does fear is the judge's entreaty to "Let me touch you" (307). The sexual implications of this whispered request activate his powerful survivor's instincts; and though the judge might help him avoid execution if he permits the "touching," the kid refuses. True to the unshakable code of masculinity, he had rather hang than submit to what the judge is suggesting. This devotion to the male code is explicitly demonstrated four pages later, after the kid has cleverly engineered his own escape from jail. A homosexual barroom patron commits the same error in judging the kid's sexual orientation that Holden has made. He mistakes the kid "for a male whore" and the kid summarily knocks him senseless "in a mudroom there where there was no light" (311). With his strong heterosexual ethic and defenses, the kid embodies the intense androcentric code that dictates his environment (and, we might add, that McCarthy at least in part endorses).

Typical of the complex networking of scenes and motifs,

the San Diego episode with the kid's rigid heterosexual ethic also reintroduces the male-to-male sexuality initiated much earlier by the Comanche Indians. Having been exposed to merchants and missionaries since the incursions of the Spanish conquistadors, the Indians long ago detected sexual schizophrenia in a culture that sent ecclesiastics to preach salvation to them on one side of the teepee and mercenaries to rape them on the other. They just as readily learned how to exploit such moral bifurcation. By the time the white scalphunters intrude, the Indians have refined their methods of psychological warfare. They quickly intuit the vulnerability of the super-heterosexual white warriors. To sodomy they add a mutilation that makes females of these enemies and that sharply focuses the cultural mortification of male-to-male sexuality. This unsexing is exemplified when the scalphunters happen upon a wagon train that apparently has been attacked by the Indians. The male victims wear "strange menstrual wounds between their legs" and have "no man's parts for these have been cut away and hung dark and strange from out their grinning mouths" (153). With such dismemberment, the Indians feminize their enemy and force him to pantomime the one sex act most abhorrent to the white man's frontier culture. In the process they also revenge themselves by exploiting the homoerotic taboos of a relentless white adversary intent on symbolically emasculating them via scalping. The Comanches and other Plains Indians had no great concern with an afterlife. As Robert H. Lowie points out, the Plains Indian felt "that the dead lived very much as they had while alive, hunting buffalo, playing games, and inhabiting the same sort of teepees as during their previous existence" (164). Counting coup and taking scalps, however, marked a male as being the bravest of the brave. Losing the scalp, obviously, had just the opposite or "emasculating" implications. We recall the dying Sproule's grudging admiration of the death-defying, super-violent Comanches who have just slain and sodomized his war buddies and mortally wounded him: "Damn if they aint about a caution to the christians" (56).

Sproule's lower-case allusion to his culture's "christianity" is strikingly ironic considering the blood-thirsty context in which it appears, but it does point to the contrast between the sexually uninhibited "savages" and ex-priest Tobin. The various sources of the conflicted "christian" sexuality that the "savage" Indians exploit are exemplified by this latter-day version of the priests who accompanied the mercenary explorers. According to the judge, "as recently as March of this year" Tobin was a "respected Doctor of Divinity from Harvard College" (306). His association with Harvard and his appellation "ex-priest" connote the two religious influences most prevalent in the settlement of the Southwestern frontier: New England Calvinism and Roman Catholicism. The Calvinist element is emphasized later when Tobin disappears from the text, but when Tobin is present the Catholicism is more accentuated. Mexican missions and other Catholic icons define the narrative landscape and constantly insinuate the Marian chastity implied by Tobin's priestly vows. Though as much a participant in the raping and ravaging of the Catholic dioceses as any other of the scalphunters, Tobin is haunted by ghosts of his lost faith. One of the narratives memorable images is Tobin in the desert "stumbling among the bones and holding aloft a cross he'd fashioned out of the shins of a ram . . . and calling out in a tongue both alien and extinct" (289-290). The dead-bone cross and the mournful pagan babble exemplify how quickly and far Tobin has journeyed from any hagiology. The "ex" of his title signifies that life amidst a hellish landscape and recent vows to the demons of violence may have redeemed him from old world piety and Harvard Presbyterianism. However, as the primitive crucifix attests, the satanic affiliations have not neutralized the Christian dogma. Its attendant sexual repressions are deeply embedded in the vows of chastity Tobin apparently endorsed as recently as last March. Though he has just reputed such vows by murdering and pillaging, his bearing of the cross and his wailing show how powerful still is his impulse to obey those vows. He is a striking personification of the church's mission into the Southwest, the corruption that accompanied it, and McCarthy's disapproval of the church.

As do all major motifs in the narrative, the ironic theological motif returns to and concludes with the kid. Wandering like Christ in the wilderness and toting a Bible "that he'd found at the mining camps" but "no word of which could he read" (312), the kid happens upon a "company of penitents" whom the Indians have violently "hacked and butchered among the stones" in the desert (315). At this late stage of the narrative, both the kid and the reader are intimately familiar with such necrotic scenes, and are ironically unmoved. This scene differs, however, in that the kid sees an old woman kneeling amid the rocks as if in prayer. Misled by the Christian icon he carries, and possibly having wandered to long in the desert with ex-priest Tobin, the kid impulsively confesses to the penitent in rhetoric reminiscent of a questing Christian knight in thrall to the Holy Virgin. He laments quixotically that "he was an American and that he was a long way from the country of his birth and that he had no family" and that he will "convey her to a safe place" (315). Predictably, the rock-hard, sun-baked landscape mocks his Marian outburst. When he lovingly touches the praying matriarch, he discovers that she is "just a dried shell" that has "been dead in that place for years" (315). The kid's epiphanic miscalculation vis-à-vis the penitent mummy is literally momentous beyond words, for immediately thereafter he disappears for seventeen years.

The mummy scene and the closing outhouse scene bracket and emphasize this seventeen-year period during which the kid is absent and the narrator is struck dumb. When the kid reappears, he is no longer "in that place" where he encountered the dead woman but on the high plains of the Texas panhandle. He is now "the man," but still without wife, children, or companions of either gender. The characters who now share the kid's "sere and burntlooking" waste (317) are even more grotesquely male and more execrable than the marauding scalphunters. Elrod the bonepicker exemplifies the Neanderthal culture that roams a landscape from which Indians, buffalo, and practically all other forms of natural life have been extirpated. Ironically, for one so seemingly inconsequential, Elrod is textually preeminent. He is the character who unites the judge's pedophilia, the kid's heterosexual truculence, and events in the impending jakes scene.

A "sullen" wretch "dressed in skins" and wearing "greenhide boots peeled whole from the hocks of some animal" (318), Elrod will never be betrayed by pietistic Marian impulses such as those which plunged the kid and the narrative into the void. Such impulses demand a particle of moral consciousness that Elrod does not possess. His shibboleth is "whore," not "virgin," and he is infuriated when he suspects that the kid is going to Griffin "for the whores" (319). Though long removed in time and space from the judge, the kid is reconnected to Holden by this grotesque brute. Elrod's anger at the possibility of the kid's visiting "whores" emanates from primitive sexual impulses that parallel the judge's perversity and that cause Elrod to be jealous. These impulses are revealed not in any utterance from Elrod, who is essentially without language, but in his fixating on the kid's necklace of blackened Apache ears. Analogous to the taking of scalps, the cutting off of ears is symbolic emasculation and has the same damning effect upon the Indian victims. Dressed in the skins of the barbarian, Elrod identifies with the "savage" Indians who recently wandered the same plains he now roams and who were themselves victims of that same civilization which has denied him. However, the ears of these savages now adorn the neck of that enemy, sign to the dimwitted Elrod that the enemy and his cultural idiosyncrasies have prevailed. That realization activates confused sexual  instincts, and Elrod is provoked to violence. Ironically, because he does not use his own ears to hear the equally violent message that the kid tries to send him, he will die.

Elrod's physical and psychological resemblance to the "savages" explains the meaning of his only private comment to the kid: "I knowed you for what you was when I seen ye" (322). Readers may first assume from the evidence of immediate context that Elrod is calling the kid a whoremonger. That accusation, however, does not explain the kid's immediate defensiveness. While his contact with women of any station has been infrequent, he has experienced whores. In the Texas coastal town when he is only fifteen the "whores call to him from the dark like souls in want" (5). Thereafter whores frequent the narrative, as in the closing episode at the Griffin brothel. Such heterosexual contact is common to the frontier life the kid has led and is explicitly approved by the male culture which directs that life. He would hardly be offended by accusations of whoring— would most likely register them as accolades to his manhood. On the other hand, as the San Diego scenes demonstrate, the kid has had several earlier experiences with male-to-male sexuality and is aggressively opposed to its forms and dangers.

Upon hearing Elrod's apparently senseless comment, therefore, the kid reacts to an insinuation that readers may not immediately perceive. The kid remembers the judge's wanting to "touch" him and his encounter with the homosexual in the San Diego barroom. Moreover, McCarthy gives a rhetorical clue to the  homoerotic inference the kid draws from Elrod's words. In the first textual allusion to the judge's perversity, the half-breed boy whom he assaults and then kills is wearing "sandals of uncured hide" (116). So too is Elrod wearing "green hide boots." This rhetorical iteration helps clarify the kid's warning to Elrod's companions: "I see him back here I'll kill him" (322). Though advised by his buddies to "hush" (321) and depart, Elrod cannot forego his dance of death. His primitive, inarticulate compulsions draw him back to the kid's camp in the night; and true to his word, the kid guns him down. Throughout his life the kid has rejected homoeroticism by flight, fist, and evasion, but Elrod forces him to take the ultimate defense against it. This drastic repulsing of an inferred sexual threat from a male completes the elaborate homoerotic vinculum among Elrod, savages, the judge, and the kid, for the homologous scene of Elrod's death anticipates and informs the imminent jakes scene. Just having murdered on the sere plains to avoid male-to-male sexuality, and perhaps distracted by that incident, the kid is all the more devastated by the judge's assault in the Griffin jakes.

The kid's literal life may or may not end in the jakes at Griffin. However, the life that he has experienced for more than thirty years in the mountains, prairies, and deserts of the Southwest does end there. The judge's assault betrays the kid individually and the landscape that has come to symbolize his freedom. The contrasts between the immense open spaces where the kid is free to defend his masculine honor and the squalid confines of the Griffin "shit house" where he literally cannot move signify the magnitude of the judge's betrayal. As A. Carl Bredahl says, spaciousness "is at the heart of the western experience" and once removed "from eastern structures and challenged by the big sky, the westerner finds himself accepting the landscape and indeed embracing it for physical and spiritual sustenance" (30). American novelists at least as early as Melville saw the spatial discrepancy as an East-West dichotomy and pondered "the political realities of the fact that closure, not wilderness, is the major given of our lives" (Bredahl 3).

In passing, we may note that McCarthy's "kid" evokes and stands in contrast to other fictive young men of the Eastern United States. Billy Budd, Henry Fleming, and even Faulkner's suicidal Quentin Compson come to mind. Moreover, McCarthy's "kid" is essentially the same age as Huck Finn and journeys west at the same time Huck heads for the territories. John Updike continues the claustrophobic Eastern fascination in comedies of manners or drawing room tragedies. Seen against such Fiction of Enclosure, McCarthy's Western-centered violence seems ironically honest and refreshing.

While McCarthy does not textually develop an East-West

conflict, he conveys it through the historicity that fills the seventeen-year narrative void. Historic discourse tells that between 1861 and 1878, institutions east of the Mississippi produced the Civil War, the assassination of Lincoln, Reconstruction, the venality of Grant's administration, and numerous other atrocities emanating from Manifest Destiny. What part the kid played in any of these distant occurrences, we do not know; but the baneful Eastern influence on the Western plains is evident. In 1861, the year in which we last see the kid prior to his reappearance on the Llano Estacado, millions of buffalo still roamed, the plains Indians still thrived, and the encroachment of the industrial East was still minimal. Like the kid, the trans-Mississippi frontier was yet youthful, tough, and essentially natural. By 1878, however, the great buffalo herds had been eliminated to feed the Eastern hide trade, the tribes had been starved into submission, and piles of bleached bones were the sole legacy of both. These bones in turn were collected by the bone pickers such as Elrod, converted to fertilizer, and soon followed the hides across the Mississippi to nourish capitalist greed and Eastern gardens. The history of this death trade is nicely symbolized in the kid's destination when he leaves the buffalo plains to encounter Judge Holden in the jakes. Fort Griffin, Texas, was actually a major Southwestern shipping point for buffalo hides destined for Eastern and European trade, before the slaughter eliminated the market and the town. Both the factual and legendary history of Fort Griffin are well known to McCarthy and any other student of Texas frontier history. Don Hampton Biggers's *Pictures of the Past* and *History That Will Never Be Repeated*, sources with which McCarthy is probably familiar, are authentic, firsthand accounts of the buffalo slaughter. They were first published in 1901 and 1902.

As seen earlier in the character of ex-priest Tobin, the Spanish Catholicism that ironically informs the pre-void narrative is replaced in the post-void text by Calvinism, a change consistent with the historic post-Civil War migration of eastern American Protestants into the Southwest. The Calvinist believed that man has dominion over nature, including heathen savages; that Satan, not God rules the wilderness; and that possessing earthly goods is a sign of God's approval. Moreover, "Calvinist" is nearly synonymous with sexual repression. These singular Calvinist traits clarify the complex relationship between the Plains Indians and the "christians" hired to exterminate them.   To the Calvinist, the trans-Mississippi West was a damned region to be redeemed from wilderness and brought into the service of God and man.   Such "redemption," as Dayton Duncan phrases the situation, "was the nation's manifest destiny" (5).

Ironically, the scalphunters and filibusters of *Blood Meridian*, operating under the guise of God's crusaders bringing Christianity to the "heathen horde" (33), neither dislike nor shun the vicious conflict that grows out of the Indian's refusal to accommodate this quaint narrow view of Calvinist religioeconomics. The judge explains the white warrior's motivation for battle when he relates the tale of the murdered traveler whose posthumous son has been "euchered" out of the right to kill his father.   The judge's parable presupposes Freud's Oedipal theory: the son directs his enmity at a father whose image stands before him as "the idol of a perfection to which he can never attain" (145) and whom he can never kill.   This instinctive fury against the unconquerable father continues indefinitely; and battling with nonchristian "savages" is one of the socially acceptable manifestations of that fury.   For men in a super-masculine culture such as that of the trans-Mississippi frontier, combat defines their humanness and they do not gladly forsake a reliable enemy.   That is why, on the desolate north Texas plains of 1878, the kid is driven back to the judge by dual and contradictory motivations: the boredom of "peace" and the shock of having murdered another human to protect his masculinity.   Holden, sooty-souled and depraved though he may be, is in 1878 the only other surviving member of the gang of Indian fighters.   He, therefore, literally personifies the safe world of violence that defined the kid as Homo Sapiens.

When the judge assaults the kid in the Griffin jakes, therefore, he betrays a complex of psychological, historical, and sexual values of which the kid has no conscious awareness but which are distinctly conveyed to the reader.   Ultimately, however, it is the kid's personal humiliation which impacts the reader most tellingly.   In the virile warrior culture which dominates the text and to which the reader has become acclimated, seduction into public homoeroticism is a dreadful fate.   We do not see behind the outhouse door to know the details of the kid's corruption.   It may be as simple as the embrace that we do witness or as violent as the sodomy implied by the judge's killing of the Indian children.   The kid's powerful survivors instinct perhaps suggests that he is more a willing participant than a victim. However, the degree of debasement and the extent of the kid's willingness are incidental. The public revelation of the act is what matters. Other men have observed the kid's humiliation. The outhouse door has been unlocked from the inside, and the urinating man and the men off the boards see what the kid and judge are doing. In such a male culture, public homoeroticism is untenable; and it is this sudden revelation that horrifies the observers at Griffin. No other act could offend their masculine sensibilities so thoroughly as to cause the shock they display. A humorous yet revealing sign of how intolerant the southwestern male was of any indications of "sissy" behavior is this report sent by a Texas ranch foreman to the ranch owner back east: "Deer Sur, we have brand 800 caves this roundup we have made sum hay potatoes is a fare crop. That Inglishman yu lef in charge at the other camp got to fresh and we had to kill the son of a bitch. Nothing much has hapened sence you lef. Yurs truly, Jim" (Forbis 22). After a life time of defending himself against the ultimate degradation, no disclosure other than "sissy" behavior could humiliate the kid so thoroughly. This triumph over the kid is what the exhibitionist and homoerotic judge celebrates by dancing naked atop the wall, just as he did after assaulting the half-breed boy.

As we see, therefore, the jakes scene is the point of convergence for the narrative elements of *Blood Meridian*. In the scene the judge proves true to his previously established character and survives to haunt the future. The repressive and destructive elements of the Christian churches are highlighted by the kid's betrayal in an "embrace" ironically reminiscent of Judas' betrayal of Christ. The filthy confines of the privy contravene the idea of freedom attributed to western spaciousness. The endemic androcentrism of the frontier, though it produces men of singular character who are violently independent, can also culminate in spiritually deadening if not physically deadly confrontations. Though we might wish to find some glimmer of light in so dark a narrative, Steven Shaviro is probably correct in concluding that as readers "We are called to no responsibility, and we may lay claim to no transcendence. *Blood Meridian* is not a salvation narrative; we can be rescued neither by faith nor by works not by grace" (113). The only possible "rescue," as McCarthy himself has suggested, is to accept that there is "no such thing as life without bloodshed." In that accepting, we avoid being one of those who "give up their souls" by refusing to acknowledge that wanton violence is the defining characteristic of the human animal.

# Toni Morrison's

## *Beloved*

Harold Bloom remarks of Toni Morrison that "her imagination, whatever her social purposes, transcends ideology and
polemics, and enters again into the literary space occupied only
by fantasy and romance of authentic aesthetic dignity" (2). Her
novels, he continues, are "candidates for entering an American
canon founded upon what I insist would be aesthetic criteria
alone" (1). Making a similar point, Jan Thurman states categori-
cally that "As culturally specific as Morrison's novels are, they
are not restrictive. They appeal to an eclectic audience, one that
is not limited by race and gender" (9). I cite these two evaluations of Morrison's art, one based on aesthetics and the other on
demographics, because I agree that the greatness of Morrison's
fiction is its aesthetic purity and its power to transcend ethnic an
cultural biases. When Morrison says that she "encourages par-
ticipatory reading" (quoted in Furman 4), she does not qualify
her invitation in any way. She wisely knows that literature and
the criticism of it cannot be Balkanized. Herself unconfined by
cultural, racial, or critical prejudices, she welcomes to her fiction
participants even as blundering as I.

Most of Morrison's fiction is marked by violence. This
distinctive violence arises from what Thurman terms a "paradox of human behavior" that compels Morrison. That paradox,
quite simply, is that "good people commit horrific acts" (5). In
none of her novels is this incongruity more clearly seen than in
*Beloved*. It is unquestionably her novel of violence. The two
sources for *Beloved* as Morrison first conceived it are the story of
the escaped slave Margaret Garner who in 1851 murdered her
children, and a photograph of a young Harlem girl whose boy
friend shot her at a dance with a silenced gun. Dying, the girl

nonetheless did not reveal that she had been shot so that her angry lover could have time to escape (Furman 68). These sources
make the point that both the historical base and the artistic inspiration for *Beloved* are violent. One source shows the female
as perpetrator of violence, the other shows her as victim. The
two sources therefore offer a fascinating philosophical dichotomy. How difficult the dichotomy was to reconcile is shown
by Morrison's decision not to confront the problem in one
novel. She wisely chose to transform the inspiration of the
Harlem photograph into *Jazz*.

It was a wise artistic decision, yet, the original two-
pronged motivation remains pertinent to *Beloved*. Despite the
polar differences between the two sources that depicted the female as both actively violent and passively victimized, Morrison
perceived a more subtle element that unified the two women.
She felt that both young women had "sabotaged" themselves for
people whom they loved (Furman 68). Sabotaged not sacrificed.
This attitude toward the women's actions in turn suggests that
Morrison saw a conflict between a woman's traditional duty to
love and her obligation to her own individual well-being or
identity. In essence, therefore, Morrison rejected the external
conflict represented by the original sources for *Beloved* but re-
tained and modified it into a psychological, subtextual configura-
tion. As we will see, this altered, subtextual conflict explains
much about Morrison's development of Sethe's character and
her general attitude toward violence.

At this juncture, we need to remind ourselves of a fact
that we have already established with Faulkner, McCarthy, and
the previous novels of violence that we have examined. Violence is a male phenomenon. Morrison, obviously, offers a contradiction to Robert Wright's truism that "the leading cause of
violence is maleness" (72). Yet, insofar as creditable theories of
violence are concerned, she is not offering an aberration. Females are indeed capable of "aggressive behavior." Luigi
Valzelli calls it "Maternal Protective Aggression." As Valzelli
explains, this type of violence is "characteristic of female animals
for purposes of defending the newborn against any potentially or
actually threatening agent" (82). It is unique to females, and is
an example of evolutionary specificity. It is, in short, a primary
trait that identifies and defines femaleness. Male violence is
more generally displaced and generated by the male's desire to
acquire females and thus disseminate his genes. This active

male violence accounts for female passiveness generally (the type passiveness we see, for example, in the story of the Harlem girl who died for her violent lover). Only the instinct to nurture and protect her children overrides this natural passivity and incites the female to acts of significant, overt violence.

Therefore, though Sethe may be an exception she is not an aberration vis-à-vis violence. Her violent action is actually located well within reputable violence theory. She does differ significantly from the type of violence that characterizes the male, but she personifies Maternal Protective Aggression. Consequently, even if the idea is difficult for us to embrace, when Sethe kills the "crawling already? baby" and attempts to kill her other children, she is asserting her femaleness and rejecting the male violence that previously has dominated her life.

We wonder perhaps why Sethe's violence is not directed at school teacher and the slave hunter instead of at her own children. Why, that is, does she not take the saw to the enemy instead of to her beloved baby? Killing her offspring contradicts the theory that clarifies and helps justify her desire to protect them at all cost. Morrison implicitly explains this paradoxical action in terms of the male violence that has so completely shaped Sethe's existence. Sethe's action follows the theory of maternal violence, but is one step removed from its tenants. That is, Sethe herself has been so brutalized that her instinct to save her children has been adumbrated by the more common and pervasive violence to which she has been subjected. In a sense, environment and acculturation overcome instinct. In the abstract, school teacher and his henchmen represent the most dreaded enemy. In reality they are four mounted, armed white men intent of capturing Sethe and her family and returning them to slavery. Sethe instantly processes both of these perceptions. She knows abstractly that the horrific confrontation has arrived. She simultaneously realizes quite pragmatically that she alone cannot stand up against the men who reify that horror. She has been rejected by a community that allows the men to reach her without warning, and the one male who is supportive and present (Stamp Paid) is not physically able to intervene or quick witted enough to realize what is about to happen. Her instinct to save the children physically, therefore, transfers to a second level of awareness: the determination to save them spiritually, or if we prefer, psychologically. Indeed, in some ways Sethe's instantaneous shifting to a different level of interpretative awareness may be an example of what James Berger terms "the Freudian logic of trauma and symptom, which seems to inform this novel" (415). Regardless of the terminology we use to describe it, however, Sethe's action indicates that she processes an immense and complex network of instinctive and experiential knowledge and responds accordingly. What attitude we individually adopt toward this unusual example of maternal protective instinct is an entirely different matter for consideration. Nonetheless, we have to acknowledge Sethe's mental processes in order to appreciate fully the central act of violence that determines every other element of *Beloved*.

As we see, then, "*Beloved*'s narrative spirals around, is ordered by, a traumatic event whose model is historical" (Berger 409). At this juncture we need to look closely at that event and the narrative matrix that informs it.

Incidental violence is pervasive and the rhetoric of violence characterizes Morrison's style throughout the narrative. More importantly, the most distressing scene of violence in American fiction forms the literal and philosophical center of the narrative. Sethe's killing of the "crawling-already? girl" and attempted killing of Buglar, Howard, and Denver begins on page 148 and concludes on page 153 of a 275-page narrative. All prior action spirals into this central scene like a vortex; all subsequent action strains to escape that vortex and twists painfully outward to the enigmatic closing. The peripheral displays of violence anticipate and counterpoint this central scene. Neither in their singularity nor in their collective impact, however, do these subordinate scenes equal the nuclear violence. The scene describes the event that the audience has been anticipating since learning that 124 Bluestone Road is "palsied by the baby's fury at having its throat cut" (5). By fulfilling that dramatic promise, the scene leaves the audience both satisfied and deeply disturbed. Satisfied that the narrative has proven reliable. Disturbed that we demanded such a detailed reckoning. Perhaps no single scene in American fiction subsumes so much narrative purpose and so many motifs as Sethe's bloody assault on her helpless children.

We as audience wander into the narrative with the transient Paul D. He activates the motif of violence, speaks for many of its elements, then closes it out. He arrives at 124 and immediately destroys the room to free it of its "evil." This capacity for violence is echoed at the end of the novel, when we learn that

Paul D served in the Civil War. Thinking he would fight for Negro freedom, he instead found himself back on the Alabama battlefields, separating dead Rebel soldiers from wounded ones (268). Within this cyclic motif of violence, even scenes that initially seem incoherent and misplaced gain credence as part of the narrative design.

That Paul D is the agent used to open and close the motif is ironic, for other than Stamp Paid he is the most placid of the many characters who populate the narrative. Beaten, chained, humiliated, battered, and abused in every possible way, he retains the characteristics that make women think of him as being "blessed": compassion, tenderness, concern, patience. We can only imagine the trauma that brought him to the one attack against a human that is alluded to: his attempt to kill the slave master Brandywine. Unlike Sethe's killing of her child, Paul D's assault on Brandywine is never detailed. Morrison keeps it distant and suppressed, thereby implying how far outside Paul D's true personality the action lies. Having had to plumb his own soul as a consequence of this one homicidal outburst, Paul D has in his lonely wanderings made peace with his demons. As a man now nearing middle-age, he personifies reason and nonviolence.. In his own way, he is as much a "Soldier of Christ" (170) as Stamp Paid. Paul D's opening and closing the motif of violence is an irony that envelopes the entire narrative structure, and one we will return to shortly.

Nearly every conceivable type of violence appears between Paul D's room-wrecking and his cadaver-hunting. Sethe's mother is repeatedly raped on the slave ship, then subsequently hanged. Sixo is burned, then shot. The Paul's are hanged. Sethe is raped by the nephews and then mercilessly whipped. Amy Denver has been abused and beaten. Stamp Paid recalls 87 lynchings that occurred in Kentucky in 1874, and the smell of human blood cooking in lynch fires. The dog "here boy" is slammed against the wall so hard he goes into convulsions. The violence of birth dominates the description of Amy Denver and Sethe's struggle to bring Denver into the world. Such scenes are constant and unrelenting. Further, the Civil War looms ominously in the background as an image of violence.

In addition to these explicit occurrences of violence, Morrison uses a rhetoric of violence to take the motif to deeper narrative levels than the concrete references alone permit. With rhetorical subtlety, Morrison forces the reader from a predominantly visceral response to a subliminal one. Several prominent examples make the point. In less than two pages (78-79) of Sethe's remembering Denver's birth, these words appear, some duplicated: hurt, pain, fire, screaming, whippings, evil, groaned, die, beat. From another page in the same episode (82), these words: dead, die, death, devil, sick. Such words may be expected in context of the Amy-Sethe episode, but in other episodes they oppose rather than complement the text. For example, before she despairs of the human condition and takes to her death bed, the holy Baby Suggs preaches a Whitmanesque sermon in which she calls for her listeners to love themselves, all their parts and all their pieces (88). However, rhetoric of violence punctuates this song of myself: despise, flay, bind, chop off, broken, break, scream. Such vocabulary runs counter to the text of Baby Suggs' joyous message and implies that violence is the true force that drives human endeavors. In the most peaceful of things, violence lurks like an evil spirit. It is a truth that causes Baby Suggs ultimately to lose her faith and decide that "There was no grace—imaginary or real—and no sunlit dance in a Clearing could change that" (89).

Later, when Paul D is viewing the newspaper photo of Sethe that Stamp Paid has shown him, the vocabulary of violence also interfuses his response: killed, maimed, burned, jailed, whipped, stomped, raped, cheated (156). The rhetoric of violence that dominates Stamp Paid's recollection of Sethe's actions is clearest in context. The italics are added:

> So Stamp Paid did not tell him how she *flew*, snatching up her children like a *hawk* on the wing; how her face *beaked*, how her hands worked like *claws*, how she collected them every which way: one on her shoulder, one under her arm, one by the hand, the other *shouted* forward into the woodshed filled with just sunlight and shaving now because there wasn't any wood. The party had used it all, which is why he was *chopping* some. Nothing was in that shed, he knew, having been there early that morning. Nothing but sunlight. Sunlight, shavings, a shovel. The *ax* he himself took out. Nothing else was in there except the shovel—and of course the *saw*. (157)

Here the rhetoric of violence contrasts with the iterated "sunlight" and the momentary innocence with which Stamp Paid views the moments before the killing. The stark isolation of "saw" is especially effective. Its meaning is ambiguous, standing simultaneously as a common hand tool and as a reference to insight. To Stamp Paid the saw is a horrible epiphany, for upon eyeing it he "sees" what is about to happen. The reader, who has already had the killing described, also suddenly realizes precisely how Sethe severed her infant's head.

Finally, the word "nigger," so taboo in modern parlance, becomes part of this rhetoric of violence. In the central violence scene, the white slavers use the expression like a verbal rapier. It is, for example, reiterated six times in one 67-word passage.

> Little nigger-boy eyes open in sawdust; little nigger-girl eyes staring between the wet fingers that held her face so her head wouldn't fall off; little nigger-baby eyes crinkling up to cry in the arms of the old nigger whose own eyes were nothing but slivers looking down at his feet. But the worst ones were those of the nigger woman who looked like she didn't have any.     (150)

In the mouths of the white slavers and repeated so often, the word becomes as violent and as vicious as a stab wound. Since the word is used elsewhere in the text with far fewer or no violent connotations (as when Paul D refers to himself as "nigger"), we see how intimately context and the rhetoric of violence are intertwined. "Nigger" is an ironic linguistic parallel to the steel saw: harmless in the proper hands but a weapon of violence when used with hurtful intent.

We might further note about this passage that the word "eyes" and references to eyes occur almost as frequently as "nigger." By juxtaposing the "seeing" motif with the slavers' racist slur word, Morrison emphasizes the moral blindness of the slavers. She makes us as audience "see" the entire scene, and without preaching, yelling, or accusing, she makes us draw contrasts between perspicacity and benightedness.

Like the bramble thicket that tears at Stamp Paid as he struggles to get to the delicious and fatal blackberries, the allusions to violence snag and prick the reader at every step. They are constant, unforgiving, and painful. Yet they lead to the genius of the central scene of violence.

The genius of this central scene is that Morrison chooses to relate it through the consciousness of the white slavers who have come to return Sethe and her children to slavery in Kentucky. Prior to this scene the reader has experienced a distant compassion, but no direct participation in the brutality that drives slavery. Having to step inside the minds of the white slavers eliminates that comforting distance. By switching to the slavers' point of view, Morrison exponentially multiplies the impact of the violence on the reader.

The "killing" chapter opens with the chilling line that immediately locates us with the slavers while leaving the impression of visitors arriving at another celebratory feast: "When the four horsemen came—school teacher, one nephew, one slave catcher and a sheriff—the house on Bluestone Road was so quiet they thought they were too late" (148). The tone is casual, calm, invested with arrogance. Unless we are careful, we overlook the apocalyptic dread of the phrase "the four horsemen." Paralleling the tone, the men are not so much actively cruel as coldly detached. Their thoughts are on another of America's defining components and the one that fathered slavery: capitalism. As James Berger recognizes, the four horsemen in *Beloved* "represent, rather, an alliance of political forces, who commit acts of political and racial violence and transgression" (410). These horsemen want Sethe and her family returned alive not because they respect life, but because "Unlike a snake or a bear, a dead nigger could not be skinned for profit and was not worth his own dead weight in coin" (148).

We borrow the eyes and share the attitude of these men when they step to the shed door to see that "two boys bled in the sawdust and dirt at the feet of a nigger woman holding a blood-soaked child to her chest with one hand and an infant by the heels in the other" (149). By this point in the narrative, we have become closely acquainted with Sethe and her children. We know their ages, their physical characteristics, and something about what motivates them. We sympathize with Buglar and Howard who have long since departed 124. We have shared the family's sorrow and the modicum of joy that has been theirs. Now we glimpse the central horror that has dictated their lives. However, we see it through the eyes of the slavers. At this most crucial moment, Sethe and the children are depersonalized, reduced to commodities. Disturbed only that they have lost their investment, the slavers back out of the shed, mount their horses, and depart. They rationalize the horror they have caused as being "testimony to the results of a little so-called freedom imposed on people who needed every care and guidance in the world to keep them from the cannibal life they preferred" (151). The slavers view themselves as caring, honorable men whose dedication to noblesse oblige has been frustrated by a savage's outburst.

Nephew, the same one who a few weeks earlier had taken Sethe's breast milk while his brother held her down, has no inkling of the motivation underlying the "nigger woman's" actions. "Hell, he'd been beat a million times and he was white. Once it hurt so bad and made him so mad he'd smashed the well bucket" (150). The ironic comparison of Sethe's near fatal beating with one that angered Nephew to bucket kicking petulance stands beyond language. Only in his hyperbolic "million times" and his trite masculine rhyme "bad" and "mad" do we glimpse the unbridgeable gulf that separates Nephew's cognition from our own. Having to share Nephew's perspective, however, reminds us of how trivial are most of our own concerns when compared to the scene we have just witnessed.

Morrison accomplishes two crucial narrative goals by having the quintessential scene of violence conveyed through the consciousness of the slave masters and their henchmen. First, she forces the reader to share the cold, compassionless guilt of the slavers. Second, she universalizes the responsibility for the institution of slavery itself. Even if we have been able to maintain an aesthetic distance from slavery during the rest of the novel, we can no longer maintain that comforting objectivity in this central scene. We have wanted the scene from the beginning of the narrative, and like a cleverly set trap, it snaps shut about us. We are there with the four horsemen, sharing their capitalistic greed and ethnic arrogance. Perhaps we too, as white readers, have shared with school teacher the delusion that uneducated, superstitious Blacks should know the "the futility of out-smarting a whiteman" (148). However, the supercilious "whiteman" has been tricked by his own greed and presumptions into a scene that we have demanded all along. Here suddenly we are purged of any trace of personal and historical naiveté that we may have brought with us into the scene. We no longer can comfort ourselves with the rationalization that slavery is historically and morally distant. It is an American phenomenon shared by us all. Three defining elements of the American character permeate the narrative: freedom, capitalism, and slavery. Here in the central scene, we suddenly realize what a violent compound those historic abstractions can form. It is hardly a comforting awakening.

Morrison's initiation of the twisting, difficult emergence

from the vortex is almost as impressive as the central scene itself. Like the shed scene, the scene immediately following it is a
"slaughterhouse" scene. We have just witnessed what horrors
occurred in the wood shed and what violence Sethe is capable of.
The next scene opens with Paul D standing outside the slaughterhouse looking at a newspaper account of the wood shed
killings and staring at Sethe's picture. "That ain't her mouth"
(154), he wails plaintively at the inexactly drawn portrait. From
eighteen years distance, and not having been present at the
killing, Paul D cannot grasp or refuses to accommodate the degree of violence depicted in the newspaper account and in Stamp
Paid's explanation of it. (Paul D cannot read.) Paul D's shocked
disbelief serves to distance us from the murder as well, letting us
move back to a more objective appraisal of what we have just
witnessed. The contextual irony holds, however, because in not
wanting to reconcile the horror of Sethe's infanticide, Paul D
turns his thoughts to pig commerce—that is, to the close ties between death and American capitalism. He himself is involved
in the slaughtering. Even as he speaks, "a little pig shit" (154)
still clings to his boots, signifying the death trade he follows.
Along with Stamp Paid he thinks of how he herds and slaughters pigs all day to feed the rapacious appetites of a growing,
prospering America. The irony seems lost of him that as he
walks to the slaughterhouse each day, he must pass the dese-
crated mounds of the Miami Indians, whose ghosts haunt the
slaughterhouse area. He too, like many other Negroes, does the
"poking, killing, cutting, skinning, case packing" (155) that feeds
the pork craving that has grown "into a mania" (155). He does
not realize that he is till a slave to American capitalism and that
others grow fat off his arduous, bloody labor.

In this scene, Morrison spares us the horrible details of the
activities inside the slaughterhouse; but here she does not want
those details and does not need them. She knows she cannot
match what has just been described to us in the wood shed. To
attempt to duplicate that scene would be anticlimax. Thus she
paints the subsequent scene with more nuance and fills it with
far less drama. Yet, juxtaposed as it is with the central killing
scene, Paul D's scene commences the retreat that diminishes our
emotional responses and permits us to analyze more objectively
what the text is trying to tell us. It is appropriate, however, that
the scene immediately following the central violence scene emphasizes capitalism, slavery, and skepticism. The slavery and

capitalism we have encountered already, but the skepticism is an element we need to keep in mind. If we are naive enough to think that Morrison's attack is simply upon American capitalism and the white man's greed that fuels it we have misread her text. Paul D's scene is a narrative road sign to avoid that misreading.

While Morrison conveys the greatest sympathy for and understanding of Sethe, she does not blithely condone her infanticide and its far-reaching consequences. Beyond slavery and past economic determinism lies personal responsibility. That is the core human trait Morrison wishes to examine, and perhaps advocate. True freedom comes solely from that trait. Lest we think that Sethe's actions are condoned, we need note that the most reasonable characters in the text repudiate Sethe. Stamp Paid obviously does not agree with her. He risks his own life in the presence of the white slavers and acts instantly on pure instinct to save Denver from Sethe's murderous rage. Had he not done so, the true heroine of the text would be absent. Ella, Stamp Paid's assistant in helping the slaves escape, denies Sethe outright. "I ain't got no friends take a handsaw to their own children," Ella assures Stamp Paid (187). The townspeople ostracize Sethe and reconcile themselves to her actions only after many years have elapsed and after Denver has proved her devotion to community values. It is in fact, Denver, not Sethe that the community re-embraces.

Appropriately, Morrison chooses Paul D to articulate the most rational and thorough denial of Sethe. He is the male most intimately and sympathetically involved with her. He has known her longest, both during and after her enslavement, and he finally comes to accept the reality of what she has done. More importantly, he has suffered tortures and humiliations commensurate with Sethe's without losing the balance and compassion that mark him as "blessed." His rejection therefore carries great weight in determining how Morrison wants Sethe to be perceived.

Remembering the Sethe of old and comparing her to the "new" Sethe, Paul D thinks "This here Sethe talked about love like any other woman; talked about baby clothes like any other woman, but what she meant could cleave the bone. This here Seth talked a bout safety with a handsaw. This here new Sethe didn't know where the world stopped and she began" (164). To emphasize his disapproval, he then tells her face to face that

"Your love is too thick" (164) and "What you did was wrong, Sethe" (165). When she argues she had no choice, he compares her to the pigs he slaughters and tells her "You got two feet, Sethe, not four" (165). What he means is that she is a human with a brain, not a pig who can't make choices. She has free will. She can accept and exercise personal responsibility, regardless of how drastic or hopeless circumstances may seem. No matter that school teacher and the nephews identified her by her animal "characteristics" (193), she is nonetheless a human with reason. She is still upright, still mobile, still conscious. Sethe cannot accept this burden of responsibility. She is devastated by what she sees as Paul D's loss of faith in her, his betrayal. He then leaves 124, not to return till after Sethe has been reduced to insanity and Beloved exorcised. Clearly her own modes of behavior have not served Sethe well. If she is to regain sanity, Paul D in his reason and patience must lead her to it.

The most telling argument against Sethe's actions are the residual effects they have on her living children. Other than the dead "crawling already? baby," the primary victim of the infanticide is Denver. Her entire life and personality are shaped by the killing of her older sister and by Sethe's subsequent management of the event. Denver is so much affected, in fact, that she exaggerates the stories that she hears from Baby Suggs and Sethe about her dead sister. Highly impressionable, she enhances the "memories" into a ghost. In that enhancement, she becomes the ghost's human facilitator. So convincing is her play-acting that she convinces Baby Suggs, Sethe, and her brothers that the spiritual reality has become corporeal. She then continues the enchantment to such a degree that a deadly (and very real) pretender takes over Sethe's home and soul. Denver is redeemed, however, because she is also the one who ultimately saves herself and her mother from the psychological enslavement into which Beloved has forced them. More than any other character in the novel, and in polar contrast to her mother, Denver acknowledges personal responsibility for her actions. That acceptance is the single most important factor in making her the protagonist of the narrative, the character who best serves to convey Morrison's dialectic.

The negative psychological impact that Sethe's violence has on Denver cannot be overstated. She is seven when the boy Nelson Lord innocently asks about what her mother did to deserve imprisonment. Hearing his question, Denver not only quits going to Lady Jones' reading lessons but plunges for two years into the silence of hysterical deafness. So afraid is she of her mother that she must shut out any word that reminds her of Sethe's violent capabilities. Denver is less than one month old when Sethe tries to kill her, and thus has no clear "rememory" of the horror that dictates her life. Only years later as a young adult can Denver articulate her life-long dread, and then only in the privacy of her own thoughts: "I'm afraid that the thing that happened that made it all right for my mother to kill my sister could happen again" (205). "She cut my head off every night. Buglar and Howard told me she would and she did. . . . I want to go to sleep but I know if I do I won't wake up" (206). Terrified, lost in silence, Denver enhances the ghost baby that has previously lingered in the memories of her mother and grandmother. Denver has heard from Baby Suggs how Sethe would not relinquish the dead baby and wash its blood from her breast, so that "Denver took her mother's milk right along with the blood of her sister" (152). She has literally drunk her dead sister's blood, a fact which makes a powerful impact on the child's developing mind. Therefore, the ghost is as much a reinvention of her own destroyed infancy as it is of her dead sister.

To give form and life to the murdered baby is the only way Denver can cope psychologically with what she fears Sethe may do to her. By resurrecting the murdered child, Denver attempts to alleviate her own extinction, the dread of nonexistence that is symbolized by her deafness. "For two years she walked in a silence too solid for penetration but which gave her eyes a power even she found hard to believe" (103). Seeing beyond the actuality of 124 Bluestone Road, Denver suddenly hears "close thunder crawling up the stairs" (103). Baby Suggs and Sethe immediately apply logical explanations to the noise. Baby Suggs thinks it is "the India-rubber ball the boys played with bounding down the stairs" or "that damn dog" (103). Sethe too thinks it is Buglar disobeying and throwing the ball down the stairs. When she looks, however, she sees Denver, not Buglar, atop the stairs. Denver's first post-deaf words are "She was trying to get upstairs." Having no idea what Denver is talking about, and surprised that she is talking at all, Sethe says incredulously "What?" The simple question shows that Sethe does not first assume that Denver is referring to the "crawling already? baby."

Denver, however, persists in her enhancement of the reborn infant. "The baby," she insists. "Didn't you hear her crawling?" (103). Sethe is befuddled, unsure how to interpret what Denver is saying: "What to jump on first was the problem: that Denver head anything at all or that the crawling-already? baby girl was still at it but more so? (103). The "more so" is crucial here, because it demonstrates that Denver's question has intensified or resurrected the "ghost" of the murdered infant. Denver is the first to give action and sound to something that was previously just a very strong, vivid memory to the two women who were present at the killing: Sethe and Baby Suggs. That is, Denver actualizes a borrowed memory. Sethe's acute sense of guilt makes her quite willing to accept the actualization.

Denver's interior monologues suggest that as a young adult she realizes who and why she enhanced the baby's spirit. Thinking back on her brief schooling at Lady Jones' and the subsequent deafness, Denver says:

> So it was good for me to learn how [to read], and I did until it got quite and all I could hear was my own breathing and one other who knocked over the milk jug while it was sitting on the table. Nobody near it. Ma'am whipped Buglar but he didn't touch it. Then it messed up all the ironed clothes and put its hand in the cake. Look like I was the only one who knew right away who it was. (208)

Once again we have the text verifying that no one other than Denver assumes a "ghost" is responsible for the common household mishaps that occur in 124. Even Sethe, more prone to emotion than reason, assumes quite rationally that her disobedient son is the culprit. So much does she believe Buglar's guilt that she whips him, which is a relatively strong response for a loving mother who has herself been beaten so severely. Denver knows her brother "didn't touch" the spilled milk jug or put his hands in the cake. She herself has caused the mischief as an additional way of reifying the "ghost."

Subsequent manifestations of the ghost are logically explained in context of Denver's enhancement process. For example, Sethe has strongly implanted the dramatic story of her birth in Denver's mind. Therefore, Denver frequently uses the image of "her birth in a canoe straddled by a white girl from whom she was named" (29). Consequently, when Denver imagines that a "white dress knelt down next to her mother and had its sleeve around her mother's waist" (29) the origin of the image is clear. The "whitegirl" is in fact Amy Denver. Since Denver cannot put an identifying face to the reluctant Samaritan who helped deliver her, Amy becomes in Denver's imagination simply a white dress. The sleeve around Sethe's waist is Amy straddling Sethe as she assists in the birth struggle. Both the image based on the birth stories and the transformed image are filled with love and caring, but the latter image ultimately grows ominous as it becomes identified with the woman Beloved. In this transferred birth image, we see not only how Denver transforms reality into the supernatural and vice versa but also how closely allied the ghost is with Denver's own self identification.

All other manifestations of the ghost child can be similarly explained by logical, real occurrences or by Denver's active participation in the reinvention of the "baby." For example, when the corporeal Beloved appears, Sethe is anxious to accept her as the adult manifestation of the murdered infant because Denver has helped condition her to such receptivity. In fact, however, Beloved is probably a killer who has escaped captivity and who is a troubled young woman. As Stamp Paid suggests, there "Was a girl locked up in the house with a white man over by Deer Creek. Found him dead last summer and the girl gone. Maybe that's her" (235). Even Sethe originally tells Denver that Beloved "had been locked up by some white man for his own purposes, and never let out the door" (119). In her own inarticulate recollections, Beloved substantiates Stamp Paid's theory. She recalls that "the man on my face is dead" (210), a memory that may refer to having killed one of her tormentors during sexual intercourse. (The face-sex association has been introduced earlier when Sethe's head is held down by one nephew while the second assaults her breast.)

Narrative closure is also explained in terms of Denver's enhancement of the baby ghost. Denver's reasons for creating the living Beloved are nullified when she is forced back to loneliness and isolation by the mutually destructive exclusive bond that Sethe and Beloved form. Thus, ironically, Denver must establish her own personality and break free of the alter ego she has created. This necessary deconstruction of her own creation is why Denver returns to Lady Jones for help, why she intercedes to prevent her mother from stabbing Edward Bodwin in Beloved's defense, and why she separates herself from Paul D and Sethe at the end of the text. If she does not do these things, she cannot become the self-sufficient, independent woman that Morrison envisions as the future salvation of a people who were so recently enslaved. Moreover, learning, community contact, and a plan for the future are instrumental in making Denver's redemption possible. These are pragmatic, commonsensical principles that contradict any suggestion that Morrison may be championing chimeras that waft out of the past to torment the present.

One other significant element of all these violence-centered relationships needs to be recognized. Morrison implies that violence and human sexuality are closely related if not indistinguishable. While this is hardly a revolutionary theory, Morrison uses it most subtly and creatively. Eroticism opens the novel and is thematic thereafter. It appears in its most palliative and most perverted manifestations, at its gentlest and at its most violent. It ranges from Paul D's compassionately kissing the "tree" scars on Sethe's back while he fondles her breasts to the nephews' taking Sethe's breast milk; from the erotic innocence shared by Sethe and Halle to the loveless "fucking" between Paul D and Beloved. Over and against each loving, life-restoring erotic relationship stands a polar counterpart that is humiliating and deadly. This polarity between peace and violence or life and death is cleverly encapsulated by one small detail in the central violence scene: Sethe's joyful, rejuvenating arrival at 124 Bluestone Road is followed exactly 28 days later by the killing of the "crawling already? baby," a time frame coincidental with the female menstrual cycle. Morrison, however, is not trying to emphasize clever sexual icons or extract artistic mileage from overworked Freudian eroticism. She has a more subtle reason for emphasizing human sexuality.

Not surprisingly, given her importance in the narrative structure, Denver is most affected by the pervasive eroticism. However, its impact on her is more apparent than real—or at least it assumes a form different from the one it first seems to possess. Insofar as sexuality is concerned, Denver is unique within the text. Sethe, by comparison, at the age of fourteen eagerly "couples" with Halle three times as soon as they are "married" (26). Eighteen years later, she just as readily couples with Paul D, consummating their relationship within hours of his arrival at 124 (20). Baby Suggs has given birth to at least eight children. Beloved's sexuality is compulsive and demanding. Denver, by contrast, remains virginal. She is hardly naive about eroticism. She knows what her mother does upstairs with Paul D and she is acutely aware of what Paul D and Beloved do in the cold shed. She watches the turtles mating by the riverside. Consistent with Morrison's ironic methodology, however, this overt sexuality and Denver's awareness of it are obvious signs of covert design. The primary narrative focus is not upon the sexuality per se but upon the fact that it is a form of slavery that Denver wisely avoids.

Because slavery is second only to violence as the dominant motif in *Beloved*, it is consistent with the narrative design that this eroticism enslaves many of the characters. It drives them to do things that are not just embarrassingly foolish (as Sethe and Halle's consummating their marriage in the cornfield and Sixo's thirty mile trips to caress his lover) but things that are unspeakably horrible (as the depraved guards forcing the Negro prisoners to fellate them and the nephews' taking of Sethe's milk). Moreover, rape and sexual assault are common in the background of the narrative (Sethe's mother being repeatedly raped on the slave ship, Ella having the grotesque half-breed child that she mercifully allows to die). Raging sexuality dominates human actions—more than money, religion education, or politics. It is as enslaving as the chains that lock Paul D to 45 other prisoners in Alfred, Georgia. Ironically, however, the eroticism is a form of slavery that Denver avoids: and once again the strings of this irony lead to the central violence scene.

As we recall, Denver dislikes Paul D. Although he treats her kindly and respectfully, she wants him out of the house as soon as he arrives, even resorting to a flagrant lie to discredit him in Sethe's eyes (56). As readers, we first assume that Denver's aversion to Paul D is motivated by jealousy. We assume that she is jealous of his coming between her and her mother, that she resents his violent outburst against the ghost, or that as an eighteen year old woman she is feeling her own sexuality and is attracted to the man "who can walk in a house and make the women cry" (273). None of these logical and apparent explanations is totally valid, however. The reason Denver resents Paul D is because of her near obsessive fixation on Halle, a father she has never seen but who has been elevated to near mythic status by Baby Suggs' continual stories about him. Again, Denver's relationship with her absent father cannot be explained in terms of conventional Freudian complexes. Her love of Halle is not a displaced erotic desire to replace her mother in her father's eyes and arms. Instead, it is motivated directly by the violence that Denver perceives as being one of Sethe's dominant "characteristics." Denver is terrified that at the slightest provocation, Sethe will behead her. As we see in the central violence scene, Denver's fear is well grounded. Thus, she fantasizes that Halle will one day arrive and deliver her to a sanctuary away from 124 Bluestone Road. In short, she dreams that her father will protect her from her mother. Thus, when Paul D arrives, Denver instantly thinks he is Halle and that her dream of salvation has finally come true. When she soon discovers that the visitor is merely one of the men from Sweet Home, her dream is permanently destroyed and her animosity toward Paul D is inevitable.

To fully understand the degree to which Denver manages and advantages the events that culminate in the central violence chapter, we need to explain the coincidental appearance of Paul D and Beloved. Inasmuch as no one has visited 124 Bluestone Road in eighteen years, the juxtaposition of these two sudden arrivals is too conspicuous to ignore. Further, this coincidence is accompanied by the subsidiary coincidence that the strange girl's age approximates that of the murdered baby if she were still living. The very conspicuousness of these coincidences warns against reading more into them than they warrant. Beloved's sudden appearance at 124 is actually no more startling than Paul D's unexpected visit. The house, after all, is on a major thoroughfare and was once a way station. Travelers and drifters have found their way to 124 for several generations. That Paul D wanders the vicinity for nearly two decades before finding it is more puzzling than that Beloved should escape captivity "over by Deer Creek" (235) and within days follow the river to 124. Further, that Beloved is approximately the same age as the murdered infant is not surprising. Paul D has already discussed how many Negroes of all ages still wander the country. Moreover, Morrison foreshadows the same-age coincidence in Amy Denver and Sethe, who are both teenagers when Denver is delivered in the old boat. No doubt many young Black women are traveling the countryside for one reason or another and any number of them could be close to the slain baby in age. The point is that the substantive and logical explanations of Beloved's coming are more cogent and convincing than any mystical or supernatural explanations. That these logical explanations are ignored in favor of supernatural ones illustrates how adeptly Denver satisfies her various emotional needs by causing the mysterious stranger to be accepted as the embodiment of the murdered baby.

Denver's motivations are unmistakable. First, she has already enhanced the spiritual presence of the murdered baby.

Second, she is disappointed that Paul D is not her fatherly savior. Third, she has long been in dread of her mother. Fourth, she craves companionship with someone near her own age and of the same gender. Taken together, these facts become the formula for Denver's revenge and the solution to her emotional needs. Because Sethe has already come to believe in the spiritual presence of "crawling already? baby," the step to believing in her tangible appearance is small. Denver immediately recognizes how willing Sethe is to accept the woman as the adult embodiment of the baby when Sethe equates her sudden desire to urinate with the breaking of her amniotic fluid. Moreover, Denver has already witnessed in the room-smashing scene how an otherwise skeptical Paul D can be led to accept spirits and evil ghosts if they further his cause. His first manly outburst ingratiates him to Sethe and immediately grants him access to her bed. His second acceptance gives him access to another lover, Beloved. (Paul D later admits to Stamp Paid that Beloved is a "bitch" [235] and that he views her just as a girl who "shot up one day sitting on a stump" [234].) Having him tormented by never knowing for sure whether Beloved is real or a ghost helps Denver alleviate her disappointment that he is not her father. That she never totally forgives Paul D and enjoys making him uncomfortable is illustrated by her double entendre reply when he asks if she really thinks Beloved was her sister: "But who would know that better than you, Paul D? I mean, you sure 'nough knew her" (267). Quick witted and perceptive, Denver takes advantage of the situation that Beloved's appearance has offered her. She is not an overtly aggressive individual, as her timidity in visiting Ms. Jones' school demonstrates. Thus she sublimates her anger (her violence if you will) into the reified spirit of the dead sister who has become her alter ego. In short, Denver seizes the opportunity to transpose her invented self into a visible form. It is an extremely clever but almost fatal move, as we have seen.

What then is Morrison's epistemology of violence? The answer lies in accepting a premise: in American culture, a mother's killing of her child is the most heinous act of violence possible. There are those who contend that the ultimate point of Sethe's infanticide is that personal freedom transcends all other values. The second greatest love is the love of freedom. The greatest love is the willingness of a mother to sacrifice a child in order to guarantee that freedom. Death is the ultimate emancipation. When circumstances render life not worth the living, fatal violence inflicted upon the most innocent of the innocent is not only a viable but a preferable act to guarantee this freedom. The argument is compelling. The slavery that Sethe experiences is horrible. So much so that it is almost extralinguistic. The choice she makes that her children are better off dead than as victims of that slavery is a hard decision to fault. The fallacy of the argument, however, is that it emanates from the same lack of logic that Morrison has warned us to be wary of. That is, the justification of Sethe's infanticide is extra-textual. Little within the text supports it.

We have already noted that all others in the text reject Sethe's act. Despite the love they feel for her otherwise, they cannot condone the infanticide. Their own feelings and society's taboo against it are insurmountable. These rejections alone are reason enough to reject the argument that seeks to validate Sethe's act. Even more compelling than the rejection of her friends and relatives, however, is Sethe's own self loathing. No one in the text rejects what she has done more vigorously than she. Her guilt literally immobilizes her till she sits "in the chair licking her lips like a chastised child while Beloved ate up her life" (250). We as readers do not have to extrapolate from clues to conclude that Sethe is mad. The sardonic narrator tells us: "If the white people of Cincinnati had allowed Negroes into their lunatic asylum they could have found candidates in 124" (250). If Sethe is so convinced that her killing of the child was the right thing (as she sometimes rationalizes), that it transcends any other kind of love or responsibility, then why is she so devoured by guilt? Guilt is the worst kind of psychological slavery; and it does not dwell in a clear conscience. It destroys a woman who has survived unbelievable hardships that would have killed others. Sethe is reduced to a filthy, sniveling infant who welcomes abuse from a madwoman whom she imagines to be the embodiment of her dead child. The cycle of Sethe's transformation from slavery, to independent freedom, back to slavery does not logically lead to the conclusion that Morrison excuses Sethe's infanticide. Sethe is violent, obsessive, guilt ridden, self-centered, with no sense of otherness. As Paul D says, "This here Sethe didn't know where the world stopped and she began" (164). Such egocentricism contradicts the community-oriented salvation that Denver personifies.

Further, nothing in the narrative supports a theological

explanation for Sethe's actions. That is, there is inadequate evidence of the presence of a Christian or even generically religious belief system to contend that Sethe thinks the "crawling already? baby" will gain "Heaven." In fact, the only church in the text is the failed dry goods shop that has been converted to the ironically named "Holy Redeemer" church (188). A passerby perfunctorily complains that Paul D should not be drinking with the church cross over his head, but other than that nothing indicates that the church wields influence over the affairs of man. Paul D sleeps in the cellar, and certainly has not been "redeemed." He is not, however, troubled by that fact.

Even Baby Suggs, holy, has no regard for organized theology. Her last sermon, before she drops into despair altogether, calls for a humanistic love of self and each other. "Love your flesh," she shouts, even the "inside parts" that the whites had "just as soon slop for hogs" (88). In short, nothing in the text suggests a viable Christian orthodoxy that would encourage Sethe to kill her child, even if she had badly misinterpreted the dogma of that orthodoxy. Approximately, only school teacher and the slave hunters are "sanctimonious," a fact suggesting that Christianity is in large part the cause of and hardly the solution to the Negro's problems. The slaughterhouse, the symbol of white man's capitalist greed, is a far more dominant presence than the church, and infinitely more influential in the affairs of the Black community.

We noted earlier that Denver is the true heroine of the narrative. That notion stands as a valid interpretation of Denver's character. However, an addendum perhaps should be noted. There is a textual "heroine" that equals or surpasses Denver as an intriguing enigma. She appears not in the text per se but in the drawings that appear on the title page and the first page of each of the three books of *Beloved*. These drawings change incrementally, and it is the end to which those changes point that we must attend.

Let us note first that the three books of *Beloved* are carefully organized. Each book begins with "124," Book One with "124 was spiteful"; Book Two with "124 was loud"; and Book Three with "124 was quiet." Not only does this reiterated sentence keep us focused on the central and crucial setting of the novel, but the changing adjectives offer some general guidelines to the action contained within each book. Further, Book One begins with Paul D's arrival and ends with his departure from 124.

Book Two begins with Stamp Paid fretting about having shown the newspaper clipping to Paul D and ends with Stamp Paid talking to Paul D. Book Three, not quite so neatly compassed, begins with Denver and ends with Beloved. Even this is a carefully orchestrated opening and closing device because, as we have seen, Denver and Beloved are closely united. Denver's personality and independence gain force in direct proportion to Beloved's deterioration and ultimate disappearance. Finally, Book One is longer by half than Books Two and Three combined; and each book decreases in proportion to the previous book by approximately one-half. (Book One is 165 pages long; Book Two is 70 pages, and Book Three is 38 pages, in the Plume paperback edition.) The point is that Morrison carefully crafted the textual structure. Thus, the drawings are meant to be an integral part of that structure rather than incidental decorations. They are technically illustrations in that they do elucidate the text they accompany.

All four illustrations share qualities of guardian figures and modern abstraction, but they differ in important ways. The title page illustration is the largest and clearest of the drawings. Its white space and black ink are nicely balanced and the design is pleasingly symmetrical. The figure is that of a Black female. She could be an angel or a girl dressed in a robe—perhaps a choir gown. Her black, curly hair is easily identified. Her eyes are open and intelligent. Her slightly drooping mouth introduces a touch of sadness or concern, even perhaps a hint of anger.

The illustration opening Book One changes dramatically. It presents a visual puzzle or a Rorschach inkblot. It is done predominately in black ink. Viewed casually, it appears to be a wide-eyed figure with angel wings and a sad mouth. Its gender is not immediately clear. However, examined more carefully, the illustration changes to a skull with prominent teeth and the angel wings seem more like flames. (The text will later influence us to think of this illustration as a female with either a necklace or scars around her neck. Also, the mouth that shifts from sad lips to skull's teeth reminds us of Paul D's plaintive refrain about Sethe's newspaper sketch: the mouth's not right.)

The illustration for Book Two is unique among the four. It is rendered in much less black ink, with white space predominating. It retains the face motif but diminishes its relative importance. The total sketch could be a totem carving or part of the decoration of a lintel, for instance. Within this sketch the face is more clearly identifiable as a mask, probably an Africa folk mask. Compared to the illustration of Book One, it is neither angelic nor morbid. The eyes remain startled and the mouth remains prominent. The surrounding decorations are floral or vegetable, with tendrils that enhance the illustration but simultaneously threaten to engulf the unprotected face.

The illustration for Book Three returns to the stark blackness of the illustration fronting Book One. Now, however, the face is distinctly that of a death mask or skull. The teeth are prominent and the eye sockets are pronounced. The eyeballs of Book One are missing. No angelic qualities are discernible, except in the black wings. Ironically, however, the figure is composed. The fear is gone from the eyes and the sad mouth has disappeared. The skull's upper and lower teeth are firmly together, but not clenched.

The ambiguity of the illustrations parallels the textual polarities: angelic, satanic; life, death; violent, content; white, black. While interesting, this parallelism is not the most important function of the illustrations. The progression (or recession) of the illustrations is more informative. Quite simply, they move toward the repose of death. Just as the three books progressively shorten, moving toward nothingness, and just as memory of Beloved fades to gray, so too do the illustrations diminish on the continuum of life and death. The steady degradation and disorganization of a social system is present in *Beloved*. Beloved is forgotten; slavery is but a memory; even the powerful reminders of *Beloved* commence to fade as soon as the covers are closed. A wide-eyed, curious girl (figure one) becomes a death skull (figure four). Taken altogether, the illustrations suggest entropy. They perhaps even suggest that the narrative is implying suicide as a viable last freedom from life's misery.

In face of such universal entropy and private dread, what is the individual to do? Morrison's answer, like her mentor Faulkner's is "endure." Perplexed and near despair from having realized that slavery of one kind or another will always hold him, Paul D pleads to Stamp Paid: "Tell me this one thing. How much is a nigger supposed to take? Tell me. How much?" Speaking as the voice of venerability and reason, Stamp Paid replies simply: "All he can, . . . All he can" (235). That simple verity encourages Paul D to take one more step in his long journey, this one leading back to Sethe. "We need some kind of tomorrow" (273) he tells her. Stuporous, she does not know what

Paul D wants or means; but she is amazed at the possible salvation suggested by the "blessed" man. We as readers are less amazed, but we are struck by the human will to endure against odds that often make death seem the only emancipation.

Marjorie Perloff gave title to a note on *Beloved* with this question: Great American Novel? Such questions are made moot by the asking, but the only reasonable answer is "yes it is and no it isn't." *Beloved* is a great American novel, but is isn't THE great American novel. The Great American Novel is as mythical a the ghost that comes to haunt 124 Bluestone Road. Such a novel has not been written and will never be written, because America is still in the making. It is redefined, if only infinitesimally, by every novel written abut it. *Beloved* adds more than most books to that redefining. It examines the one component of American history that makes it unique and that molds the American character: slavery. Morrison's masterpiece conducts the examination with unusual intellect, emotion, and artistry. In that sense, *Beloved* most certainly is an eminent guide to where we have been, where we are, and where we will be as a nation. While not as dark in its prognosis as *Blood Meridian*, it does not encourage dreams of a paradise regained. It teaches that Americans are a violent race and that any modicum of personal tranquillity comes only from blind luck and a constitution able to endure and inflict violence in extremis. By conveying that message as perhaps no other novel has done, *Beloved* is a great American novel.

# Hubert Selby, Jr.'s *Last Exit to Brooklyn*
## and
## Bret Easton Ellis's *American Psycho*

It is rather easy, as many critics and readers have done, to dismiss Hubert Selby, Jr.'s *Last Exit to Brooklyn* (1964) and Bret Easton Ellis's *American Psycho* (1991) as trash, filth, pornography, or whatever other term finds favor with readers in the throes of moral and intellectual absolutism. *Time* magazine, in its October 30, 1964 review of *Last Exit*, implied Selby was a borderline psychotic and called the book scatological trash (199). Roger Rosenblatt, in a December 1990 review of *American Psycho* in the *New York Times Book Review* insisted not only that it be condemned but urged that it not be published at all. John Irving calls Rosenblatt's essay "a piece of writing prissy enough to please Jesse Helms" (25). Admittedly, both novels assault conventional sensibilities and neither is a work of art in the same sense, say, that *Light in August* is art. Neither gives us a character comparable to Joe Christmas, whose violence may offend but whose complexity creates new moral questions each time we recall his tormented life. *Last Exit* and *Psycho* expand our understanding of neither humanity in general nor of the individual characters they present to us. Other than reiterating that the human animal is an egocentric brute, Selby and Ellis say little that increases our awareness of self or our empathy for our fellow creatures. At best their novels are socio-psychological tracts that are interesting on various levels but compelling on none. Yet, they offer a fitting closure to a study of the American novel of violence.

The two novels are very similar. Both are set in New York City and deal with characters who are aberrations from the standard American middle-class. These characters are drug users and alcoholics who spend much time in bars and eating establishments. No vestige of any traditional cultural institutions is visible in their lives. They do not serve in the military, go to church, or concern themselves with political issues. They show no benevolence as parents, friends, or colleagues. Most do not work at productive occupations. Selfishness, arrogance, vanity, and idleness mark their personalities. They look for someone to hate and for excuses to be cruel. Whether they are homosexual or heterosexual is a mute point, for ultimately all expressions of their sexuality are vicious and deadly. Though for different reasons, both sets of characters end up in the same nihilistic state. Moral anarchy is complete; political anarchy seems near at hand. They depict the absolute worst consequence of a post-industrial urban life made grotesque by the new technology. When we finish reading the novels, we are left with the same degree of puzzlement. How did these creatures get so morally vacuous, cruel, destitute? To what degree is society to blame? Is their condition predestined by genetics? How much, if at all, are we meant to care about what James B. Lane terms "the offal of post-industrial society" (302)?

A notable difference between the two narratives—more superficial than essential—is that the people of *Last Exit* have never been "up" the scale of civilization with access to art, leisure, technology, and the endless supply of nonessential goods on which Capitalism thrives. The "last exiters" are the raw material of humanity. Only the thinnest veneer of machine age culture separates them from the Neanderthals. On the other hand, the idlers of *American Psycho* have been as high as society's ladder reaches. They epitomize Thorstein Veblen's theory of the leisure class, made grotesque by postmodernist excess. They are glutted by possessions—the most expensive automobiles, clothes, wines, furniture, and fine art. (We recall Patrick Bateman's upside down 6x4 foot naked woman, painted by David Onica.) They need not work except to have reason to hang out together, drink their cappuccino, J&B, and imported waters, and purchase the endless supply of gadgets and gizmos produced by workers such as those we meet in *Last Exit*. In the final accounting, however, Bateman and his kind are no further away from the Neanderthal's world than Vinnie, Abe, Tralala and the rest of the low-brows we see in Selby's novel. It would be comforting to believe that circumstance and economics make these people the way they are; but nothing in *Last Exit* and

*American Psycho* suggests that. The best and the worst examples of human beings that American capitalist economics can produce end up at the same place. No difference is discernible between the animalistic lust that leads to Tralala's gang bang and the vicious sex and torture that Patrick Bateman enjoys. He and his running mates are compelled by the same selfishness that makes Abe Washington let his kids suffer from malnutrition so that he may drive his Cadillac and "look good."

More than all these traits, the attribute that the two novels share above all others is violence. We would be hard pressed to determine which author has devoted himself most completely to depicting violence in its most extreme manifestations, with the most gut-wrenching rhetoric.

Ellis delays the outbreak of his heinous violence for approximately 130 pages. Selby, however, lets us know immediately and emphatically that the locus and force of his novel are violence and sex, which are indistinguishable. Violence in *Last Exit to Brooklyn* is not focused on one central scene but is endemic to the milieu that Selby creates. As the novel opens, the regular loafers at the rundown diner called the Greeks attack a drunk Southern soldier:

> They formed a circle and kicked. He tried to roll over on his stomach and cover his face with his arms, but as he got to his side he was kicked in the groin and stomped on the ear and he screamed, cried, started pleading then just cried as a foot cracked his mouth, Ya fuckin cottonpickin punk, and a hard kick in the ribs turned him slightly and he tried to raise himself on one knee and someone took a short step forward and kicked him in the solarpleuxus and he fell on his side, his knees up, arms folded across his abdomen, gasping for air and the blood in his mouth gurgled as he tried to scream, rolled down his chin then spumed forth as he vomited violently and someone stomped his face into the pool of vomit and the blood whirled slight in arcs and few bubbles gurgled in the puke as he panted and gasped and their shoes thudded into the shiteatinbastards kidneys and ribs and he groaned and his head rolled in the puke breaking the arching patterns of blood and he gasped as a kick broke his nose. . . .     (17)

The whore Tralala later joins the loafers in brutalizing another soldier whose wallet she has stolen:

> Before they left Tralala stomped on his face until both eyes were bleeding and his nose was split and broken

> then kicked him a few times in the balls.  Ya rotten
> scumbag, then they left and walked slowly to 4th av-
> enue and took a subway to manhattan.         (97)

Tralala herself is subsequently brutalized in a gang-bang that she initiates and that takes two and one-half pages to describe.  The scene's closing passages are representative:

> . . . finally a sort of line was formed everyone yelling
> and laughing and someone yelled to the guys on the end
> to go get some beer and they left and came back with
> cans or beer which were passed around the daisychain
> . . . and more came 40 maybe 50 and they screwed her
> and went back on line and had a beer and yelled and
> laughed and someone yelled that the car stunk of cunt
> so Tralala and the seat were taken out of the car and
> laid in the lot and she lay there naked on the seat and
> their shadows hid her pimples and scabs and she drank
> flipping her tits with the other hand . . . and Tralala
> cursed and spit out a piece of tooth and someone shoved
> it again and they laughed and yelled and the next one
> mounted her and her lips were split this time and the
> blood trickled to her chin . . . and the kids who were
> watching and waiting to take a turn took out their dis-
> appointment on Tralala and tore her clothes to small
> scraps put out a few cigarettes on her nipples pissed on
> her jerked off on her jammed a broomstick up her snatch
> and bored they left her lying amongst the broken bot-
> tles rusty cans and rubble of the lot and Jack and Fred
> and Ruthy and Annie stumbled into a cab still laughing
> and they leaned toward the window as they passed the
> lot and got a good look at Tralala lying naked covered
> with blood urine and semen and a small blot forming on
> the seat between her legs as blood seeped from her
> crotch. . . .                              (112-114)

Though Selby's violence may appear as random examples of postmodern unmotivated malignancy, there is design to the violent episodes.  The assailants in each of these violent scenarios are depicted in groups.  They are the pack against the lone victim.  This phenomenon dispels any possibility that human violence is a deviation from the norm or an exceptional trait limited to certain individuals.  The pack mentality proves that violence is the basic instinct of the human animal and that other members of the species are most often the victims of that collective viciousness.  Pack mentality supersedes any regard for individual members of the species.  This truth is demonstrated later when the same loafers from the Greeks turn against Harry Black.

Though Harry has participated in assaults with them and has long been one of their drinking and whoring companions, they do not hesitate to beat him in a prolonged attack that leaves him almost dead. They then celebrate with the same gleeful satisfaction they have shown after previous such attacks.

Tralala's willing participation in her own violation and death offers a different perspective on the group violence. Throughout the novel, other women accept and enjoy violence expressed as sexual passion. In some cases, the women actively encourage such sexual assault. In this respect, Tralala is typical. The difference is that her participation is extreme and the entire sexual process has been made grotesque by a society from which all traditional values and patterns of behavior have been extirpated. Aside from establishing that she finds her own identity and worth in her sexuality, Tralala's participation suggests that her instincts orient her to men who are violent and aggressive. One of the reasons for her attack on the soldier who seeks return of his identification card is that he asks or begs, rather than simply charging in and taking what is rightfully his. Neo-Darwinian sociologist especially argue that the underlying purpose of violence is to gain access to females, to mate, and to therefore deposit one's genes in the species. Selby would not argue with this premise, as the harsh naturalism of his text indicates. Thus, when Tralala willingly allows the violent gang to assault her in the guise of sexual pleasure, she is, ironically, following right instincts if not right reason.

Sex and violence are indeed two sides of the same drive to copulate with the most violent, and thus most able mate. The horrible outcome of Tralala's instinctive drive, as Selby sees it, results because modern industrial society and its resultant environments have distorted the form and purpose of otherwise normal behavior. In this specific instance, the culprit is alcohol, which alters the senses of both victim and assailants. Selby uses alcohol as a symbol of the larger, more encompassing evils of the post-industrial world. This evil is suggested by the fact that many of Tralala's assailants are soldiers from the nearby army base—soldiers who have recently fought in World War II and who, we assume, are prepared to fight again to keep the world safe for capitalistic democracy and the kind of behavior demonstrated by the gang-bang. Tralala's fate, Gilbert Sorrentino says, "seems to me so utterly sad, so crushing, that it is unutterable. She doesn't do this as a 'gig,' or for money, she does it (God help us) out of a feeling of pride in herself, her worth and 'know-how' as a whore. In her mind, she had not defiled her body, nor do those who take advantage of her offer, defile theirs" (342). Sorrentino is correct. To Tralala's way of thinking, she is following right instincts and cannot, therefore, be going against nature. Ultimately, it is not nature that betrays her, but a society that has distorted nature's original balance between violence and procreation. If indeed Selby's novel is "a step out of the Dark Ages in the history of American realism" (305), as James B. Lane contends, the violence contained in scenes such as  Tralala's is what makes it so.

Ellis's violence erupts more unexpectedly than Selby's, exploding from a milieu where, because of our economic stereotyping, we do not expect it to appear.  For approximately 130 pages, Ellis delineates this boring, non-violent milieu of the idle rich crowd.  It is a story of 1980s yuppies with Wall Street jobs and the neurotic, vacuous women they run with.  Patrick Bateman, the "psycho," is the first-person narrator.  A graduate of Harvard and Harvard business, Bateman is from a wealthy family and does not have to "work." He does, however, hold some kind of job at a place called Pierce & Pierce or P&P. He usually has a Walkman stuck in his ear, and seems obsessed with *Les Misérables*, a  TV talk show called *The Patty Winters Show*, and movie videos.  He devotes entire chapters to reviews of record albums, in a chatty, *Entertainment Weekly*-ese.  He is also obsessed with clothing and possessions, giving explicit details of what people wear, how apartments are furnished, and how much things cost. Internally void, Patrick is acutely aware of his external surroundings.  His lengthy prologue to violence details characters and a setting so superficial and irrelevant to our lives that we are bored to numbness reading about them.  If we have read reviews on *American Psycho* or heard tales of its lurid publishing history, we begin to wonder what possibly could be offensive about the text other than its absolute, total monotony. Once he has lured us into his malaise, however, Ellis detonates his first narrative bomb.

Walking on Twelfth Street near an antique store, Bateman comes across a Negro bum and his small mongrel dog. He first befriends the man, in what seems to be just another expression of his insincere, superficial social conscience.  Suddenly, however, Bateman erupts:

> He starts nodding helplessly and I pull out a long, thin
> knife with a serrated edge and, being very careful not to
> kill him, push maybe half an inch of the blade into his
> right eye, flicking the handle up, instantly popping
> the retina. . . . I grasp his head with one hand and
> push it back and then with my thumb and forefinger
> hold the other eye open and bring the knife up and push
> the tip of it into the socket, first breaking its protective
> film so the socket fills with blood, then slitting the
> eyeball open sideways, and he finally starts screaming
> once I slit his nose in two, lightly spraying me and the
> dog with blood, Gizmo blinking to get the blood out of
> his eyes. I quickly wipe the blade clean across the
> bum's face, breaking open the muscle above his cheek.
> Still kneeling, I throw a quarter in his face, which is
> slick and shiny with blood, both sockets hollowed out
> and filled with gore, what's left of his eyes literally
> oozing over his screaming lips in thick, webby strands.
> Calmly, I whisper, 'There's a quarter. Go buy some
> *gum*, you crazy fucking *nigger*.' Then I turn to the bark-
> ing dog and which I get up, stomp on its front legs while
> it's crouched down ready to jump at me, its fangs bared,
> immediately shattering the bones in both its legs, and
> it falls on its side squealing in pain, front paws sticking
> up in the air at an obscene, satisfying angle. I can't
> help but start laughing and I linger at the scene,
> amused by this tableau. When I spot an approaching
> taxi, I slowly walk away.                    (131-132)

Now we are rejuvenated. We are suddenly interested in Ellis's
text and in the pathetic life of Patrick Bateman. Once Ellis taps
into our own violent instincts, he plays them as Holden
Caulfield imagines playing women like a sexual violin. After
this scene with the hapless bum, Ellis's violence is unrelieved.

Most of his scenes of rapes, tortures, and murders are too
long to quote in their entirety, but this edited version of his attack on Bethany, a girl friend from Harvard, gives some indication of the explicit rhetoric and violence that fill the rest of
*American Psycho*. Other scenes are just as explicit and even
more vicious:

> I drag her back into the living room, lying her across
> the floor over a white Voilacutro cotton sheet, and then
> I stretch her arms out, placing her hands flat on thick
> wooden boards, palms up, and nail three fingers on each
> hand, at random, to the wood by their tips [with the
> nail gun]. . . . I keep shooting nails into her hands until
> they're both covered—nails bunched together, twisted
> over each other in places, making it impossible for her

> to try and sit up. . . . Finally, in agony . . she starts
> pleading, or at least tries to, the adrenaline momentar-
> ily overpowering the pain. 'Patrick oh god stop it
> please oh god stop hurting me. . . .' The fingers I
> haven't nailed I try to bite off, almost succeeding on her
> left thumb which I manage to chew all the flesh off of,
> leaving the bone exposed, and then I Mace her. . . . I oc-
> casionally stab at her breasts, accidentally (not really)
> slicing off one of her nipples through the bra. . . . I take
> advantage of her helpless state and, removing my
> gloves, force her mouth open and with the scissors cut
> out her tongue, which I pull easily from her mouth and
> hold in the palm of my hand, warm and still bleeding,
> seeming so much smaller than in her mouth, and I throw
> it against the wall, where it sticks for a moment,
> leaving a stain, before falling to the floor with tiny
> wet     slap. . . . The I fuck her in the mouth, and after
> I've ejaculated and pulled out, I Mace her some more.
>
> (245-246)

To analyze such scenes would in itself be a bit psychotic, though we can glimpse in them the manifestation of desires that Bateman has up to now repressed. He is sick of hearing Bethany talk, for instance. Thus, he cuts out her tongue. Yet such expli- cation hardly explains passages that are themselves so purely vi- olent and so primordial that they defy intellectual discourse. If Ellis has put his fiction beyond art, he certainly has put it beyond textual criticism.

That failure of textual criticism has been proven by ana- lysts who seem to have overlooked (either willfully or other- wise) one extremely important factor in Ellis's narrative. Ellis gives a subtle but hardly subliminal admonition against such oversight. We need first to recognize, as Laura E. Tanner has done, that Bateman's thinking is greatly influenced by "stereo- types appropriated from bad movies and melodramatic novels" (104). More precisely, Ellis borrows from Alfred Hitchcock's movie *Psycho*. The horrific milieu and the protagonist's name come from that classic horror film. A novelist names a protago- nist Patrick Bateman and uses the word "psycho" in a title only if he expects the audience to make associations with Norman Bates, the psychotic hero of Hitchcock's masterpiece. We need next to recognize the importance of the pun contained in the re- iterated segment of the names Bates and Bateman. "Bates" warns us that Ellis is baiting us throughout the narrative. Bate- man himself likes to "bait" people—with his money, with his clever repartee, with his fancy apartment. He loves to set other characters up for rebuttals ranging from sarcastic replies to ax attacks. The outrageous example of this "bait" mentality is the episode in which he imagines using a trapped rat and cheese to torture one of his female victims (327). The "bate" pun and the baiting motif, therefore, should warn us that Ellis intends that we see something more than clever word play and disgusting sexual images in his narrative.

Tanner, one of the few critics with temerity enough to approach *American Psycho* without hysteria pro or con, offers some intelligent analysis of a novel that she rightfully sees as an extension of the "capitalist mentality" (96). Tanner overlooks, however, the significance of the trap that Ellis has baited. Nowhere in her discussion does she acknowledge that the horrendous crimes Bateman details to us might never happen in reality. They may be in his head, his imagination. The imaginary status of the murders seems obvious in the narrative. Bateman talks of carrying bodies around in taxicabs, stashing them in a unit he owns in Hell's Kitchen, and other details that are simply incredible. He physically, practically could not accomplish such deeds. The undeniable evidence that he is relating imaginary events, however, is that victims he has just killed and dissected, such as Luis Carruthers, later appear alive and well (292). Moreover, when Bateman "confesses" to murder at the New Club, Harold Canes rejects the bait. He knows the horrible story is nothing more than a joke (386f). If we still miss the point that Bateman is imagining his horrors, then he himself tells us in what is probably the most revealing passage in his painful tale. Readers of Ralph Ellison's *Invisible Man* will recognize Ellis's source and thus Bateman's psychological dilemma:

> . . . there is an idea of a Patrick Bateman, some kind of abstraction, but there is no real me, only an entity, something illusory, and though I can hide my cold gaze and you can shake my hand and feel flesh gripping yours and maybe you can even sense our lifestyles are probably comparable: *I simply am not there.* It is hard for me to make sense on any given level. Myself is fabricated, an aberration. I am a noncontingent human being.          (376-377)

Bateman then closes his narrative by confessing that the automated teller machine has started speaking to him, saying "Cause a Terrible Scene at Sotheby's" or "Kill the President," and that a park bench followed him for six blocks (395). If we are to believe that Bateman is rational and that his reports of rape and torture are real, then we must also believe that he is reporting fact here. As the novel ends, however, Bateman is back with the same in(s)ane friends with whom he begins his narrative, pursuing the same superficial life that first caused him to start fantasizing. He and his friends are the consummate product of the mass market mentality, the ideal consumers dreamed of by the *New Yorker* and *Gentleman's Quarterly*. Tanner states the case well when she says that "*American Psycho* pushes the capitalist mentality to an extreme that renders visible the machinery at work beneath its apparent magic" (96). The sign at Harry's, warning that THIS IS NOT AN EXIT (399) lets us know that Bateman will not escape this life of the Absolute Surface and that his deadly fantasies will continue.

When Tanner argues that Bateman is a "monster" (112), however, she blurs the point of Ellis's satire of this 1980s "non-contingent human being" and his sad commentary on fin de siè-cle American culture that deadens and incarcerates the individual. Bateman is no monster at all. He is quite typical of a society obsessed with "stuff" and media status. Who in America, like Bateman, does not dream of appearing on a popular daytime talk show such as *The Patty Winters Show*? His fascination with serial killers proves only that he shares interests with millions of other celebrity-obsessed Americans and TV executives who grant instant fame to the Ted Bundys and Jeffrey Dahmers of the world. In other words, Bateman is disturbingly normal, if "normal" is defined by the democratic process of the majority rule. As Cynthia Ozick says:

> Even Jeffrey Dahmer, the cannibal sadist who kept boys' body parts in his kitchen refrigerator, is not so very anomalous in the context of what can happen in ordinary neighborhoods: a little girl imprisoned in an underground cage; children tormented, starved, beaten to death; newborns bludgeoned; battered women, slain wives, mutilated husbands. Domesticity gone awry.
>
> (114)

Especially because his sadism is imagined, we can convict Bateman of nothing that ordinary, everyday, good citizens are not guilty of. Bateman, like all of us, is free to imagine any horror that he chooses. Such imagining is one of the last sanctuaries against a society that has become impersonal and brutal beyond reason—but not beyond our wildest imagining. The imagining of such horrors, in fact, is what Ellis himself does when he creates the horrors that he transfers from his own imagination to Bateman's. Ellis is a postmodernist Edgar Bergen to Bateman's Charlie McCarthy. Therefore, if Bateman is a monster, Ellis is a worse monster still. If Ellis's imaginary crimes are punishable, then all art is monstrous. Creation itself becomes an abomination.

In passing, we should note that Ellis contrasts form and function to heighten the intensity of the violence he portrays. *American Psycho* is a traditional novel in form and narrative management. It has a beginning, a middle, and an end, is chronologically ordered, and makes use of no grammatical or syntactical devices that are not readily identifiable. That is, its setting is realistic, its time frame standard, its dialogue straightforward, and its characters ordinary humans. Compared to a novel such as William Burrough's *Naked Lunch*, which follows no rules or conventions in construction or content, *American Psycho* is a "well made" novel. That, of course, is part of its horror. We are led into the trap of a conventional narrative that unleashes very unconventional descriptions of violence. The same point could be made of Cormac McCarthy's *Blood Meridian*, but even McCarthy's narrative bloodbath does not rival Ellis's sadistic viciousness for shock and disgust.

There remains one element of both *Last Exit* and *American Psycho* that needs to be addressed: their eroticism. No other fiction in American literature erases the distinctions between violence and eroticism so completely. Consequently, no other novels have drawn such ire and fire. Much of the reason behind such violent reaction is that we refuse to admit an erotic response to the sadism that Selby and Ellis depict. To deny such a reaction, however, is critically and morally disingenuous. Attempts at outright censorship such as the one promulgated by Roger Rosenblatt are flagrant and outrageous. We can disparage them and feel, rightfully so, a satisfactory intellectual righteousness. However, even to discuss the novels in terms of "capitalism," "sociological statements," or "art" implies a form of self-censorship. Adopting such contexts for discussion guarantees a parallax view of the crucial issues that Selby and Ellis force before us. Such an oblique approach to the texts is dangerous because it suggests a refusal to acknowledge that violence as much as sex compels us.

Such neo-Calvinistic prudery diminishes if not negates the very arguments we might raise in defense of the two novels' right to exist as published texts. John Irving, refuting Rosenblatt's "prissy" review of *American Psycho*, returns to *The Scarlet Letter* and Hawthorne's admonition against censorship both literal and psychological. Appropriately, Irving entitles his attack on censorship and repression "Pornography and the New Puritans." Censoring our own emotional reactions to literature, it seems, is the deadliest form of the Puritan repression that Hawthorne warned against. Granted, such sadism as Selby and Ellis depict is hardly pleasant. Having to face the human potential for malevolence seldom is. The fine print at the bottom of our biological contract with nature is that sexuality is violent and violence is sexual. Taken in balance, they form the instinct that keeps the species current. The reader's responsibility, both Selby and Ellis imply, is to realize the degrees of separation that distinguish sexuality from brutality. In that narrow zone of separation lie culture and civilization.

　　*Last Exit* and *American Psycho* illustrate what happens when that separation is nonexistent. Both manage to move out from behind the "art of fiction" that historically has been the novel's sanctuary. Flushed from cover, they reveal the rawest, most honest appraisal of society's animalistic heritage. In depicting this brutal lineage, as Gilbert Sorrentino admits, Selby writes with no style and no elegance (337). More to the point, Norman Mailer quickly recognized that despite his success otherwise in *American Psycho*, Ellis "does not translate his materials into art" (159). Neither novel is "art" in the traditional sense, because one of the major lessons both authors seek to teach is that "art" is a curtain behind which we hide our violent humanness. We recall that the human animal is the only animal that kills, maims, and otherwise causes pain to his fellow humans on a regular, massive basis, for no especial reason and for no overt gain. These two novels, more so than any other in this study, validate the truth of this gratuitous human violence beyond any reasonable doubt. If the previous novels have not convinced us that Homo Sapiens is an animal, and a very violent one at that, then *Last Exit to Brooklyn* and *American Psycho* certainly will.

　　Both Selby and Ellis make sure that no artifice stands between us as readers and the horrific truth they wish to explore. *Last Exit* and *Psycho* are indeed not art; and that is precisely why they offer the ideal closure to a study of the American novel of violence. At the beginning of the twentieth century Norris showed us, in the words of Jerome Loving, that the human battle was "generally the interior struggle in which the 'brute' of prehistoric man fought with his better, socialized self" (x). Through their own conscious artlessness Selby and Ellis show that art, the historic last line of defense between culture and the brute, has been eradicated.   The socialized self has lost the struggle.

# Summary Conclusions

This discussion began with William Faulkner's *Light in August* because it initiates the modern novel of violence in America and is the artistic catalyst for many subsequent novels. The dilemma that marks postmodernist fiction is born in the freedom-control paradox that Faulkner instigates when he sets individuals such as Joe Christmas and Joanna Burden loose to cope with their overwhelming animal instincts. Moreover, though Frank Norris vaguely hints at the connection, Faulkner is almost strident in advocating that sex and violence are inextricably joined. While writers such as Sherwood Anderson recognized the Freudian significance of that connection before him, Faulkner was the first to analyze in fiction the two fundamental drives and thus to show how deadly they become when they act as mutual catalytic agents upon each other in the cauldron of human motivations.

James M. Cain's *The Postman Always Rings Twice* (1934) borrows from various sources, including Faulkner, Hemingway, Raymond Chandler, and newspaper headlines. It is composite fiction that continues and extends the eroto-violence that Faulkner introduced. In the process of writing such a sadistic thriller, Cain fabricated a sardonic, unencumbered narrative style that proved more influential than the story it conveyed. That desolate style, which serves as the matrix for graphic eroto-violence, distinguishes *The Postman Always Rings Twice* and explains the influence that it had on subsequent novels of violence.

Katherine Anne Porter shares with Cain a distinct, identifying style and the narrative technique of injecting sudden violence into mundane lives. Porter's style is used almost as a character in her fiction, creating a conflict between content and narrative form that is dramatically ironic. The gem-perfect style of *Noon Wine*, superimposed over instinctual violence, creates a subliminal tension that vibrates at the least stimulus. The style suggests the presence of a controlling narrative intelligence that has no equal in the lives of the people it depicts. Moreover, Porter does not permit that extraneous intelligence to transfer osmotically to the dramatis personae of her tale. She, more so than Faulkner, suggests in *Noon Wine* that her characters are damned by a Southern environment that stimulates the violent instinct to action. Rural and isolated, the Southerner is cut off from those cosmopolitan influences that the abiding narrative intelligence seems to possess. Thus separate, the natural violence that is in fact shared by all humans becomes distorted because the characters lack alternative outlets and the acuity to deal with violent stimuli when they occur. Such people are nevertheless subject to the pressures of laws, both social and legal, that proscribe violence but offer no guidance toward amelioration or empathy for transgressors who give in to their violent instincts. Such an attitude toward individual violence seems to imply a pro-urban bias for Porter, though little else in her fiction evinces that bias. Some of the urbane, or at last comparatively sophisticated characters of her other fiction (*Ship of Fools* for instance) do not prove that the violent instinct is tempered in the cosmopolite. More probably, Porter would argue that aestheticism, not shallow cosmopolitanism, is the ultimate antidote to violence and brutish behavior generally.

Hemingway develops an attitude toward violence that seems to arise out of the same conflict between intelligence and the violent instinct that we see in Porter. Like Faulkner, however, Hemingway recognizes the positive elements of violence. Both writers see aggression and defensive violence as being preferable to mindless passivity. However, both also realize that violence has to be moderated by intelligence less it destroy the individual and potentially the species. They imply that intelligence leads to the moral codes needed to offset the destructiveness of violence but that intelligence and violence are constantly at odds. Were such intelligence and the resulting ethics common among individuals, then human society could avoid the devastation of interspecific wars. However, more individuals lack than possess the difficult balance between intelligence and ethics. Consequently, the future of Homo Sapiens is not especially promising.

Neither Hemingway nor Faulkner specifies what this intelligence is or its sources. On one level they seem to attribute it to the randomness of heredity and genetics. As some individuals are taller than others, so some are more intelligent and thus more prone to what society defines as ethical behavior. On another level Hemingway and Faulkner imply that this socially preferred behavior develops from such conventional sources as reading, discourse shared with other "intelligent" people, and introspection. Neither is interested in arguing exactly what separates an Adolph Hitler from a Manhatma Ghandi, though ultimately they do suggest that some people are simply more moral and less violent than others. It would be overstating the case to say that this rather finely tuned attitude toward human violence is Hemingway and Faulkner's legacy to other authors of novels of violence. Nonetheless, in one form or another, as we see in Porter, Vonnegut, and others, it is an attitude shared by many of these authors.

With *In Cold Blood* Truman Capote takes fiction down an intellectual path less traveled. He removes the veil of fictionality from the violent personality. That is, while his style and narrative control are traditional fiction, his personae are "real." Instead of trying to make fiction imitate life, Capote forces life to imitate fiction. It is a clever ploy that prevents the reader from rejecting either the fantasy or the reality of violence. When reading such super-vicious novels as Ellis's *American Psycho*, some readers avoid the gruesome violence by reminding themselves that the blood, guts, and gurgling screams are fiction— that is, lies. The illusion keeps the reader's sanity and sense of superior distancing intact. Though this violence does not rival *American Psycho* or several other novels of violence for sheer intestine-churning graphics, Capote nonetheless closes the psychic escape routes to the reader. By all the standards we use to judge "reality," the events related in *In Cold Blood* are real. Moreover, they are so convincing that we know that they speak for us either as perpetrator or victim. Such clever merging of fact and fiction produces a "novel" of violence unlike any other.

The chronological hiatus between *For Whom the Bell Tolls* and *In Cold Blood* is marked by the publication of many potential novels of violence. Almost exclusively these were the war novels of World War II that Frederick J. Hoffman analyzes in *The Mortal No: Death and the Modern Imagination*, which I have already mentioned. These war novels were numerous, and many of them are good examples of the genre. Though some of these novels contain incidental scenes of violence (William Hoffman's *The Trumpet Unblown* comes quickly to mind), they do not have graphic violence as their central focus and do not display the rhetoric of violence. We might expect war novels to be more gut-wrenching and overtly violent than novels that depict our domestic routines, but that is not the case. None of these novels rivals, say, Hubert Selby, Jr.'s depiction of domestic violence in *Last Exit to Brooklyn* for absolute viciousness and aggression.

What we might conclude from such nonviolent "war" novels is problematic, though a likely explanation is that the "real" war itself was so traumatic that the authors (all veterans) realized the limitations of discourse and language when they tried to fictionalize it. For eons before human beings were linguists, they were mute blood-thirsty warriors; and the newly developed art of language simply cannot articulate the primordial mysteries. This peculiar failure of language to connect with primitive instinct is what Kurt Vonnegut (also a veteran) tries to clarify in *Slaughterhouse-Five*, a war novel that acknowledges from the beginning that it will clarify nothing about World War II, Vietnam, or any other war. This linguistic failure is what Vonnegut wants to address. The ersatz science fiction that overlays his failed narrative creates the absurdist, postmodernist mishmash that proves his point that language malfunctions on every possible level—whether the words be lullabies, love talk, or presidential commands to obliterate cities. Vonnegut writes with violence at the core of his design to show that no language can depict the reality of violence. The resulting narrative is an interesting artistic sleight of hand that takes the "war novel" into new generic territory.

While Vonnegut adapts the venerable war novel genre to the new era, Toni Morrison adapts the equally venerable ghost story to the one horrendous and protracted act of violence that distinguishes the United States from ever other modern, post-industrial state: slavery. *Beloved* is also the only novel of violence in which a female persona operates as central character of violence. *Beloved* is distinguished by this act of violence that shatters all our stereotypes about maternal "love" and the female protective instinct. To have a mother kill her child as an act of love forces us into difficult reappraisals of the conventional wisdom pertaining to violence, love, motherhood, family and American history, among other things. Morrison is an admitted disciple of William Faulkner, but she moves the issues of maternal love, violence, and slavery onto a place where Faulkner obviously could not travel. When she combines ghost story, slave narrative, and postmodern attitudes toward violence, Morrison creates a singular example of the American novel of violence.

Cormac McCarthy takes yet another venerable genre and regenerates it with postmodernist violence. The "Western" (and American fiction generally) will not be the same again after *Blood Meridian*. The western, as developed by Owen Wister, the dime novels, and countless pulp novels, has traditionally been violent; but the typical "Western" violence is formulaic, clean, and lacking in graphic power. That is, we hear the shot, a man is dead, somebody is lynched, we hear another shot or two, and then domestic order is restored. The blood, gore, screams, moans, and other graphic horrors of human-to-human violence are absent from the conventional Western. The audience expects such pristine violence. The genre would not have reached the popularity and influence it enjoys were it not defined by such implied violence.

McCarthy takes this traditional genre with its conventions and affixes to it the graphic blood-spilling, gut-splattering viciousness that had been purged from it at birth. He questions how a culture could consciously distort historic reality to elevate frontier adventurers and cowboys to mythic status. By removing the violence from the Western experience, historians and fictionists ironically denied the humanizing quality of the experience. By denying violence, we deny our humanity, both as individuals and as a culture. That denial, McCarthy warns, robs us of soul and purpose. He makes that statement in a prose style that ironically echoes Irving, Melville, Hawthorne, Faulkner, and other shapers of American fiction but that is nonetheless uniquely his own. Given the quality of his prose, the scope of his subject, and the uncompromising honesty of his violence, McCarthy creates what is arguably the purest example of the novel of violence yet written by an American.

What distinguishes *Billy Bathgate, Last Exit to Brooklyn* and *American Psycho* as American novels of violence is that, like McCarthy, each author grafts overt, graphic violence to a defining element of American culture so that he might comment on the postmodernist American individual. Doctorow takes the gangsterism of the 1920s and 1930s, which has become a cliché in American fiction—as seen in works as diverse as *The Great Gatsby* and the television series "The Untouchables." He re-energizes the cliché and the stereotypes it suggests by grafting to it a rhetoric of violence and explicit scenes of violence that were either forbidden to or simply missing from the earlier, defining gangster texts. By so doing, he elevates the type into a significant statement about American culture, not so much in the Depression but more so during the 1980s and 1990s.

Hubert Selby, Jr. has at the heart of *Last Exit to Brooklyn* the social and economic disparity of American capitalism immediately after World War II. That heart, however, beats only faintly, since Selby is no neo-Marxist, post-Depression propagandist. He simply takes as his starting point the stark reality of the economically depressed, intellectually under endowed, and semi-barbaric lower classes of a post-industrial urbane environment. He is not especially upset that such a class exists in the city that epitomizes the world's greatest economic and military power. The New York lower classes simply fascinate him as a natural phenomenon. In the tradition of Stephen Crane, but not of Upton Sinclair, Selby is less concerned with social reform than he is enthralled by the utter animalistic viciousness that characterizes such citizens. Crane, too, touched on the violence that characterized the mass of humanity that had come to town and sold their souls to the machine. Selby, however, makes that violence the center of his concern. His narrative is less a traditional novel and more a miscellany of disjointed, terrible vignettes connected not by human compassion but by violence, misery, and the accident of shared urban geography. Freed from most of the censorious elements that muted Crane and earlier portrayers of the underclass, Selby puts the fiction of social reform into a new form and language.

*American Psycho* is in some respects a violent corrective to Selby's portrait. If Selby leaves the slightest suggestion that money would solve the problems of the chronic underclass by making them sanguinary and thus less violent, Ellis emphatically dispels that humanistic fallacy. Ellis goes to the opposite end of the economic spectrum to show the hollow, superficial "yuppies" of the 1980s who feed off the poverty and misery of the workers we see in *Last Exit*. If Selby's Brooklynites are the waste products of the industrial revolution, Ellis's idle rich New Yorkers are the ones who stand on top of the ash heap. These people have become so much like the technological gadgetry and clever machines they admire, that only absolute violence can remind them of their human-ness. Ellis attacks the selfish mindlessness of the Gen-Xers and connects the twin instincts of sex and violence in a most overtly violent and mean tempered narrative that takes the novel of violence into uncharted waters.

One crucial question that arose as I began this study was whether these novelists of violence ultimately express an articulated philosophy of violence. That is, as Americans, as writers fascinated by violence, and as creative personalities, do they concur on any one explanation or find any one single theory of human violence feasible? The temptation to place all the novelists into the same philosophical assembly is great. Yet, the single truth on which the fictionists agree with the theorists vis-à-vis violence is that the human instinct to violence is hard wired by genetics and cannot be changed. The authors agree that the human drive to violence has not altered significantly since the days of the primordial slime. What has altered, obviously, is society's reactions to violence and the artist's depictions of that violence. The common factor that our discussions of the American novels of violence have uncovered, therefore, is that the American novelist is more interested in recording the changes than in theorizing about causes. A priori, the American novelist acquiesces in the fact that no one theory can explain the origin or cause of human violence. Violence is a primal motivator, beyond language and absolute analysis. Past that one consensus opinion, no one view or philosophy of violence encompasses all the authors.

We can conclude too, contrary to what Henry James and others might suggest, that the art of fiction is an effort to sublimate the violent instinct that dominates the species. Art is the highest form of sublimation, but it is also perhaps the most vulnerable defense against the instinct that it attempts to counteract. The impulse to create and the impulse to kill are so closely allied, as we see in Capote's *In Cold Blood*, that the barrier between them is more like a membrane than a wall. As novelist Louis Bagley recently noted in the *New Yorker*, murderers and novelists have much in common. "Fantasies: we write them, they act them out" (*New Yorker*, August 4, 1997, 92). The aesthetic grandeur of art and art's subsequent vulnerability create a precarious balance between order and chaos. This precariousness explains why the artist is so fascinated by violence in all its forms and manifestations. Few incentives, if any, compete with violence as a reason to create art.

All the novels we have discussed, to one degree or another, demonstrate how art is a thin shield between overt violence and the ability of human beings to live together for a relatively long period of time with their devices for sublimating violence in place. This latter phenomenon is what we call civilization. The novels show too that once the values implied by art (love, compassion, faith, empathy) are abraded to razor thinness by various forces, the violent instinct re-erupts. Hemingway's *For Whom the Bell Tolls* exemplifies this eruption of the violent instinct, both on an individual and societal plain. Bret Easton Ellis's *American Psycho* is the aberrant extreme of this truth. All the novels show that violence is void of moral restraints and, once released, is inhibited by no value judgments. We see this phenomenon displayed from Faulkner to Ellis, with varying degrees of separation and clarity.

The novels demonstrate, too, a deviation from the conventional moral attitudes toward violence. Both the earlier fiction of violence and previous studies of violence generally assume that violence is "bad" or "evil." That assumption is more difficult to defend when tested against the novels in this study. Some of the novels clearly work on the assumption of violence as evil—Cain's *The Postman Always Rings Twice* and Porter's *Noon Wine* being perhaps the two most apparent examples. Cain especially assumes that violence, coupled with its cousin impulsive sexuality, is detrimental to the social order and deserving of punishment. Even Faulkner, while less condemnatory of violence, nonetheless punishes Joe Christmas severely for his violent outbursts. As we move further into the postmodernist era, however, equating violence with evil becomes less apparent. As we have argued, Capote is clearly more sympathetic with the killers than with the killed. Vonnegut is simply bemused by, but not judging of the absolute violence of which the human being is capable. By the time we reach Ellis's *American Psycho*, we see that horrific violence is personally gratifying and unpunished. In this progression, at least, the artists have inadvertently paralleled the theorists. Especially the neo-Darwins hold that violence is a human's way of reasserting his right to participate in the genetic configuring of future generations. Thus, they argue, violence is a positive manifestation of evolutionary law. Even gang violence, seen in this light, is explicable and biologically if not morally positive. While the novelist of violence hardly espouses so concrete an argument, indications are that recent artistic attitudes have lessened or removed the stigma once attached to violence. The attitudes range from viewing violence as a pragmatic necessity to viewing it as a self-gratifying right. In the middle of the spectrum is the view that violence is particularly acceptable if it serves a goal broader than mere individual satisfaction. None of these attitudes presumes moral judgment against violence.

What accounts for this progression in the degree to which violence is depicted in the novel of violence and changes in the implied authorial attitudes toward violence? Several philosophical and at last one pragmatic factor answer this question.

The pragmatic factor is quite simple: the relaxation of editorial restrictions and federal court decisions against censorship. Writers such as Faulkner, with works such as *Sanctuary*, severely tested what editors would allow and courts would tolerate. Faulkner's timing is interesting, because the modern legal approach to censorship began in the 1930s, when the federal courts ruled that James Joyce's *Ulysses* was not pornographic and could be sold in the United States. In clearing *Ulysses*, the courts stipulated that the mere use of words considered "dirty" did not make a book dirty. Perhaps the most important ruling against censorship came in 1962, when William Burrough's *Naked Lunch* was cleared of obscenity charges. Since then, the barriers of censorship have gradually fallen. During the 1970s the federal courts determined that obscenity would be determined by contemporary community standards—a criteria that has proven so nebulous as to preclude most forms of censorship.

Thus freed from the tyranny of the moral minority, and perhaps with some desire to shock the Little Old Lady from Dubuque who once squelched their eroto-artistic impulses, American novelists since World War II have intensified the level of violence and sexuality in their fictions. What was daring in Faulkner has become commonplace and what was unthinkable to Faulkner has become avant garde.

The philosophical explanations for the increase in and severity of the violence depicted in the American novel are more nebulous and thus more problematic.

One such explanation is a postmodernist twist to an old theory: Darwinian evolution. Though we have traditionally viewed violence as negative and socially destructive, that view

may be erroneous and itself culturally stifling.  Instead of being
"evil," violence may be a positive force in Homo Sapiens move
toward "perfection."  Though its positive results are obscured by
the vast time and space in which evolution operates, and
though we may not understand its benefits at close range, its end
purpose may indeed be benign.  A corollary to this argument,
therefore, if we accept this neo-Darwinian view of violence, is
that as an evolving animal we are moving toward a more intelligent understanding of the violent instinct.  By removing violence from the category of "evil" and "destructive," we perhaps
can learn to live with it more comfortably and utilize it more
constructively.  Consciously or unconsciously, the American
novelist nudges us in that direction.

    Another agreement is that mass communications have
demystified violence, or at least removed it from the realm of
the intensely personal to the realm of the distant and imagined.
That is, in the eons before the advent of radio, and especially before television and computers in the postmodernist era, violence either had to be experienced directly or viewed first hand.
This was true whether the violence be war, lynchings, fist fights
animal brutality, or whatever.  The pain inflicted was perceived
immediately and its reality was never in doubt.  The blood
smelled and the moans and screams were authentic.  With some
degree of irony, it was the "story," told either orally or recorded
later through the miracle of print, that first began to distance us
from violence.  Instead of having to experience it first hand, as
either victim, viewer, or villain, we could experience it vicariously.  Yet, no matter how effective the teller, the tale of violence was never as powerful or as convincing as the violence itself.  As this distancing factor increased as the methods of communication improved, our experiential relationship with violence continued to diminish.  Regardless of how many wars we
fought or how many felonies were committed nation wide, few
Americans were in fact confronted by the kind of violence that
defines a novel of violence.

    At some point we crossed a line.  We became so desensi-
tized to actual violence that its mystique, its horrors if you will,
became nullified.  The ultimate irony of this distancing via mass
communication is that after we had crossed the line of nullifica-
tion, the novelist of violence reclaimed the right to reintroduce
the most graphic forms of primitive violence back into the cultural mix—a phenomenon we see most clearly in novels such as

*Blood Meridian* and *American Psycho.* Thus, just a it was the story teller who first made it possible for us to experience violence vicariously rather than first hand, it was the story teller who tried to use the art of story telling (i.e., fiction) to force a new awareness of cultural violence. Though the experience is still vicarious, the limits have been pushed back so close to the original type of first hand violence that the experience is almost virtual. Writers such as Selby, McCarthy, and Ellis get as close as one can to actual violence without having oneself splattered with blood or traumatized by death rattles. That phenomenon represents an interesting and exciting cycle for the teller of violence vis-à-vis actual violence.

As before, there is a corollary to this phenomenon. As mass communications have advanced, they have created generations of children who move away from traditional attitudes toward violence. Even if church, school, and parents teach them that violence is "wrong" or "bad," movies, television, and other forms of electronic communications show them graphically that violence is a common human response to problems both minor and major. Moreover, these mass media show children that violence can be humorous, satisfying, and an effective way to establish power and respect within cultural milieus. In most cases, the attitude imparted by the mass media triumphs over the contrary attitudes of the conventional moral and philosophical systems that disparaged violence. These attitudes formed as children become modes of cultural responses as the children become adults. Consequently, society becomes more tolerant of violence. This tolerance may lead to the benign results that the neo-Darwinists envision or it may lead to the absolute destruction of the planet, a consequence that Kurt Vonnegut satirizes with a repressed horror. More likely, the ultimate results will fall at a point somewhere between those two extremes because one of the cultural ironies of violence is that it is a moderating, not an annihilating instinct.

The residual influence of childhood experiences with violence has a significant impact on the adult author's fiction making, especially fiction making that produces novels of violence. An axiom of psychology is that role playing is normal behavior in children. Freud argued long ago that the "child" in us is what makes us creative, inquisitive, imaginative. Subsequent investigations of human behavior, both those that support Freud and those that do not, have substantiated this "child" phenomenon.

However, some argue that when such role playing is extended into adulthood, it is deemed psychosis—a loss of contact with reality. With that thought in mind, we might ask to what degree does the creation of fiction differ from childhood role playing or make believe, since both actions are the conscious choice to remove oneself from "contact with reality." The answer, I think, is "not much." The normal role playing of the average child and the fiction making of the imaginative adult are essentially the same process, albeit highly modified by experiential and theoretical knowledge.

If there is any one "lesson" to be learned from the modern American novel of violence, it is that violence lies at the heart of American culture. It defines our heritage—through slavery, civil disobedience, the settlement of the West, and numerous wars. As the words of H. Rap Brown remind us, "Violence is as American as cherry pie."

# Works Cited

Allen, William Rodney. *Understanding Kurt Vonnegut.* Columbia: University of South Carolina Press, 1991.

Armstrong, Nancy and Leonard Tennenhouse, eds. *The Violence of Representation: Literature and the History of Violence.* New York: Routledge, 1989.

"The Banning of Billy Pilgrim," *The Christian Science Monitor* (June 2, 1971), 681.

Bell, Vereen M. *The Achievement of Cormac McCarthy.* Baton Rouge: Louisiana State University Press, 1988.

Berger, James. "Ghosts of Liberalism: Morrison's *Beloved* and the Moynihan Report." *PMLA* 3 (May 1996), 408-420.

Biggers, Don Hampton. *Buffalo Guns and Barbed Wire: Two Frontier Accounts by Don Hampton Biggers.* A combined reissue of *Pictures of the Past* and *History That Will Never Be Repeated*, first published in 1901 and 1902. Lubbock: Texas Tech University Press, 1991.

Bloom, Harold. *Modern Critical Views of Toni Morrison.* New York: Chelsea House Publishers, 1990.

"Borderline Psychotic," *Time*, 84 (October 30, 1964), 119.

Bredahl, A. Carl, Jr. *New Ground: Western American Narrative and the Literary Canon.* Chapel Hill: University of North Carolina Press, 1989.

Brown, Norman O. "The Excremental Vision," in *Swift: A Collection of Critical Essays.* Ed. Ernest Tuveson. Englewood Clifts, New Jersey: Prentice-Hall, 1964.

Cain, James M. *The Postman Always Rings Twice.* New York: Vintage Books, 1978.

Caldwell, Erskine. *Tobacco Road.* New York: New American Library, 1959.

Capote, Truman. *In Cold Blood: A True Account of a Multiple Murder and Its Consquences* (1965). New York: New American Library, 1980.

Chamberlain, Samuel. *My Confession: Recollections of a Rogue.* New York: Harper & Brothers, 1956.

Chase, Richard. *The American Novel and its Tradition.* Garden City: Doubleday & Company, 1957.

Clark, Walter Van Tilburg. *The Ox-Bow Incident* (1940). New York: Time Incorporated, 1962.

Clarke, Gerald. *Capote: A Biography.* New York: Simon and Schuster, 1988.

Clerc, Charles and Louis Leiter, eds. *Seven Contemporary Short Novels.* 2nd edition. Glenview: Scott, Foresman & Company, 1974.

De Bellis, Jack. "Visions and Revisions: Truman Capote's *In Cold Blood*." *JML* 7 (September 1979), 519-536.

Doctorow, E. L. *Billy Bathgate*. New York: Random House, 1989.

Donoghue, Denis. "Dream Work." *The New York Review of Books*. June 24, 1993, 5-6.

Duncan, Dayton. *Miles from Nowhere: Tales from America's Contemporary Frontier*. New York: Viking, 1993.

Ellis, Bret Easton. *American Psycho*. New York: Vintage Contemporaries, 1991.

Eron, Leonard D. "Introduction" in *Aggressive Behavior: Current Perspectives*. Ed. Husemann L. Rowell. New York: Plenum Press, 1994.

Faulkner, William. *Light in August*. New York: Random House, 1959.

Fawcett, Barbara, Brid Featherstone, Jeff Hearn and Christine Toft, eds. "Introduction" in *Violence and Gender Relations: Theories and Interventions*. London: Sage Publications, 1996, 1-5.

Fiedler, Leslie. *Love and Death in the American Novel*. New York: Criterion Books, 1960.

Forbis, William H. *The Cowboys*. Alexandria, Virginia: Time-Life Books, 1973.

Fowler, Dougls. *Understanding E. L. Doctorow*. Columbia: University of South Carolina Press, 1992.

Frohock, W. M. *The Novel of Violence in America*. 2nd edition. Dallas: Southern Methodist University Press, 1957.

Fromm, Erich. *The Anatomy of Human Destructiveness* (1973). New York: Henry Holt and Company, 1992.

Graham, Hugh Davis and Ted Robert Gurr, eds. *The History of Violence in America: Historical and Comparative Perspectives*. New York: F. A. Praeger, 1969.

Haas, Robert. "Disney Does Dutch: *Billy Bathgate* and the Disney-fication of the Gangster Genre" in *From Mouse to Mermaid: The Politics of Film, Gender, and Culture*. Eds. Eliabeth Bell, Lynda Haas and Laura Sells. Bloomington: Indiana University Press, 1995, 72-85.

Heller, Joseph. *Catch-22* (1961). New York: Dell Publishing Company, 1970.

Hemingway, Ernest. *For Whom the Bell Tolls* (1940). New York: Charles Scribner's Sons, 1968.

Hersey, John. *The War Lover*. New York: Alfred A. Knopf, 1959.

Hoagland, Edward. "Kurt Vonnegut Singing in the Bath." *The New York Times Book Review* (March 15, 1981), 3 & 33.

Hoffman, Frederick J. *The Mortal No: Death and the Modern Imagination*. Princeton: Princeton University Press, 1964.

Holman, C. Hugh. *A Handbook to Literature*. 4th edition. Indianapolis: Bobbs-Merrill Educational Publishing, 1980.

Hoopes, Roy, ed. *The Baby in the Icebox and Other Short Fiction*. New York: Holt, Rinehart and Winston, 1981.

Howe, Irving. *William Faulkner: A Critical Study*. 2nd edition. New York: Vintage, 1952.

Hungerford, Harold. "Past and Present in *Light in August*." *American Literature* 55 (May 1983), 183-198.

Iannone, Carol. "E. L. Doctorow's 'Jewish Radicalism.'" *Commentary* 81:3 (1985), 53-56.

Irving, John. "Pornography and the New Puritans." *New York Times Book Review*, March 29, 1992, 1, 24-25, 27.

Jones, Howard Mumford. "The Soul of Spain." *Saturday Review of Literature* XXIII (October 26, 1940), 5, 19. Reprinted in *The Merrill Studies in For Whom the Bell Tolls*, ed. Sheldon Norman Grebstein. Columbus: Charles Merrill Publishing Company, 1971, 2-5.

Kazin, Alfred. *On Native Grounds* (1942). Garden City: Doubleday Anchor Books, 1956.

Kowalewski, Michael. *Deadly Musings: Violence and Verbal Form in American Fiction.* Princeton: Princeton University Press, 1993.

Lane, James B. "Violence and Sex in the Post-War Popular Urban Novel: With a Consideration of Harold Robbins's *A Stone for Danny Fisher* and Hubert Selby, Jr.'s *Last Exit to Brooklyn.*" *Journal of Popular Culture* 8 (1974), 295-308.

Leiter, Louis. "The Expense of Spirit in a Waste of Shame: Motif, Montage, and Structure in *Noon Wine*" in *Seven Contemporary Short Novels*. Eds. Charles Clerc and Louis Leiter. Glenview: Scott, Foresman and Company, 1969, 186-219.

Lentricchia, Frank. "Last Will and Testament of an Ex-Literary Critic." *ALSC Newsletter* 2:4 (Fall 1996), 1, 3-6.

Loving, Jerome. "Introduction" in *McTeague: A Story of San Francisco*. Oxford: Oxford University Press, 1995, x-xxviii.

Lowie, Robert H. *Indians of the Plains*. Lincoln: University of Nebraska Press, 1982.

Madden, David. *James M. Cain*. New York: Twayne Publishers, Inc., 1970.

Marling, William. *The American Roman Noir: Hammett, Cain, and Chandler*. Athens: The University of Georgia Press, 1995.

McCarthy, Cormac. *Blood Meridian: Or the Evening Redness in the West*. New York: Vintage International, 1992.

McGinnis, Wayne D. "The Arbitrary Cycle of *Slaughterhouse-Five*: A Relation of Form to Theme" in *The Critical Response to Kurt Vonnegut*. Ed. Leonard Mustazza. Westport, Connecticut: Greenwood Press, 1994, 114-122.

McMurtry, Larry. *Lonesome Dove*. New York: Pocket Books, 1985.

Morrison, Toni. *Beloved*. New York: A Plume Book, 1987.

Oates, Joyce Carol. "Man Under Sentence of Death: The Novels of James M Cain" in *Tough Guy Writers of the Thirties*. Ed. David Madden (Carbondale: Southern Illinois University Press, 1968), 110-123.

Ozick, Cynthia. "Dostoeyevsky's Unabomber: Raskolnikov Lives On." *The New Yorker* February 24 and March 3, 1997, 114-121.

Perloff, Marjorie. "*Beloved*: Great American Novel?" *ANQ* 5:4 (October 1992), 229-231.

Pilkington, Tom. "Fate and Free Will on the American Frontier: Cormac McCarthy's Western Fiction." *Western American Literature* 27:4 (Winter 1993), 311-322.

Porter, Katherine Anne. "Noon Wine" in *Seven Contemporary Short Novels*. 2nd edition. Eds. Charles Clerc and Louis Leiter. Glenview: Scott, Foresman and Company, 1974, 324-371.

—. "The Necessary Enemy" in *The Collected Essays and Occasional Writings of Katherine Anne Porter*. New York: Delacorte Press, 1970, 182-186.

Selby, Hubert, Jr. *Last Exit to Brooklyn*. New York: Grove Press, 1964.

Sepich, John Emil. "The Dance of History in Cormac McCarthy's *Blood Meridian*." *Southern Literary Journal* 24:1 (Fall 1991), 16-31.

—. *Notes on Blood Meridian* (Louisville, Kentucky: Bellarmine Press, 1993).

Shaviro, Steven. "'The Very Life of the Darkness': A Reading of *Blood Meridian*." *Southern Quarterly* 30:4 (Summer 1992), 111-121.

Stegner, Wallace. "Walter Clark's Frontier" in *Walter Van Tilburg Clark: Critiques*. Ed. Charlton Laird. Reno: University of Nevada Press, 1983.

Stigliano, Tony. "Jean-Paul Sartre on Understanding Violence" in *Crime and Social Justice: Crisis in Theory and Social Policy* 19:1 (1983), 52-63.

Tanner, Laura E. *Intimate Violence: Reading Rape and Torture in Twentieth-Century Fiction*. Bloomington: Indiana University Press, 1996.

Thurman, Jan. *Toni Morrison's Fiction*. Columbia, South Carolina: University of South Carolina Press, 1996.

Toch, Hans. *Violent Men*. Revised edition. Cambridge: Schenkman, 1984.

Tokarczyk, Michelle M. "The City, *The Waterworks*, and Writing: An Interview with E. L. Doctorow." *Kenyon Review* 17:1 (Winter 1995), 32-35.

Unrue, Darlene Harbour. *Understanding Katherine Anne Porter*. Columbia: University of South Carolina Press, 1988.

Valzelli, Luigi. *Psychobiology of Aggressions and Violence*. New York: Raven Press, 1981.

Vaughan, J. N. "Books of the Week." *Commonweal* XXXIII (December 13 1940), 210. *The Merrill Studies in For Whom the Bell Tolls*, ed. Sheldon Norman Grebstein. Columbus: Charles Merrill Publishing Company, 1971, 2-5.

—. "Books of the Week." *Commonweal* XXXIII (December 13 1940). Reprinted in *The Merrill Studies in For Whom the Bell Tolls*, ed. Sheldon Norman Grebstein. Columbus: Charles Merrill Publishing Company, 1971, 210.

Vieira Nelson H. "*Evil Be Thou My Good*: Postmodern Heroics and Ethics in *Billy Bathgate* and *Bufo & Pallanzani*." *Comparative Literature Studies* 28:4 (1991), 356-378.

Vonnegut, Kurt, Jr. *Slaughterhouse-Five: or The Children's Crusade*. New York: Delacorte Press, 1969.

Wolman, Benjamin B. "Foreword." Eds. Leonore Loeb Adler and Florence L. Denmark. *Violence and the Prevention of Violence*. Westport, Connectictu: Praeger, 1995, xv-xx.

Woodward, Richard B. "Cormac McCarthy's Venomous Fiction." *The New York Times Magazine*, 19 April 1992, 28-31, 36, 40.

Wright, Robert. "The Biology of Violence." *The New Yorker*, March 13 1995, 68-77.